Community Archives, Community Spaces: Heritage, memory and identity

Community Archives, Community Spaces: Heritage, memory and identity

Edited by
Jeannette A. Bastian and Andrew Flinn

facet
publishing

Published by Facet Publishing,
7 Ridgmount Street, London WC1E 7AE
www.facetpublishing.co.uk

Facet Publishing is wholly owned by CILIP:
the Library and Information Association.

British Library Cataloguing in Publication Data
A catalogue record for this book is available from the British Library.

ISBN 978-1-78330-350-2 (paperback)
ISBN 978-1-78330-351-9 (hardback)
ISBN 978-1-78330-352-6 (e-book)

First published 2020

Text printed on FSC accredited material.

Typeset from editors' files by Flagholme Publishing Services in
10/13 pt Palatino Linotype and Open Sans.
Printed and made in Great Britain by CPI Group (UK) Ltd, Croydon, CR0 4YY.

Contents

List of figures

Contributors

Karen Adams is Wiradjuri and is the Director of the Indigenous Unit in the Faculty of Medicine, Nursing and Health Sciences at Monash University, Australia. Karen has a nursing background, working in areas of aged care, communicable diseases and managing Aboriginal health services. She has a Master's in Applied Epidemiology and her PhD focused on social network analysis and child health. Her research has largely focused on equity and she has an interest in adaptable health workforces that can respond to needs of Indigenous peoples. She believes having equitable representation of Indigenous peoples in the health professions is critical to this.

Janet Ceja Alcalá is Assistant Professor of Archives at the School of Library and Information Science at Simmons University in the US. Her research and teaching focus on cultural heritage archives, community engagement and moving image preservation. She holds a PhD in Archival Studies from the University of Pittsburgh, a Master's in Film and Media Preservation from the University of Rochester, and a Bachelor's degree in Film Studies from the University of California, Santa Barbara.

Sarah Baker is a Professor of Cultural Sociology at Griffith University, Australia. Her recent work explores the community heritage sector and the institutions collecting, preserving and documenting popular music's past. Her books include *Community Custodians of Popular Music's Past: a DIY approach to heritage* (Routledge, 2017), *Curating Pop: exhibiting popular music in the museum* (Bloomsbury, 2019) and the edited collections *Preserving Popular Music Heritage: do-it-yourself, do-it-together* (Routledge, 2015) and *The Routledge Companion to Popular Music History and Heritage* (Routledge, 2018).

Jeannette A. Bastian is Professor Emerita at the School of Library and Information Science, Simmons University, Boston, Massachusetts, where she directed their Archives Management program. A former Territorial Librarian of the United States Virgin Islands, she holds an MPhil from the University of the West Indies and a PhD from the University of Pittsburgh. Her books include *West Indian Literature: an index to criticism, 1930–1975* (G. K. Hall, 1981), *Owning Memory: how a Caribbean community lost its archives and found its history* (Libraries Unlimited, 2003), *Community Archives: the shaping of memory* (ed., Facet Publishing, 2009), *Archives in Libraries: what librarians and archivists need to know to work together* (Society of American Archivists, 2015) and *Decolonizing the Caribbean Record: an archives reader* (Litwin, 2018). She was elected a Fellow of the Society of American Archivists in 2019.

Lauren Booker (Garigal clan and Dharug, Western Sydney) is a researcher and archivist with a particular focus on Indigenous communities' relation to and representation in collecting institutions. She worked as the Collection Officer and Project Assistant for PARADISEC, assisting projects with endangered language communities to digitise recorded cultural material for cultural/language revitalisation and organise appropriate digital archives. Lauren was a 2017 Churchill Fellow and her current research focuses on histories of collection and display of Ancestral remains and the issues of archival preservation of cultural materials.

Zelmarie Cantillon is a Postdoctoral Research Fellow in the School of Humanities, Languages and Social Science, Griffith University, Australia. She is co-editor of the *Routledge Companion to Popular Music History and Heritage* (Routledge, 2018) and author of *Resort Spatiality: reimaging sites of mass tourism* (Routledge, 2019). Her current research focuses on the intersections between urban identity, cultural heritage and community wellbeing.

Michelle Caswell is Associate Professor of Archival Studies in the Department of Information Studies at the University of California, Los Angeles (UCLA), where she directs the UCLA Community Archives Lab (https://communityarchiveslab.ucla.edu). She is the co-founder of the South Asian American Digital Archive (www.saada.org), an online repository that documents and provides access to the diverse stories of South Asian Americans. She is the author of the book *Archiving the Unspeakable: silence, memory and the photographic record in Cambodia* (University of Wisconsin Press, 2014), as well as more than three dozen peer-reviewed articles on archives, communities and social justice.

Aziz Choudry is Associate Professor and Canada Research Chair in Social Movement Learning and Knowledge Production in the Department of

Integrated Studies in Education, McGill University, Canada, and Visiting Professor at the Centre for Education Rights and Transformation, University of Johannesburg, South Africa. He has been involved in a range of social, political and environmental justice movements and organisations since the 1980s. Among other books, he is author of *Learning Activism: the intellectual life of contemporary social movements* (University of Toronto Press, 2015), editor of *Activists and the Surveillance State: learning from repression* (Pluto Press, 2018) and co-editor of *Reflections on Knowledge, Learning and Social Movements: history's schools* (Routledge, 2018).

Jez Collins is the founder of the Birmingham Music Archive C.I.C. The BMA is a cultural and creative arts organisation that employs citizen and community archiving practices to capture, document and celebrate the musical culture of Birmingham. It develops associated projects such as exhibitions, tours, talks, youth and community focused projects and broadcast media (film and radio). Jez is a co-director of Un-Convention, a global grassroots music network based in Manchester, is leading on the formation of the Birmingham Music Coalition and is a Trustee of the National Jazz Archive, UK. He also sits on the Community Heritage and Archive Group advisory board.

Joanne Evans, Associate Professor, is the recipient of an Australian Research Council Future Fellowship (FT140100073) and is co-ordinator of the Records Continuum Research Group in the Faculty of Information Technology, Monash University, Australia. Through her fellowship she has established the interdisciplinary Archives and the Rights of the Child Research Program to address the lifelong identity, memory and accountability needs of childhood out of home care. This involves the exploration of participatory design and research strategies to develop dynamic evidence and memory management frameworks, processes and systems supportive of multiple rights in records and recordkeeping.

Shannon Faulkhead is a Koorie woman from Mildura, Australia. She has a PhD from Monash University, Australia, and her research concentrates on Koorie peoples' knowledges: the location, its position within the broader Australian society and collective knowledge as reflected through narratives and records. Shannon's multi-disciplinary research has centred on community and archival collections of records. Being the recipient of the Finkel Fellowship has provided Shannon with opportunities for greater exploration and development in the area of Indigenous archiving.

Andrew Flinn is a Reader in Archival Studies and Oral History at University College London, UK. He is the vice chair of the UK Community Archives and Heritage Group and joint co-ordinator of the Archives Cluster in the University of Gothenburg/UCL Centre for Critical Heritage Studies. He received his PhD from the University of Manchester in 1999. Prior to UCL he worked at the People's History Museum in Manchester and the British Museum. His research interests include community-based heritage practices and DIY/participatory approaches to knowledge production aiming at social change and transformation. Relevant publications include (with Duff and Wallace) *Archives and Social Justice* (Routledge, forthcoming 2019), 'Working with the Past: making history of struggle part of the struggle' in *Reflections on Knowledge, Learning and Social Movements* (Choudry and Vally (eds), Routledge, 2018) and 'Community Archives' in the *Encyclopedia of Archival Science* (Duranti and Franks (eds), Rowman & Littlefield Publishers, 2015).

Anne J. Gilliland is Associate Dean for Information Studies in the Graduate School of Education and Information Studies at the University of California, Los Angeles (UCLA). Her interests relate broadly to the history, nature, human impact and technologies associated with archives, recordkeeping and memory, particularly in translocal and international contexts. Her recent work addresses recordkeeping and archival systems and practices in support of human rights and daily life in post-conflict settings, particularly in the countries emerging out of the former Yugoslavia, and in forcibly displaced communities; as well as the role of community memory in promoting reconciliation in the wake of ethnic conflict.

Claire Hall is a first-generation tauiwi (non-Māori) New Zealander of Scottish and Irish descent. Claire is an author, historian and Māori language advocate. She manages the Te Reo o Taranaki archive, Te Pūtē Routiriata, teaches and records oral history. Over the past decade, Claire has supported Taranaki whānui (descendants of the eight tribes of the Taranaki region) to tell their own stories and independently care for their tukuihotanga – tangible and intangible cultural heritage. She is writing a master's thesis on the intergenerational transmission of memory in whānau (family) archival collections.

Paul Long is Professor of Media and Cultural History in the Birmingham Centre for Media and Cultural Research, Birmingham City University, UK. His recent research on popular music history, heritage and archives has taken a practical turn with the co-curation of the exhibition *'Is There Anyone Out There?' Documenting Birmingham's Alternative Music Scene 1986–1990* (Parkside,

2016) and his involvement in the *Home of Metal* heritage events and exhibitions for 2019. He is currently writing *Memorialising Popular Music Culture: history, heritage and the archive* (Rowman and Littlefield Publishers) for publication in 2020.

Honiana Love (Te Ātiawa, Taranaki Iwi, Ngāti Ruanui, and Ngā Ruahinerangi) is the Pou Ārahi – Strategic Advisor, Māori, at Ngā Taonga Sound & Vision, where she works with iwi and Māori around the use of their collections. Prior to this she was a Senior Adviser, Māori at Manatū Taonga, Ministry for Culture and Heritage. She has over 25 years of archival experience, including working as an archivist at Archives New Zealand and Te Reo o Taranaki, and as a librarian. She is passionate about connecting people with their tūpuna and taonga. 'My iwi, hapū and whānau are at the heart of who I am.'

Raphaël Nowak is a cultural sociologist and postdoctoral research fellow at the Griffith Centre for Social and Cultural Research, Australia. He is the author of *Consuming Music in the Digital Age* (Palgrave, 2015), co-editor of *Networked Music Cultures* with Andrew Whelan (Palgrave, 2016), and co-author of *Curating Pop* with Sarah Baker and Lauren Istvandity (Bloomsbury, 2019).

Michael Piggott is a semi-retired archivist consultant and researcher based in Canberra, Australia, and during 2018–19 was a Senior Research Fellow with Deakin University. He is also Chair, Territory Records Advisory Council; and in 2017 completed a five-year term as President, Friends of the Noel Butlin Archives Centre. Between 1972–2008 he worked for the National Library of Australia, the Australian War Memorial, the National Archives of Australia and the University of Melbourne. He was made an AM in the Queen's Birth-day Honours in 2017. A selection of his published writing appeared as *Archives and Societal Provenance: Australian essays* (Chandos, 2012).

Désirée Rochat is a community worker and educator in Canada who has had the chance to learn from Montreal youth and other workers over years of involvement. She develops pedagogical material and educational projects for the community sector and is a PhD candidate in the Department of Integrated Studies in Education at McGill University. She is also involved in numerous projects for the preservation and promotion of archives in Montreal community-based organisations, especially of Caribbean communities. Her research interests include community education, histories of diasporic activism/community and their pedagogical potential, and community-based archives.

Kanokporn Nasomtrug Simionica is a Lecturer at Loei Rajabhat University, Thailand, teaching courses in Library and Information Science. She completed her PhD at the University of Liverpool, UK, in Archives and Records Management. Her research interests include community archives and tangible and intangible cultural heritage documentation.

Rebecka Taves Sheffield is a Senior Policy Advisor for the Archives of Ontario, Canada, and a member of the Recordkeeping Strategies Unit. She has taught at the Simmons School of Library and Information Science in the US and at the University of Toronto iSchool. She has previously served as Executive Director of The ArQuives: Canada's LGBTQ2+ Archives, where she began as a volunteer archivist in 2007. Rebecka holds a graduate degree in information studies with a specialisation in archives and records management. She completed a PhD at the University of Toronto iSchool in collaboration with the Mark S. Bonham Centre for Sexual Diversity Studies.

Tamara Štefanac is Director of the Croatian Railway Museum in Zagreb and also manages collections of museum and archival material. She holds a PhD from the University of Zadar, Croatia. Through her everyday practical experiences in museum work, she has developed her research interests in topics relating to the processing and description of archival material held in museums as well as the conceptualization and uses of archival material in different contexts.

Kirsten Thorpe (Worimi, Port Stephens NSW, Australia) is a PhD student in the Faculty of Information Technology, Monash University, and a researcher at the Jumbunna Institute of Indigenous Education and Research, University of Sydney. Kirsten's research interests relate to Indigenous self-determination in libraries and archives. She has worked on numerous projects that have involved the return of historic collections to communities and advocates for a transformation of practice to centre Indigenous priorities and voice in regard to the management of data, records and collections. Kirsten is an advocate for building and supporting the development of local digital keeping places.

Narissa Timbery is a PhD student in the Faculty of IT and Monash Indigenous Centre, Monash University, Australia, exploring the development of an Aboriginal community archival system of the virtual 3D models of the

Monash Country Lines Archive, with the support of a scholarship from auDA (.au Domain Administration). Narissa is a Koori woman whose family is from the Yuin Nation, on the NSW South Coast. She is passionate about archives that relate to Aboriginal and Torres Strait Islander Peoples and has a strong desire to connect families and archival material in a way that best suits their needs.

Marjorie Villefranche is the Executive Director of La Maison d'Haïti in Canada. Her work over the last 40 years has been devoted to fighting for the rights of immigrants and against racism, sexism, discrimination and all forms of social exclusion. She has developed many educational programs for immigrants, illiterate adults, women and children, and has taken part in different advocacy campaigns over the years. She also produced three documentaries: *Port-au-Prince ma ville*, *District 67* and *Petites mères*. A committed feminist, she was a spokeswoman of the March of Bread and Roses, and a representative for Quebec at the National Organisation of Immigrant and Visible Minority Women. For her work, Marjorie Villefranche received the Woman of Merit Award from the YWCA Foundation in 2008, the 2010 Solis prize from the City of Montreal, and was named Personality of the Week by La Presse and the CBC/Radio Canada in May 2012.

Kristen Young is a community archivist currently based in Montreal, Canada. She received her Master's in Information Studies at McGill University's School of Information Studies in 2016. As a diasporic individual with a background in History at the University of Toronto, Kristen is interested in the intersection of archives, history, memory and identity and how they interact in community environments. Kristen has been and is currently involved in various archiving projects in Montreal-based institutions that promote preservation and the importance of local history within Caribbean and minority communities.

Acknowledgements

Andrew would like to thank for their inspiration and knowledge all the many people working in and responsible for independent, autonomous and community-led archives in the UK and internationally, including (but by no means exclusively) over the years all those involved with the National Museum of Labour History/People's History Museum, the Working-Class Movement Library, the Marx Memorial Library, the Black Cultural Archives, Alda Terracciano, Tola Dabiri, Judith Garfield at Eastside Community Heritage, Ajamu X, Glenn Jordan, Mary Stevens, Stefan Dickers at the Bishopsgate Library and Archive, Eve Hostettler and Sharon Messenger.

In addition he would like to thank his many colleagues in the Community Archives and Heritage Group, including but again not exclusively, Jane Golding, Jack Latimer, Sue Hampson, Judith Harvey, Alan Butler, Jez Collins, Laura Cream, David Mander, Elaine Davis and Vic Gray. And also the many inspiring community archivists who spoken and presented at all the Community Archives conferences we have organised since 2006.

Jeannette would like to acknowledge the encouragement and enthusiasm of her graduate students in the School of Library and Information Science at Simmons University whose thoughtful discussions about and research into the evolving issues of community archives have greatly influenced and shaped her thinking.

Andrew and Jeannette are grateful for the enthusiastic responses from the contributors to this volume and would also like to recognise the support for this volume over a number of years from the editorial staff at Facet, including Helen Carley, Damian Mitchell and Michelle Lau.

Introduction

Jeannette A. Bastian and Andrew Flinn

> The activity of 'archiving' is . . . always a critical one, always a historically located one, always a contestatory one, since archives are in part constituted within the lines of force of cultural power and authority; always one open to the futurity and contingency – the relative autonomy – of artistic practice; always . . . an engagement, an interruption in a settled field, which is to enter critically into existing configurations to re-open the closed structures into which they have ossified.
>
> (Hall, 2001, 89–92)

This dynamic vision of the 'activity of archiving' proposed by Stuart Hall a decade ago is being vigorously addressed today by community archives, not least through their challenges to traditional archival theory and practice. As the essays in this volume demonstrate, the practice of community archiving is not only a compelling and diverse international endeavor in its own right, but presages shifts in archival development as society increasingly engages with records and with people whose lives and histories have often seemed to exist beyond and outside the mainstream.

From exploratory beginnings in the twentieth century, community archives as discrete and identifiable entities burst upon the archival world, belatedly receiving recognition and interest from the archive and heritage professions in the early decades of the twenty-first century with a forceful momentum that to date shows no signs of abating. Community-based informal archives, frequently staffed by volunteer and non-professional archivists, had long existed in a variety of venues but the concept of community archives was largely unexplored and unfamiliar to archivists. The ad hoc and highly diversified natures of community archives were often not recognised as archival repositories. Their content, often focused on marginalised and undervoiced segments of the population and often not manifest in standard records formats, did not meet the normative standards of archivists generally focused on institutional records and the acquisition of prestigious collections and were dismissed as ephemeral. Neither did they invite sustained study by archivists increasingly focused on redefining their own profession in light of the challenges posed by digital environments, even though the social affordances of these same digital technologies were a significant factor in boosting the uptake and visibility of community archive and heritage activities that had previously gone under the radar.

The origins of community archives are obscure but it does seem clear that in a wide variety of guises, community archives have existed ever since groups of people have felt the need to affirm themselves and their own identities within or apart from the wider society. Historical societies, municipal centres, local history rooms, religious organisations, community and cultural centres are only a few of the various settings that seek to establish and express the identity of a group whether it be it a town, a region, an affinity, an ethnicity, a belief, an occupation or interest. Records, in all their many modalities and forms, follow from the articulations and actions of people and so become the natural and organic expressions of any group of people wishing to express and proclaim themselves both within their own group and to the outside world.

The term 'community archives' itself as a specific designation came into general use in the twentieth century to characterise a non-traditional archival collection specifically tied to a particular group, often one that may be undocumented or under-documented by traditional archival institutions. A search through the professional English language literature identifies usage of the phrase as early as 1942 when an article in *Library Journal* places 'community archives' within the sphere of the public library. The article, 'Libraries as Community Archives in Wartime', emphasises the archival obligations of libraries in documenting the wartime activities of their particular community, encouraging individuals involved in World War 2 to create an archive of their own particular war experiences within the public library. The author writes that 'every type of library has its archival function in wartime. The public library can keep the record of the activities of the community and of the war's impact on it. The college and university library can keep similar records of the wartime history of the institution, its faculty, students and alumni' (Barr, 588).

Charting a trajectory of literature on community archives reveals that over time community archives have responded to and fulfilled a spectrum of community needs. From roles as chroniclers and documenters of community engagement in war; as archives outside institutional spaces such as the Lesbian Herstory Archives founded in 1973 established (and still continuing) in a private residence; as local collectors and historians of places distant and removed from larger regional centres; as counter narratives to 'official history books and institutions of public culture' (Eales, 1998, 11) as in efforts to encourage community archives among marginalised and undocumented groups in South Africa in the 1990s; to the social justice advocates of today in the first quarter of the twenty-first century, community archives react to the societal callings of their time. In 2001, the British *Public Library Journal* took note of the growing community archives movement asserting that:

> Community Archives have become a grass roots movement – there is no funded coordination (though undoubtedly there should be). It is not something that is being organised from the top down, it is simply seeding all over the country as people hear of the idea and want to do it in their own locality.
>
> (Pearson, 2001, 39)

This ever-modulating role suggests close and enduring affinity between communities, their heritages and the records that underpin the telling of those heritage narratives, an affinity and informal relationship that archivists often set aside, preferring to put archives into neat and manageable boxes rather than deal with that often sprawling messy relationship on its own terms. But it is through this relationship between people and their records that community archives – by becoming spaces that accommodate multiple voices in multiple modalities and visions – represent a further step in the evolution of archival thinking, one that moves away from formalised hierarchical structures towards a recognition of community archives as a repudiation and disruption of formal definitions.

In 2007, at the Sharing Community Memories conference in the United Kingdom, Andrew Flinn, offered the following definition of community archives:

> Community histories or community archives are the grassroots activities of documenting, recording and exploring community heritage in which community participation, control and ownership of the project is essential. This activity might or might not happen in association with formal heritage organisations but the impetus and direction should come from within the community itself.
>
> (Flinn, 2007, 153)

Even so, despite growing exposure within the archival community as well as the publication of at least 20 journal articles in the archival literature between 1980 and 2009, when *Community Archives: the shaping of memory* – a precursor to the current volume – was itself published in 2009, the concept of community archives was still an ambiguous outlier on the archival spectrum. The editors of that volume not only struggled to define the concept but struggled to find examples, assembling a potpourri of possibilities that mingled a number of different perspectives on what community archives could be or become. It seemed that despite the long history of community-based archives, for archivists, the concept was still marginal, loosely defined and incidental to archival work.

But change was in the air! Today, a decade later, community archives are recognised entities within the archival world and the use and critical exploration of the term is increasingly international. Still diversified, it is their diversity that defines them, and they are often seen as bridges between the traditional representations of the formal archives and the representations of the many marginalised groups that do not appear in those archives.

Since 2009, the literature on community archives has grown exponentially. Over 60 articles have appeared in English language archival journals and over 20 theses or dissertations have been produced. While much of the research and academic writing on community archives seems to have coalesced more specifically around social justice issues, as the essays in this volume demonstrate, community archives continue to respond to a diverse range of needs while at the same time rejecting some traditional tenets of archival practice in favour of approaches that speak to these needs. Niamh Moore perhaps defined it best when describing community archives as boundary objects, spaces for collaborative thinking and working, best understood 'not as an inadequate professional archive, but rather as an archive tailored to its location' (2016, 29).

In many ways, community archives, by becoming spaces that accommodate multiple voices in multiple modalities and visions, represent a further step in the evolution of archival thinking, one that moves away from formalised hierarchical structures towards a more fluid set of constructs that locates people and groups as they define themselves at the centre of archival concerns.

The editors of this second volume on community archives believe the time is right, the level of debate and thinking more mature and the voices more plural, for an in-depth engagement with archival thinking and practice. We take the view that community archives and the practice of community archiving sit within an archival and recordkeeping multiverse that is holistic and inclusive. While community archives are frequently viewed as boundary objects, offering a reproach and alternative ways of thinking and doing to the practices of traditional and mainstream archives and heritage bodies and indicating pathways to more participatory, more democratic, more pluralised recordkeeping theory and practice, they also share many of the same characteristics, motivations and meaning-making with more traditional archives. Following Cook (2013) and others, we suggest that the study of community archives is best viewed in ways that recognise difference and pluralism of approach but also transcend easy but ultimately unhelpful binaries, such as between professional and non-professional, mainstream and community, personal and organisational, evidence and memory, collecting and archiving.

Building on the earlier volume, the chapters in this book consider the history of community archiving and the emergence of what we might loosely call a 'community archives movement', while looking towards the future. Through three theoretical essays and seven case studies this book pursues several goals: to continue to build upon and expand the theoretical framework for community archives, while also demonstrating how this framework extends traditional archival practice; to explore, through case studies, interpretations of community archives that push the boundaries of what we think of as community archives – in fact to suggest that there may be no boundaries to these synergies between people and their ability to unite around the records and the ability of records to unite them; to envision community archives as a further step in the archival continuum that learns from past practice and accommodates new strategies.

The first section of the book – three chapters – is intended as a theoretical exploration of various aspects of community archives. Rebecka Taves Sheffield offers an 'optimistic' view of the sustainability of community archives, analysing issues and concerns as well as suggesting positive actions. Michelle Caswell, focusing on the quality of affect suggests ways in which this critical community value can be integrated into traditional archival practice. Michael Piggott interrogates community archives in parallel with the records continuum, considering whether these two theoretical frameworks are analogous or disparate and what they can offer one another.

The second section offers seven case studies that indicate the broad reach of community archives, both geographically and topically, while demonstrating the variety of interpretations of community archives themselves. In Thailand (Nasomtrug Simionica), community archives are aligned with cultural heritage with an emphasis on intangible heritage. In New Zealand (Hall and Love), the Māori community works towards synergy between indigenous records and a colonial legacy, while in Canada (Rochat et al.), Maison d'Haïti functions as an advocate and educator for Montreal's Haitian community. Developing new models for archiving becomes critical as communities form around non-traditional records such as music (Long et al.) and trauma and healing as in Indigenous Australian communities (Evans et al.). Community-based scholarship by forging partnerships that work towards social justice (Ceja Alcalá) and community entities as counterbalances to official narratives (Gilliland and Štefanac) offer still additional perspectives on the many and disparate roles of community archives and specifically where archivists and educators fit into these structures.

As a totality, the chapters in this second volume on community archives expand our understanding of this phenomena, showing the diversity of the movement but also indicating a sea change in the notion of archiving itself. The official master narratives and the smaller but insistent voices of those omitted from that narrative may seem to be in opposition, but, as Stuart Hall suggests, critical interventions into a continually contestatory field help to open up otherwise closed and exclusionary narratives. These interventions in the aggregate can be woven into more inclusive human stories if archivists are willing to take up the challenge by rethinking their practice and re-adjusting their theories.

References

Barr, P. (1942) Libraries as Community Archives in Wartime, *Library Journal*, **67**, 588.

Bastian, J. and Alexander, B. (eds) (2009), *Community Archives: the shaping of memory*, Facet Publishing.

Cook, T. (2013) Evidence, Memory, Identity, and Community: four shifting archival paradigms, *Archival Science*, **13** (2–3), 95–121.

Eales, K. (1998) Community Archives: introduction, *South African Archives Journal*, **40**, 11–16.

Flinn, A. (2007) Community Histories, Community Archives: some opportunities and challenges, *Journal of the Society of Archivists*, **28** (2), 151–176.

Hall, S. (2001) Constituting an Archive, Third Text, **15** (54), 89–92.

Moore, N., Salter, A., Stanley, L. and Tamboukou, M. (2016) *The Archive Project: archival research in the social sciences*, Routledge.

Pearson, C. (2001) A Community Captured, *Public Library Journal*, **16** (2), 39.

PART 1

Analytical Essays

CHAPTER 1

Archival optimism, or, how to sustain a community archives

Rebecka Taves Sheffield

Whatever the experience of optimism is in particular, then, the affective structure of an optimistic attachment involves a sustaining inclination to return to the scene of fantasy that enables you to expect that this time, nearness to this thing, will help you or a world to become different in just the right way. But, again, optimism is cruel when the object/scene that ignites a sense of possibility actually makes it impossible to attain the expansive transformation for which a person or a people risks striving; and, doubly, it is cruel insofar as the very pleasure of being inside a relation have become sustaining regardless of the content of the relation, such that a person or a world finds itself bound to a situation of profound threat that is, at the same time, profoundly confirming.

(Berlant, 2011, 2)

Introduction

What does it mean to sustain a community archives? We know that constituting an archives is a special moment, one that consciously brings together the corpus of our documentary heritage, however fraught with lacunae, into a space where it can be cherished and deeply considered by ourselves and others. We know that the early moments of an archives are often sparked by a desire to build a heritage that better reflects who we are and what we want to be as a community. We know that our nascent archival practices are often the most exhilarating activities as a community archives begins to take shape. But what happens next? What happens after this excitement gives way to a recognition that archival work is labour, that it requires an investment of time and money and that our community's ideas about who we are and what we want to be change over time? What if the banality of collecting, cataloguing and indexing has discouraged everyone but the most dedicated champions of the archives? What happens when the champions bow out?

Drawing from both archival studies and queer theory about the archive as a site for cultural reproduction, this essay will focus on how communities sustain and nurture archival projects over time. Here, I conceptualise sustainability as both a practical challenge and an ideological exercise, producing imbricated, overlapping and distinct sets of demands. I introduce the concept of archival optimism as a way to understand the reasons why communities contribute labour, often without compensation, and invest in sustaining archival practices that tell as much about this community's past and present as it does about their promissory stake in an imagined future.

Archival optimism

Lauren Berlant (2001) writes that optimism is a force that moves us beyond our individual lives and out into the world, bringing us closer to 'satisfying something' that we cannot create on our own, a 'way of life, an object, a project, concept or scene' (1–2). Berlant's writing on optimism is an intervention on, what she claims, is the pessimistic nature of queer theory. In queer theory, she writes, authors dwell on negative affects, such as shame and melancholy, to describe how queer folks have been systematically removed from or kept out of normative civil society. As a result, much of queer theory grapples with the feelings that arise from such persecution or erasure and from the inability of queer folks to access means of biological and cultural reproduction. Some, such as Lee Edelman (2004) and Leo Bersani (1987; 2008), go so far as to claim that the exclusion of queer folks from the means of reproduction has resulted in a situation in which queerness exists only in the realm of the present, without a sense of a collective past or future.

Berlant is nevertheless critical of this overarching pessimism because it fails to account for the ways in which queer folks not only resist such exclusions, but also consistently disrupt the status quo simply by failing to live within its expectations. Such pessimism also dismisses the ways in which the congealment of queer identities – most prominently gay and lesbian – have actually produced and reproduced queer cultures, within and outside of sexual communities. To take but one example of queer reproduction, the rainbow flag has now become a symbol for gay pride recognised around the world. This symbol did not arise out of nothing and has cultural currency beyond the present. If, as Berlant notes, optimism is what pushes us to work together toward something larger than our individual selves, and with a sense of the past and future, then this must also be a catalyst for the founding of an archives and the force that drives queer communities to engage in archival practices that strive to preserve evidence of a past for the benefit of a queer future. The archives is a site of queer cultural reproduction.

To build on Berlant's work on queer optimism, archival optimism might be imagined as a broader concept that draws from a lineage in queer theory but is not tied necessarily to queer communities. That is, archival optimism is the notion that we engage collectively in archival work because we have a sense of confidence in a future that will recognise the shared heritage that we build and include those who respect our determination to preserve this heritage, even if the experiences and opinions of those documented in the records diverge from our own.

Archival optimism is emphasised in archival theory's insistence that history provides a context for the present – as enshrined in the Shakespearean phase 'what is past is prologue', which is engraved on the US National Archives Building in Washington, D.C. Canadian archivists take pride in the fact that the only statue ever raised in Ottawa to honour a civil servant is that of National Archivist Sir Arthur Doughty, who claimed in 1924 that 'Of all national assets, archives are the most precious. They are the gift of one generation to another, and the extent of our care of them marks the extent of our civilisation' (quoted in Cook, 2009, 171). As Terry Cook (2009) recalls in his essay, 'Remembering the Future', Doughty's words appear on posters and mugs found in many archivists' offices throughout the country. Archival optimism is archivists' joie de vivre, our raison d'être, the fuel that lights our way through the meticulous and difficult labour of archival work. It is the knowledge that we toil for a greater purpose. Derrida might call this *mal d'archive*, but we tend to think of archival work not as a sickness but as a desire to better understand who we are and communicate this knowledge beyond our temporal limits. To return to queer theory, archival optimism aligns with Elizabeth Freeman's (2010) notion that neither pure nostalgia nor a purely futural orientation that depends on forgetting will provide a meaningful or transformative understanding of the present. Rather, archives resist this forgetting as a way of opening up future discussions that require a grappling with the past.

Archival optimism neatly describes the sense that the resources we invest in building and sustaining archives as apparatuses that support archival practices are worthwhile. What this does not do is to actually describe those necessary resources or provide any insight into how communities manage these resources over time. As I've noted in the introduction to this chapter, sustaining a community archives is both a practical challenge and ideological exercise. The remaining discussion will dig deeper into these challenges and return to the concept of archival optimism to break apart the ways in which sustainability is as much about labour, money and expertise, as it is about managing the sometimes conflicting and always fraught ideas about who constitutes a community, its shared understanding of its history and its desire for a collective future.

Space, money and expertise

The practical challenges that impact the sustainability of community archives do not vary significantly from those of other cultural heritage institutions. Community archives require space, whether this is physical or virtual or, more likely, a combination of both. At a minimum, they need some financial investment to support the purchase of archival supplies and other technologies, as well as operational costs. In addition, community archives require an investment of human resources with a variety of expertise – archiving is a labour-intensive practice and making collections available requires yet another kind of labour and skill set. Space, money and expertise are therefore a trifecta of necessary resources that need to be carefully managed and delicately balanced in the event that one is more easily acquired than another. An archiving initiative that is well funded, for example, but lacks expertise, can result in collecting practices that are unsustainable beyond its early stages. Expertise alone is not enough to sustain an archives, which requires capital to support its operations and collecting practices as well as space to keep collections. In this section, I will offer a brief discussion of how these practical challenges have been understood by community archives and some of the strategies that these organisations have developed to cope with these challenges.

Finding and maintaining dedicated space for archival work is an important and ongoing task for community archives. As Diana K. Wakimoto, Debra L. Hansen and Christine Bruce (2013) note in their article 'The Case of LLACE: challenges, triumphs, and lessons of a community archives', research on community archives has found that these initiatives tend to be established when there is a real or perceived failure on the part of traditional collecting institutions to adequately and accurately reflect the experience of the community. As a result, many community archives are established in spaces that reside outside of the recognised archival system, for example in community centres, bookstores, private homes or academic offices, or carve out space in existing institutions. The Lavender Library, Archives and Cultural Exchange (LLACE), for example, considered working with the Sacramento Public Library before its founders established an independent space on B Street in Sacramento, California.

Danielle Cooper's (2017) dissertation work on LGBT collecting organisations describes several examples of archives that have started in homes as personal collections but have since grown into important community organisations. She suggests that even archives that start as self-documentation projects signify a 'commitment to collecting personal records and artifacts towards wider societal benefit' (Cooper, 2017, 83). The ArQuives: Canada's LGBTQ2+ Archives (formerly the Canadian Lesbian and Gay Archives) was founded in the back room of a bookstore run by co-founder Jearld Moldenhauer, who also co-founded the community news magazine The Body Politic (Sheffield, 2015). Much has been written about the founding of the Lesbian Herstory Archives (LHA) in the home of co-founder Joan Nestle (Thistlethwaite, 1998; Corbman, 2014; Cooper, 2017). Situating archival practices within a domestic environment was not only a consequence of practicality – founders and 'archivettes' could work on collections in a comfortable environment after their paid work or on weekends – but this decision also aligned with the LHA's political stance as a non-institutional archives. Today, the LHA resides in a home in Park Slope, Brooklyn, that is always occupied by a live-in caretaker who is responsible for day-to-day activities such as turning on the lights, collecting mail and answering the phone.

Wakimoto, Hansen and Bruce (2013) note that uncertainty about access to or suitability of facilities can have a great impact on the capacity of a community archives to sustain its momentum and thrive. A recent crisis at the Sexual Minority Archives demonstrates the extent to which precarious space can impact the sustainability of a community archives. The archives, which operated out of a rented home in Northampton, Massachusetts, for more than four decades, was nearly shut down completely when the homeowners decided to sell the property (*The Rainbow Times*, 2017). After a successful fundraising campaign, the archives and its curator, Ben Powers, were able to find a new home for the collections a few miles away in the city of Holyoke.

My own research on the development of the history of the June L. Mazer Lesbian Archives uncovered similar struggles to secure dedicated and adequate space for its collection (Sheffield, 2015). The archives was established in the home of co-founder Cherrie Cox, near San Francisco, California, but later moved to Los Angeles when the collections outgrew the space and capacity of volunteers. At the time, the energies of the local lesbian community were focused on the AIDS epidemic and most community spaces had been dedicated to the care of those living with AIDS or activities aimed at mitigating the outbreak of the disease. As a result, an archives that started as a way to document the activities of Bay Area lesbians was removed from its originating community and re-imagined as a Southern California collecting institution.

For many grassroots community archives, financial investment also remains a key challenge. If archival practices remain small in scope, they may continue self-funded by participants. As Wakimoto, Hansen and Bruce note, the LLACE operated without a budget for some time, relying mostly on small donations from community members or volunteers who would 'chip in' to buy necessary supplies to catalogue and house the materials that they collected (2013, 445). As a long-term volunteer at the ArQuives, I found myself picking up supplies or paying for photocopying on behalf of the archives without any expectation that I would be reimbursed. Many other volunteers did the same. As community archives grow, however, they will need to seek out broader community support. Research on lesbian and gay archives reveals a variety of community fundraising tactics aimed at supporting the archives (Sheffield, 2015). These include 50/50 tickets sold at bars and clubs, ticketed events such as concerts or dances, or donations from more mature community organisations. The ArQuives, for example, relied heavily on financial support from Pink Triangle Press, which published *The Body Politic*, and often gave the archives free space for its work. That community members would support an archival project through personal and business donations shows the extent to which the broader community values documentary heritage and believes in the work of the archives. Community fundraising is also an exercise in archival optimism, especially when archivists take money from community members who do not directly participate in the archives, but who see the value of this work for those involved and for an imagined collective future.

Relying on community members to 'chip in' is nevertheless risky, as support may be unpredictable or unreliable over time. One sustainability strategy adopted by several long-standing community archives has been to formalise as a non-profit charity. This allows the archives to access financial resources, such as the United Way and employee contribution matching, and the ability to issue tax receipts for cash and in-kind donations. The capacity to issue tax receipts is designed to encourage support for such organisations; however, the process of becoming recognised as a charity usually requires that the archives incorporate with a structured governance system and published set of by-laws. There is also a lengthy application process that is not always successful. Not all community archives will mature to the point that they are able to formalise in this way.

In other instances, a community's approach to archival practices may not be appropriate for a more bureaucratic structure on its own or without another supporting structure, for example oral history projects and storytelling through blogs. Perhaps more significantly, communities that engage in archiving as an explicitly political project may find that the restrictions imposed by revenue agencies for the purpose of maintaining charitable status hamper or in some cases contradict the mission or spirit of the archives. Depending on the jurisdiction, for example, charities may be explicitly prohibited from engaging in political activities, including lobbying efforts or supporting partisan causes.

Still, acquiring charitable status has been fruitful for some community archives. Formalising also has benefits by demonstrating stability and creating a sense of governance transparency and accountability of the organisation to the community it serves. To succeed as charities, community archives must also develop thoughtful, productive fundraising strategies that provide a good return-on-investment for donors. This is often challenging for community archives, which tend to lack expertise in fundraising or managing development programs. Fundraising also takes away human resources from other archival tasks, such as processing and providing reference services.

Over the past two decades, and alongside the proliferation of digital technologies, many communities have adopted online spaces to engage in archival practices. For emerging and/or marginalised communities, the use of online spaces can remove some of the barriers to collecting that exist for physical collections (Ormond-Parker and Sloggett, 2012). Data stored on hard drives require less real estate and can be more easily integrated into personal homes or other community spaces without causing too much physical disruption. Records can also be stored in the cloud using any number of digital platforms, such as hosted Omeka or Mukurtu sites. Virtual or digital archives can also meet the needs of communities that are increasingly geographically dispersed and facilitate entirely new forms of outreach and reference engagements.

Two archival projects, the Digital Transgender Archives (DTA) and the Archives of Lesbian Oral Testimony (ALOT), exist primarily online, offering digitised and born-digital collections in an open-access platform accessible through any internet-enabled device. Anthony Cocciolo (2014) warns, however, that digital space is also precarious and, more often than not, communities that leverage free or low-cost digital technologies risk losing their work if and when the technologies fail or become obsolete. Communities have to not only consider the sustainability of their archival practices, but also the platforms on which this work is done. KJ Rawson (2013), founder of the DTA, also acknowledges that, although the public facing archives is wholly digital, the work of digitising analogue materials, managing digital records, and making these available on the web is done at a laboratory space provided by the College of the Holy Cross, where Rawson is appointed as an associate professor. Likewise, ALOT is provided server space by Simon Fraser University, where director Elise Chenier is a professor in the Department of History (2010). ALOT also employs a grant-funded project archivist, who requires desk space within the university library.

The relationships between DTA and ALOT and their respective host institutions demonstrate the extent to which an academic apparatus can provide some infrastructural and financial support to community archives. Faculty members can potentially adopt existing IT infrastructure and take advantage of staff support if available. They can also access grants and other funding opportunities to help support archival projects, assuming that this activity is relevant to their academic research. Reliance on academic labour raises additional concerns about the sustainability of hosted projects beyond the capacities of their faculty champions (see Mercado, 2013; Chenier, 2010). After all, it is unclear how the archives would continue if either Chenier or Rawson were to step back from their respective roles.

Whether tied to a research agenda or not, archival labour is difficult to sustain. Cataloguing materials and developing access tools take time and effort that can be mundane and tedious. Working with the members of a community to document shared experiences and/or identify important documentary heritage requires additional dedication of resources. This kind of labour can be exhilarating. Caswell et al. (2017) found that community archives founders, volunteers and staff tend to feel excluded from and/or misrepresented by mainstream collecting institutions. As a result, the labour that they contribute to building a more representative archives results in significant positive impacts. The experience of 'seeing oneself in history' actually produces an ontological change in those that participate in the archives, by creating a sense of solidarity with those who share their own history and heritage (Caswell et al., 2017, 17).

Archival work also produces collections of records that have symbolic and affective value that affirms and validates personal and community identities. In addition, contributing to archival work has a social impact that brings together a group of people through their engagement with the archives, but also because archives reveal social connections between and among people documented in the records. Caswell et al. (2017) describe the positive benefits of archival labour as three dimensional, 'I am here,' 'we were here' and 'we belong here,' all overlapping to create a sense of representational belonging (Caswell et al., 2017, 5). This understanding of archival labour as having immediate benefits for those undertaking this work complements the idea of archival optimism, which might provide a fourth future oriented dimension, 'we have hope for our future'.

While much archival labour might be described as pleasurable, working with records of your own community – particularly when this community has experienced trauma or marginalisation – can produce a range of negative impacts as well. Returning to the concept of archival optimism, archival work might be described as a 'labour of love', an expenditure of physical and affective labour for the benefit of an imagined future community. Nevertheless, this work might be undervalued by the very community it purports to represent. Community expectations also change over time or differ from those participating in the archives. As Rabia Gibbs (2012) reminds us, communities are not homogenous and, even within self-identified groups, there is the potential that some members will continue to feel marginalised, a sustainability concern that is the focus of the next section of this chapter. Even if the work is compensated or valued, it can be difficult to sustain because of the emotional burden that it creates.

Anna St. Onge (2016) has pointed to the work of Cathy Caruth (and others) who have written about the ways in which archivists are affected by their exposure to records that document difficult histories, issues of marginalisation and traumatic experiences, even if these experiences are not shared by the archivists themselves. This exposure results in vicarious trauma and can reduce capacity to engage in archival practices or even bring about the complete burnout of archivists if not addressed and managed appropriately. Although St. Onge is focused on the experiences of professional archivists, her work resonates with community archivists as well, many of whom work with records that document trauma within their own communities and where the emotional impact is at least one degree closer to the individual. Caswell and Cifor (2016) have advocated for the incorporation of a feminist ethics of care that repositions archivists as 'caregivers, bound to records creators, subjects, users, and communities through a web of mutual affective responsibility' (23). Even with this shift in thinking about archival work as having an emotional or affective component and the development of methods to recognise risk factors for vicarious trauma, sustaining archival practices can take a toll on those involved.

Sustaining momentum through challenging times

If archival optimism is the thread that draws communities together to engage in archival practices, even against the odds, what happens when communities pull apart? What if a community begins to recognise, through the changing present, that its future may not unfold in ways previously imagined? José Esteban Muñoz (2009) warns us that the 'future is only the stuff of some kids' (95). In other words, the most visible demographic assume that the future will be populated by those who look like them and think like them, that they will share similar experiences and desires, that they will want to archive the same kinds of records with the same tools and interpret existing collections in anticipated ways. As society changes, however, so do the communities that engage in archival practices. One approach to archiving can give way to another. This transition not only signifies a change in technological and cultural sensibilities, but also in the coalescing dynamics of the community that originally led to the establishment of the archival project. Thus, while archives are material in the sense that they preserve records that inform us, they are simultaneously rhetorical projects that persuade, affect and impress upon us what past generations want us to know about them. In an effort to sustain these projects across generations, communities must develop strategies to negotiate changing community culture, priorities and goals. In addition to material resources, communities must take efforts to sustain their archives as rhetorical projects amidst ideological and philosophical crises. How do these crises and our responses to them impact our community archival practices? How can community archives serve as spaces where voices from the past, present and future are simultaneously alive and speak to one another for the purposes of expansive transformation? For the remaining section of this chapter, I will offer some additional insight into the immaterial ways in which community archives have sustained themselves over time.

One of the ways to respond to changes in community expectations is to embrace the archival practices that are under scrutiny with an even tighter grasp. While on one hand reinforcing long established approaches to collecting can be seen as digging ones heels in or refusing to acknowledge emerging and sometimes conflicting community identities, cleaving to the practices that originated with the founders and champions of the archives can also provide some clarity around the goals of the larger project. Michelle Caswell (2014) draws from Guayatri Spivak to argue that communities often organise around identity-based categories, such as race, ethnicity, sexuality and gender expression. Archives established within the context of such identities draw strength from a practice of strategic essentialism, which supports political action by creating solidarity through a shared heritage. The danger, Caswell warns, is that the benefits of strategic essentialism rely on coherent categories of identity that are 'contingent and that very often they have been constructed and imposed by the powerful' (41). She goes on to explain that the paradox of strategic essentialism is that 'our deployment of these [identity] categories for discrete political goals must ultimately seek their dismantling' (41).

Caswell's warning resonates with the work of the LHA, which was established as a way to provide a safe space for lesbian women to deposit their records and for lesbians to access a documentary heritage that provided a sense of representational belonging. Although the archives is open to all visitors, its collecting practices and programming remains focused on the needs of lesbians. Yet, the category of lesbian does not necessarily describe the myriad expressions of sexuality and gender identity that have emerged since the LHA's founding in 1974. Rather than amend their collecting practices, LHA's coordinators continue to collect records by, for and about lesbians with the understanding that, at some point in the imagined future, the socio-political and economic systems may change enough to make it no longer necessary for lesbian women to require a separate safe space for their documentary heritage. In other words, the LHA operates only as long as it is needed for a community of people who identify as lesbians, a category that the LHA has, in part, helped to define. The sustainability mechanism of the LHA is, in fact, its imagined end.

Maintaining a focus on a particular identity category is not always a successful strategy for community archives, nor does it encourage horizontal participation from those who feel excluded from this identity. While at the ArQuives, I came to understand the work of collecting and organising records as a social activity much like a form of crafting. As David Gauntlett (2011) has argued, crafting can be a way for communities to create a sense of shared identity as individuals work together to make something. In the case of the ArQuives, people came together to make an archives. Collecting practices were generally undertaken by a small group of dedicated volunteers, mostly white, cis-gay men, who conducted their work in routines developed over time and with particular meaning to this group. Even though the ArQuives was envisioned as a community space, its collecting practices reflected and privileged, what Elizabeth Kaplan (2000) has called, the 'self-perceptions, aspirations, divisions and anxieties' of its founders and champions (127). Like knitting or quilting, archival practices might be passed along to newcomers who will incorporate their own traditions and develop entirely new approaches to community documentation. This assumes, however, that newcomers feel welcomed and valued within the archives, even if they do not ascribe to any of the foregrounded identity categories. Even the name of the organisation could be perceived as alienating to a younger generation. The ArQuives, which was known for nearly two decades as the Canadian Lesbian and Gay Archives, only changed its name in 2019 in response to pressure from those who do not identify as lesbian or gay, and from trans and non-binary folks who do not always see their own experiences reflected in the archives. Considering this history, the ArQuives has tended to attract a homophilous community of volunteers, unintentionally complicit in the reification of particular identity categories through the sublimation of others. At the time of this writing, it is too early to assess the impact of the name change.

The homophily that persists at the ArQuives is not unique. Kaplan (2000) surveyed the archival practices at the American Jewish Historical Society (AJHS) and found that, much like the ArQuives, the organisation was established as a way to gather together documents to help construct a coherent community identity. In bringing together documentary evidence of Jewish life in the United States, the AJHS validated a very particular ethnic identity, even though founders were aware of the vast differences among, for example, those who had emigrated from Germany and those who came from other parts of Europe. In addition, founders recognised the impact of socio-economic class and language differences among Jewish Americans. Collecting practices nevertheless obscure many of these differences. Much like Caswell (2014), Kaplan recognises that a coherent albeit essentialist identity can be used strategically to attain particular political goals. At the same time, Kaplan calls on archivists to recognise the impact that this essentialism has on our collections whereby we end up collecting what we are and becoming what we collect. For identity-based archives that attract participation from community members with similar approaches to archival practices, essentialist collecting can produce a kind of archival homophily, which is difficult to overcome. If collections continue to highlight the interests of some and underrepresent others, those who do not see themselves reflected in the records may also see little value in the community archival practices as a whole.

The strength of a coherent identity supported by a community archives suffers from, what Berlant calls, cruel optimism. To put this into alignment with the notion of archival optimism, cruel optimism is a product of 'optimistic attachments' to practices that have been successful in the past and continue to be fruitful in the present, but which cannot be sustained into the future because they make it impossible to achieve the kind of expansive transformation that is the ultimate goal of the project (Berlant, 2011, 2). For community archives developed around a particular identity, cruel optimism manifests through those homophilous practices that have contributed to material improvements for the community, but through which transformative change is not possible. An archives established in the wake of the gay liberation movement, for example, will struggle to meet the needs of a contemporary queer community who does not necessarily see themselves reflected through the archives, despite benefitting from its existence.

Archivists have already started to brush up against the problems of cruel optimism. Christine N. Paschild (2012) found that the efforts spent on grappling with community identities can distract from the practical work required to actually create, manage and make accessible a collection of archival records. While she does not eschew the idea that community archival practices can enhance connections between and among members of this community, she questions the usefulness of identity as a unifying concept. In her discussion of the Japanese American National Museum (JANM), Paschild draws from Brubaker and Cooper, who argue that there are limits to the utility of identity as a social construct. She writes that, the 'stretching of identity has impoverished the term of all usefulness' because it conflates affinities and affiliations that would otherwise be 'infinitely elastic' into a hard shell of identity that has the potential to set up entirely new forms of exclusionary practices (133). She also notes that the ways in which identity is typically used 'emphasises a theoretical position that is constructed and relative but consistently and firmly located within the actual marginalised communities with the most at stake in resistive or interventional action' (133).

As a result, the construction of a shared heritage based on community identity rarely allows for recognition of diversity within the community and, furthermore, does little to challenge the marginalisation that continues to occur. If the community does achieve some or all of its discrete political goals, those members who feel most aligned with a central identity may no longer need such a hard shell. If the archival practices have grown up around this identity, however, and resist intervention and re-imagining, they may become unsustainable. At one end of the spectrum, marginalised communities may not be able to sustain collections because they lack the practical and ideological resources to do so; at the other end, communities that have become increasingly status quo may find that their practices create collections that are so extensive that they require care beyond their capacities.

One possible way to move beyond cruel optimism is for community archives to focus less on the product of archival work and more on collective practices. In this way, community archives become spaces where past, present and future intersect, and where making and connecting in the present is foregrounded. This focus can also open up possibilities of developing practices and programming that actually confront the archives' own gaps and biases and which acknowledges community diversity without devaluing the important work of those who have come before. This programming might include, for example, workshops and healing circles where those who feel excluded from archival practices are encouraged to occupy the archives and speak about the impact of this exclusion and where community archivists agree to listen without reacting. More formalised community archives can also issue open calls for volunteers to serve in governance roles and encourage participation from younger and underrepresented community members by providing paid internships and structured mentorship. Archivists might also offer expertise or space to emerging communities who would not otherwise participate in established archival practices, without expectations that records produced by these communities will be integrated into the larger collections. Most importantly, community archivists must acknowledge that, as their practices and collections develop over time, they may actually become status quo, a consequence of changes to the socio-political and economic systems that adapt to include particular identities while further marginalising others. These others may not be willing or even interested in picking up the torch and carrying it forward.

Conclusion: archival optimism beyond community

So what happens when no one is willing to pick up the torch? Or the identity at the centre of archival practices becomes so fraught that it can no longer coherently support political goals? One possibility is that the archives ceases to exist. Collections are left in basements or to degrade in the hands of community members. Another possibility is that the archives develop some nimbleness in their programming, incorporating a present perspective in addition to the typical past and future perspectives. At the ArQuives, archival optimism has been fueled by the fear that histories of gay men and lesbians can and have been erased from our documentary culture. The founding members of the archives were acutely aware that a flourishing homosexual community in Weimar Germany had been rendered forgotten by the Nazi regime until it was rediscovered in the early 1970s through oral histories and the meticulous reconstruction of documentary heritage (Sheffield, 2015). This fear of erasure produced an urgency among community archivists who brought together documentation of their own experiences to preserve for future generations so that this kind of history would never be lost again. Until recently, this anti-fascist collecting frenzy seemed not only outdated but also rather quaint in a contemporary Canada, where many political leaders proudly participate in pride parades and human rights for gay men and lesbians are enshrined in law. In order to attract new investment in the archives, the ArQuives has been creative: producing gallery programs, partnering with elementary teachers to support public school curriculum, delivering historical walking tours and hosting a variety of community events that broaden the archives' appeal beyond its collections to its symbolic position as the authority on LGBTQ history. The ArQuives has also grown its financial support beyond the community to earn provincial and federal grants, secure investment from major banks and other corporate funders so that it is now able to employ a full-time executive director and archivist. How long the ArQuives will be able to adequately care for its collections without infrastructural support from an academic institution or public archives is unknown at this time, but it is clear that the organisation is now too big and too important to the Canadian archival system to simply allow the torch to be dropped.

Perhaps the most optimistic view of sustainable community archiving practices is that they will continue to unfold in ways that make the most sense and have the greatest benefit for those who undertake them. If this is true, however, it also suggests that community archives are only sustainable insofar as they are meaningful to the people who support them. To aid this conclusion, it may be helpful to distinguish between community archival practices and the collections of records these practices create. While practices occur in the present and can be altered and enriched to support the needs of a dynamic community, the records produced by these practices might not be so mutable. While it might be understood that our interpretation and use of these records change over time, the Western approach to archiving is inclined toward a stasis form of preservation in which records are kept as long as possible in the context and structure in which they are created, thus enhancing their trustworthiness over time. This non-indigenous approach to recorded or documentary heritage is contrary to an indigenous worldview that, according to David Throsby and Ekaterina Petetskaya, considers both the process and the knowledge created through this process as part of the preservation of heritage (2016, 119–140).

If sustainability is the goal of community archiving practices, then the product of these practices might actually prove a burden to sustainability. In other words, to sustain connecting and making, the community might have to give up some of its crafts to make room for new ones. This is where community archives and the traditional or mainstream archival system might diverge in both practice and philosophy.

Elizabeth Crooke (2010) has argued that community heritage organisations tend to diverge in practices and composition but appear to share a desire to remain autonomous and to maintain heritage without the intervention of the mainstream heritage sector. At the same time, Mary Stevens and Andrew Flinn (2010) have suggested that, although community archivists share a desire to control the ways in which they engage in archival practices, this does not preclude a need to partner with a larger or more robust institution to ensure that these practices can sustain themselves over time. Stevens and Flinn anticipate the work of Chenier and Rawson, developing community archives within the auspices of academic institutions, and they also open the door for new kinds of partnerships that community archives might pursue to ensure that their collections are well managed.

In 2009, the June L. Mazer Lesbian Archives entered a partnership with UCLA to hand over more than 90 archival collections to be digitised, housed and made accessible to researchers through the university's library system (McHugh, 2014). The donation of collections was, in part, to ensure that they would be stewarded for future generations, but also to open up more space at the Mazer's West Hollywood location to continuing engaging in community archival practices. Handing materials over to a repository designed for the care of archival records actually allows the community archives to sustain its practices while at the same time ensuring the survival of the collections these practices have produced over time. While no one would deny the value of the records themselves, the Mazer's champions have made the conscious decision to foreground archival practices in the present as a way to remain meaningful to those who continue to find value in the archives. Although some may perceive the process of integrating community-build collections into a larger repository as assimilationist, it may also be part of a transformational goal to intervene on a documentary heritage that has previously excluded, obfuscated or censored this community. Wherever the collections end up, the practices that surround them can continue to develop, shaped by socio-political and economic structures and, most importantly, the interests and affinities that bring communities together in the first place.

References

Berlant, L. (2011) *Cruel Optimism*, Duke University Press.

Bersani, L. (1987) Is the Rectum a Grave?, *October*, **43**, 197–222.

Bersani, L. and Phillips, A. (2008) *Intimacies*, University of Chicago Press.

Caswell, M. (2014) Inventing New Archival Imaginaries: theoretical foundations for identity-based archives. In Daniel, D. and Levi, A. S. (eds), *Identity Palimpsest: archiving ethnicity in the U.S. and Canada*, Litwin Books.

Caswell, M. and Cifor, M. (2016) From Human Rights to Feminist Ethics: radical empathy in the archives, *Archivaria*, **81** (1), 23–43.

Caswell, M., Mignoli, A. A., Geraci, N. and Cifor, M. (2017) 'To Be Able to Imagine Otherwise': community archives and the importance of representation, *The Journal of the Archives and Records Association*, **38** (1), 5–26.

Chenier, E. (2010) Hidden from Historians: preserving lesbian oral history in Canada, *Archivaria*, **68**, 247–269.

Cocciolo, A. (2014) *Youth Deleted: saving young people's histories after social media collapse*, International Internet Preservation Consortium General Assembly, 19–23 May 2014, Paris, France. www.thinkingprojects.org/youth_deleted_iipc.pdf.

Cook, T. (2009) Remembering the Future: appraisal of records and the role of archives in constructing social memory. In Blouin, Jr, F. X. and Rosenberg, W. G. (eds), *Archives, Documentation and Institutions of Social Memory: essays from the Sawyer Seminar*, University of Michigan Press.

Cooper, D. (2017) Personal Touches, Public Legacies: an ethnography of LGBT libraries and archives, Dissertation, University of York.

Corbman, R. F. (2014) A Genealogy of the Lesbian Herstory Archives, 1974–2014, *Journal of Contemporary Archival Studies*, **1** (1). https://elischolar.library.yale.edu/jcas/vol1/iss1/1

Crooke, E. (2010) The Politics of Community Heritage: Motivations, Authority and Control, *International Journal of Heritage Studies*, **16** (1–2), 16–29.

Edelman, L. (2004) *No Future: queer theory and the death drive*, Duke University Press.

Esteban Muñoz, J. (2009) *Cruising Utopia: the then and there of queer futurity*, New York University Press.

Freeman, E. (2010) *Time Binds: queer temporalities, queer histories*, Duke University Press.

Gauntlett, D. (2011) *Making is Connecting: the social meaning of creativity from DIY and knitting to YouTube and Web 2.0*, Polity Press.

Gibbs, R. (2012) The Heart of the Matter: the developmental history of African American archives, *The American Archivist*, **75** (1), 195–204.

Kaplan, E. (2000) We Are What We Collect, We Collect What We Are: archives and the construction of identity, *The American Archivist*, **63** (1) (2000), 126–151.

McHugh, K.A. (2014) Preserving the legacy of lesbian feminist activism and writing in Los Angeles. In McHugh, K.A., Johnson-Grau, B. and Sher, B. (eds), *Making invisible histories visible: A resource guide to the collections of the June L. Mazer Lesbian Archives*, UCLA Center for the Study of Women.

Mercado, M. L. (2013) *On Equal Terms? The Stakes of Archiving Women's and LGBT History in the Digital Era,* Women's History in the Digital World, 35, https://repository.brynmawr.edu/cgi/viewcontent.cgi?article=1035&context=greenfield_conference.

Nestle, J. (2003) *A Restricted Country*, Cleis Press.

Ormond-Parker, L. and Sloggett, R. (2012) Local Archives and Community Collecting in the Digital Age, *Archival Science*, **12** (2), 191–212.

Paschild, C. N. (2012) Community Archives and the Limitations of Identity: considering discursive impact on material needs, *The American Archivist*, **75** (1), 125–142.

Rawson, K. J. (2013) Rhetorical History 2.0: toward a digital transgender archive, *Enculturation*, **16** (9), http://enculturation.net/toward_digital_transgender_archive.

Sheffield, R. (2015) The Emergence, Development and Survival of Four Lesbian and Gay Archives, Dissertation, University of Toronto.

Stevens, M. and Flinn, A. (2010) New Frameworks for Community Engagement in the Archive Sector: from handing over to handing on, *International Journal of Heritage Studies*, **16** (1–2), 59–76.

St.Onge, A., Holland, J. and Robichaud, D. (2016) *It's Nothing, I'm Fine: acknowledging emotion and affect in archival practice*, The Archives Association of Ontario annual conference, Thunder Bay, Ontario, 13 May 2016, https://yorkspace.library.yorku.ca/xmlui/handle/10315/31366.

The Rainbow Times (2017) *Sexual Minorities Archives Celebrate Grand Re-Opening at New Home in Holyoke*, https://www.therainbowtimesmass.com/

sexual-minorities-archives-celebrate-grand-re-opening-new-home-holyoke.

Thistlethwaite, P. J. (1998) 'A Home of Our Own': the construction of the Lesbian Herstory Archives. In Carmichael, Jr, J. V. (ed.), *Daring to Find Our Names: the search for lesbigay library history*, Greenwood Press.

Throsby, D. and Petetskaya, E. (2016) Sustainability Concepts in Indigenous and Non-Indigenous Cultures, *International Journal of Cultural Property*, **23** (2), 119–140.

Wakimoto, D. K., Hansen, D. L. and Bruce, C. (2013) The Case of LLACE: challenges, triumphs, and lessons of a community archives, *The American Archivist*, **76** (2), 438–457.

CHAPTER 2

Affective bonds: what community archives can teach mainstream institutions

Michelle Caswell

Within an archive you're throwing in all this raw material that for generations afterward can be used to make new meanings, to make new words, to have new definitions of certain experiences, certain identities, that if you don't get in there will just be lost forever . . . Having worked as an oral historian before, for me the most concrete thing that I could see . . . what mattered most, was for someone to realize that as ordinary as they thought their experience was, as regular they thought their life history has been, say the person was female, the person was low caste, the person has never been asked by their husband or any male in their family, 'What mattered to you? Why did you remember this?' . . . For many of them, for a little American boy to come ask them, 'What happened to you when you had to leave home?' 'How did that feel?' And to have that second of recognition, and of value for their story in and of itself, as an end, was incredible to experience, and also, the way that they would react was infectious and the way that their daughter would join and start chipping in her own part of the story. And the daughter would ask her own questions, the daughter would ask things she didn't know about her mother, and all of the sudden, you have the whole family there asking grandma about all of these things. And all of the sudden I'm like, outside of the space, I'm still the oral historian sitting back in my chair and watching the discussion that has unfolded around grandma, but the idea of an archive I've now left behind with this family, that now values asking grandma, maybe a difficult question, maybe about something that's kind of traumatic, but knowing that she has something to share, and has wanted to share for a long time, but nobody has ever asked her…. That's something that's infectious, and propagates through society, propagates through groups, it doesn't matter if I have the high minded goal of the archive expanding the breadth of South Asian experience, and how we define it in America, it's more important to get to 10–15 people in the course of a year, and have those people go out and ask other people their stories and communicate their stories and feel that the stories are worth sharing.

(Zain Alam, musician/former oral historian, 1947 Partition Archive)

Introduction

In a 2014 article in *Archival Science*, I identified five key principles that distinguish community-based archives from their mainstream counterparts: participation, shared stewardship, multiplicity, archival activism and reflexivity (Caswell, 2014a). Building both on Gilliland's work recognising the importance of emotion in formulating community archives (2014) and Cifor's work on affect theory (2016), this chapter names an additional principle – that of *valuing affect* – and delineates how, through their appraisal and outreach strategies, community archives value the affective impact of records on the communities they serve and represent.

Drawing on my experiences as a co-founder, former board member and volunteer archivist for the South Asian American Digital Archive (SAADA) (www.saada.org), this chapter uses the organisation's 2016–2017 project Where We Belong: Artists in the Archive (SAADA, 2017a), as its primary site to investigate how community archives value affective impact in their appraisal and outreach practices. In this regard, this piece builds theory through thick description enabled by participant observation of a single case. At the same time, it is important to acknowledge that the case study examined is situated physically, socially, culturally and politically within a specific community within the United States; the author wishes to make no claims of generalisability, particularly across international lines, and is curious about the degree to which the assertions from this study resonate with or diverge from other cases in other communities in other contexts.

Within archival studies, the past decade has seen an increase in interest in identity-based community archives, that is, spaces (both physical and digital) where individuals and communities that have been oppressed due to white supremacy, capitalism, hetero-patriarchy and/or ableism take it upon themselves to document their shared history. As my prior research posited, these identity-based community archives counter the symbolic annihilation of marginalised groups and have a tremendous affective impact, asserting a sense of belonging for groups who have been placed on the margins (Caswell, Cifor and Ramirez, 2016). Such symbolic annihilation occurs because mainstream archives have, by and large, focused on documenting elitist history at the expense of people of colour, white women and LGBTQ people.

At the same time, many archivists working for mainstream, predominantly white American institutions lament their failure to attract members of marginalised communities as users of archives. Yet, as this chapter argues, mainstream archives will continue to attract only those users from dominant groups unless significant efforts are launched to change top-down appraisal and outreach practices. This chapter contends that mainstream archives have much to learn from community archives practices and discourses, namely a shift in attention to the affective or emotional impact of archival appraisal and outreach practices on marginalised communities.

After a brief overview of literature on community archives and affect, this chapter traces how affect was a primary consideration in a single community-based archives project, using the experience of working with SAADA as a lens through which to develop theory on affect and community archives. I then suggest ways in which mainstream archives can learn to value the affective impact of archival work on marginalised communities. I posit first that mainstream archives should consider the affective value of representation in records when making appraisal decisions, that is, factoring in the ways in which records emotionally resonate with marginalised groups. This recommendation diverges significantly from standard appraisal practices that rely on documenting functions or evidential values rather than emotional impact in users. Secondly, I argue that outreach strategies that explicitly value affect, as first developed by community archives, can be employed by mainstream institutions to break down barriers, repair extractive colonialist legacies and smash narrow conceptions of archival users that prioritise academics over community members. While acknowledging that community-based practices are diverse and best seen as a continuum rather than as a clear break from mainstream practice, I conclude with an assertion that both types of institutions are crucial for ending oppressive representations of marginalised communities in archives.

Community archives and affect: definitions and literature review

While notions of community are always context-dependent, Flinn, Stevens and Shepherd (2009) define community as 'any manner of people who come together and present themselves as such, and a "community archive" is the product of their attempts to document the history of their commonality' (75). Adding to this definition, I posit that 'marginalised identity-based community archives' is a more accurate term because it distinguishes those archives coalescing around a marginalised identity from other organisations, such as more traditional neighborhood-based historical societies, which often arise from the desires of dominant groups to preserve their power (Caswell, 2014b). Power – who has it and who does not, historically and contemporarily – is central to this definition; it is only groups who have been left out of, misrepresented in, and disempowered by mainstream historical practices who form community archives (Caswell, 2012). In this way, the most accurate term to describe the phenomenon of interest is, in fact, 'marginalised identity-based community archives', yet, given how unwieldy this term is, this chapter will use the less precise 'community archives' as a stand in. Such archival communities can materialise around marginalised ethnic, racial or religious identities (Kaplan, 2000; Daniel, 2010; Caswell, 2014b), gender and sexual orientation (Barriault, 2009; Sheffield, 2015), economic status (Flinn and Stevens, 2009) and physical location, when such location is closely associated with marginalised identity (Flinn and Stevens, 2009).

These community archives are framed as grassroots alternatives to mainstream repositories through which communities can make collective decisions about what is of enduring value to them, shape collective memory of their own past and control the means through which stories about their past are constructed. In maintaining varying degrees of independence and encouraging participation, these archives strive to provide a platform in which previously marginalised groups are empowered to make decisions about archival collecting on their own terms. Flinn, Stevens and Shepherd (2009) found that political activism, community empowerment and social change were prime motivating factors for those who volunteer at these organisations.

In this chapter, I suggest that the differences between community archives and mainstream institutions are seen less as hard-and-fast boundaries and more as a permeable continuum of distinguishing values and practices (Caswell, 2014a). As such, mainstream institutions can learn from, incorporate and exhibit community-based archival values and practices if they actively strategise to do so. Furthermore, such practices and values are always contextual, culturally-dependent and shifting; what one community values or practices in their archives may not be what another community values or practices.

The archival profession and archival studies as an academic field are only now beginning to address this burgeoning community archives phenomenon, with Cook (2013) declaring that the recent emphasis on community constitutes a paradigm shift in the field akin to previous conceptual guideposts like evidence and memory. In the realm of practice, the rise of community archives has meant reframing the functions of appraisal, description and access to align with community-specific priorities, reflect contingent cultural values and allow for greater participation in archival decision-making (Shilton and Srinivasan, 2007; Krause and Yakel, 2007; Huvila, 2008; Caswell, 2012; Caswell, 2014b; Caswell and Mallick, 2014). As Zavala, Migoni, Cifor, Geraci and Caswell (2017) found across sites in Southern California, community archives have compelled shifts in dominant models of practice to reflect community values and agency in archival management, particularly regarding custody, sustainability and governance.

Community-based forms of practice have also led to conceptual challenges being raised in archival theory. For example, Bastian (2003) has suggested expanding the core archival concept of provenance to include descendants of the subjects of records, while Wurl (2005) echoed this theoretical shift by advocating for ethnicity as a form of provenance. The Pluralizing the Archival Curriculum Group (PACG, 2011) called for an incorporation of local and indigenous ways of knowing and being into archival theory and practice in line with community-centric values and practices.

In the 2014 article referenced earlier, I proposed five principles that commonly guide community-based archival work: participation, shared stewardship, multiplicity, archival activism and reflexivity (Caswell, 2014a). These principles draw attention to the ways in which community archives generally encourage participation in archival labour from the communities they serve and represent; conceptualise their relationship to materials as one of mutually responsive caregiving rather than a formal legal transfer of custody; acknowledge multiple and conflicting views, as well as a multiplicity of formats; are explicitly political in orientation; and foster a culture of self-reflection and evaluation. These principles were meant to be flexible, heuristic guideposts rather than universal laws and were, in the case of the article, meant to shape the policies and practices of self-declared 'human rights archives' towards a more 'survivor-centered' archival praxis (Caswell, 2014a).

Recent work has begun to investigate the affective impact of community archives on identity and representation (Caswell, 2014b; Caswell, Cifor and Ramirez, 2016; Caswell et al., 2016). This research leveraged the concept of 'symbolic annihilation' from the field of communications, which describes the ways members of marginalised groups are absent, under-represented or misrepresented by mainstream media and archives (Caswell, 2014b). My research team and I developed a tripartite framework for measuring the impact of community archives: ontological impact (in which members of marginalised communities get confirmation '*I am here*'); epistemological impact (in which members of marginalised communities get confirmation '*we were here*'); and social impact (in which members of marginalised communities get confirmation '*we belong here*') (Caswell, Cifor and Ramirez, 2016). We also proposed the concept of 'representational belonging' to denote the ways in which community archives can empower people who have been marginalised by mainstream media and memory institutions to have the autonomy and authority to establish, enact and reflect on their presence in ways that are complex, meaningful, substantive and positive to them in a variety of symbolic contexts.

Such research builds explicitly on recent groundbreaking work on affect in archival studies. In a 2016 *Archival Science* special issue on affect and archives, Anne Gilliland and Marika Cifor draw on a large body of humanities and social science literature to explore the psychological and physiological responses to records from individuals, communities and archivists. In that same issue, Cifor (2016) posits that a focus on affect and archives catalyses us to consider the body, asserting, 'Affect is a force that creates a relation between a body and the world' (Cifor, 2016, 8). She further explores several cases of feminist and queer communities whose recordkeeping and archiving practices question dominant neoliberal structures by valuing affect. Gilliland's VIA (Voice, Identity, Activism) framework (2014) explicitly names honoring emotions as a hallmark of community archives, which serves as the conceptual starting point of this chapter.

SAADA and the 'Where We Belong: Artists in the Archive' Project

SAADA is a US-based community archives that I co-founded in 2008 with Samip Mallick, who has since served as the organisation's executive director. SAADA documents, preserves and provides access to the rich history of South Asians in the United States. We broadly define South Asian American to include those in the United States who trace their heritage to Bangladesh, India, Nepal, Pakistan, Sri Lanka and the many South Asian diaspora communities across the globe. We have a particular emphasis on collecting materials related to early South Asian immigration to the US, to anti-South Asian race riots, to labour, student and religious organisations, to political involvement, and to artists and intellectuals. We collect materials that are not just celebratory in nature, but reflect the diverse range of South Asian American experiences from the turn of the 20th century to the present.

SAADA is a post-custodial online-only archive and has no central physical location. Volunteers digitise historic materials and collect born-digital sources, describe them in a culturally appropriate manner, link them to related materials in the archives and make them freely accessible online to anyone in the world with an internet connection. After digitisation, the physical materials are returned to and remain with the individual, family, organisation or repository from which they originated.

The organisation has undertaken several projects that aim to uncover and digitise historic materials, generate new records and encourage the use of materials already in the collection. For example, with support from a National Endowment for the Humanities Common Heritage grant, SAADA organised two digitisation day events in the Los Angeles area in 2016 in which community members brought materials to be digitised to pop-up SAADA stations in public libraries. SAADA's participatory First Days Project (www.firstdaysproject.org) encourages immigrants from anywhere in the world to record brief narratives about their first 48 hours in the United States (Caswell and Mallick, 2014). SAADA's Road Trips project (http://roadtrips. saada.org) helps redefine the American road trip by enabling community members to submit photographs and stories about the time they and their families spent travelling across the country by car; such stories of mobility have taken on added significance in the country's current xenophobic climate. Finally, the organisation's magazine *Tides* (www.saada.org/tides) context-ualises the more than 3,000 records in SAADA's collection by publishing articles that draw on, explicate and add layers of meaning to the materials.

As SAADA's collection has grown, staff and board members have been thinking about how best to conduct archival outreach in a post-custodial environment where we have little direct contact with our users and hear only anecdotally about our impact. We are particularly interested in marketing the collection to non-traditional user groups like activists and artists. Inspired by Kathy Carbone's work (2015) on the City of Portland's Archives and Record Center's artist-in-residency program and my own research team's work on symbolic annihilation and South Asian American history (Caswell, Cifor and Ramirez, 2016), SAADA launched the Where We Belong: Artists in the Archive project in 2016 with a generous grant from the Pew Center for Arts and Heritage. The funding enabled us to launch a discovery process whereby we selected five South Asian American artists working across a range of media and genres to create new works of art inspired by records in SAADA. One of the explicit goals of the project was to counter the symbolic annihilation of South Asian Americans by creating new artistic representations that re-contextualise the community's history. After an intensive in-person weekend retreat in October 2016, the five selected artists began working on their pieces, which were then presented to the public at a well-attended daylong event at the Historical Society of Pennsylvania in April 2017.

Following the success of that event and seeking to expand its reach nationally, SAADA staff organised local community gatherings based on the project on 5 August 2017, the fifth anniversary of a white supremacist shooting at a Sikh gurdwara in Oak Creek, Wisconsin. SAADA staff created an easily-accessible event kit for those gatherings (SAADA, 2017b) that represented the works of each of the artists involved in the project, raised key discussion questions linking representation in archives and art with contemporary politics and encouraged participants to create new works of art based on their own experiences with the archives. The event kit was widely publicised on SAADA's website, via SAADA's social media accounts (such as Facebook and

Twitter) and via the organisation's listserv. Participants were encouraged to use the hashtag #wherewebelong to amplify their own discussions. At least 15 groups across the country signed up to engage in these community conversations, which expanded the reach of the Pew-funded project into community members' homes across the country. The project continues to have an afterlife as the organisation explores new ways to engage artists and the artwork created for the program, as well as encourage the ongoing use of the event kit.

Valuing affect in appraisal: the story of the Sharanjit Sing Dhillonn Collection

In Spring 2016, I heard from one of my students in UCLA's media archives program that she was working on digitising some home movie reels for a class project that might be of interest to SAADA. When she sent me a link to the digitised footage, my eyes widened, my jaw dropped and I started jumping up and down with excitement. What I saw on the screen was silent footage of a bearded and turbaned Sikh man marrying a sari-clad white woman in Norman, Oklahoma, in 1959. As I kept watching, I saw 12 years of their daily lives together unfold on the screen: first one baby, then a second; the man, now clean-shaven and devoid of turban, having fun with the children; the children, celebrating birthdays, learning to walk, taking baths, enjoying a coke, sharing an ice cream cone, dressing up like cowboys. In short, I saw what I previously might have considered to be the impossible: everyday footage of South Asian American family life in middle America in the 1950s.

These 40 minutes of footage complicates our understanding of South Asian American history. In 1923, a US Supreme Court decision denaturalised Indian immigrants, barring them from citizenship and causing the once-burgeoning community to return to India. We usually think of the time between 1946, when the Luce-Cellar Act imposed a restrictive 100-person a year quota on Indian immigration, and 1965, when US immigration policies opened up, as being a kind of dead space for the community. The footage shows a previously unknown continuity of South Asian American stories. But even more importantly, in showing South Asians as average Americans in the 1950s and 1960s, the footage invokes a visceral response: we simply never see South Asian Americans depicted in this way on the screen during this time period. It is a representation that catalyses affect.

SAADA's Executive Director, Samip Mallick, also had an emotional reaction to seeing the footage for the first time. 'When I first saw the home movies I was amazed. It felt like I was glimpsing a piece of history that I never thought I would see. I actually hadn't thought that there would be home movies from the South Asian community from that period in time. And seeing these home movies made me wonder what other kinds of materials there must still be out there sitting in someone's basement or attic,' he said, continuing:

> There is something so relatable in the mundane experiences recorded in these home movies. They are the kind of images that you could imagine any family having. Yet, these images are incredibly important, by the very fact that these are the home movies of a turbaned Sikh man and a white woman in Oklahoma during a time when interracial marriages were not just rare, but also illegal in many parts of the country; this was all happening nearly a decade before the U.S. Supreme Court ruled in Loving v. Virginia to prohibit anti-miscegenation laws. So these home movies are not just of great importance to the South Asian American community and its history, but our awareness and knowledge of the diversity of the American experience as well.
>
> (S. Mallick, personal communication, 12 January 2018)

We both knew instantly, and viscerally, we wanted to acquire these records. Of course they fit within the scope of SAADA's collection policy, but the appraisal decision was, above all else, an affective one. In placing value on the way the collection increases the representational belonging of South Asian Americans, SAADA elevates the materials and their place in a larger community.

With the help of my students, we soon tracked down the origins of the footage. The home movies belonged to Bibi Dhillonn, an administrator at UCLA. Her father, Sharanjit Singh Dhillonn, came to the US from India to pursue master's degrees in chemical engineering and mathematics at the University of Oklahoma. In 1958, Sharanjit met his wife, Dorothy, who was also studying at the University of Oklahoma. After their 1959 wedding, the couple had four children, soon moving from Oklahoma to rural California, where Sharanjit got a job as a chemical engineer at Borax. After a racist attack at a gas station, Sharanjit cut his hair and beard and stopped wearing the customary Sikh turban. He was an avid fan of film and photography and an amateur filmmaker.

His daughter, Bibi Dhillonn, had been looking for a way to digitise the three home movie reels her father had left behind in order to share them with her siblings. She reached out to UCLA's Film and Television Department, which referred her to our media archives program. As luck would have it, the student assigned to the project also knew about SAADA's mission and scope. Like many archival collections, this one was acquired through serendipity.

After contacting Bibi, we soon learned that, in addition to the home movie reels, Sharanjit also left behind a scrapbook of photographs and ephemera that document his time at the University of Oklahoma, including records of his founding of the school's first international club, local press coverage that depicted him as 'exotic' and photographs from a harem-themed costume party he organised. Bibi was willing to have these materials included in SAADA and, after she signed our donor agreement form, I organised a group of UCLA students to quickly digitise the scrapbook and describe the materials, which are now freely available in SAADA (www.saada.org/collection/sharanjit-singh-dhillonn-materials).

Valuing affect in outreach

In October 2016, at the initial meeting of the artists selected to participate in SAADA's Where We Belong project, the musician Zain Alam discussed the type of records he was interested in engaging for the project. Alam, an artist who composes under the recording project Humeysha, a graduate student at Harvard and a South Asian American Muslim, is no stranger to archives, having worked for a year at the 1947 Partition Archives collecting oral histories about the division of India and Pakistan. He explained:

> I think one of the things that has always attracted me most about archives, the archives of social and personal histories, is that beyond the image of archives being these vast repositories of statistics and politics and political dealings, diplomatic things, is that an archive like [SAADA], or an archive like the Partition Archive . . . is that the everyday and the specific can sometimes say a lot more about our condition and the circumstances of identity and the evolution of representation than some big survey or some big pile of statistics.
> (Z. Alam, interview with author, 12 September 2016)

Alam also clearly expressed the importance he places on representation. Describing his formative experiences growing up in the Southern US state of Georgia in the 1990s and early 2000s without any South Asian American role models in music or popular culture, he said, 'somebody who looked like us, who was of South Asian descent, was never at all within the spectrum of people I could possibly encounter [in American popular culture]. And you just kind of accept that . . . that's just reality.' Yet, he also expressed hope that he would help change that lack of representation:

> If one younger brown boy comes up to me and says, 'I've never seen a brown boy play guitar before, and to see you do this really makes me want to do the same thing.' . . . If he goes and decides to do something creative that he felt encouraged

to do because he saw this, there's really nothing else. That's the whole world. That's everything and that's what's meaningful about work like this.

(Z. Alam, interview with author, 12 September 2016)

Based on Alam's interest in the everyday, his understanding of the value of complex forms of representations and his brief mentioning of an interest in composing a score to accompany moving images, Mallick and I instantly thought he would be a perfect match for the Dhillonn footage, which had not yet been posted on the SAADA site.

When Mallick and I sent Alam the footage, he too had a visceral reaction. 'The moment I watched these videos I knew they were what I had to work on,' Alam told the audience at the April 2017 SAADA event. On Public Radio International, Alam elaborated: 'It almost didn't seem real. Like it was a miracle that this [marriage] could have happened so long ago. But it wasn't a "miracle". It could also be described as just a very normal American community in Oklahoma where two people fell in love' (Tseng, 2017). In a 2018 email to the author, Alam further described:

> My first reaction to the Dhillonn footage was of surprise. To this day I think most South Asian Americans are surprised when they see a marriage that crosses ethno-religious lines, or other norms like class and sexuality. Many who've been in such relationships (including myself) have dreaded the moment they will have to reveal their true selves to their families, and wonder when this will no longer be the case. To see such a wedding unfolding – with both white and Punjabi families present – in warm and hazy video tones was my first surprise. I couldn't look away from it the moment I began watching . . . it had set back my mental clock – in a visceral, deeply felt way.
>
> (Z. Alam, personal communication with author, 16 January 2018)

Alam quickly got to work composing an original score for the silent Dhillonn footage and ultimately decided to remix excerpts of the historic home movies with contemporary news footage covering white supremacist violence against Sikhs and South Asian Americans writ large. The resulting 9-minute multimedia piece, 'Lavaan', juxtaposes a moving homage to Sharanjit and Dorothy Dhillonn's marriage and the striking beauty of everyday family life in the 1950s with the contemporary rise in hate crimes and xenophobia, suggesting an almost wistful longing to return to a time of intimacy and security. (The piece can be viewed here: www.saada.org/wherewebelong.) Yet, as Alam explained in his public presentation of the piece at the April 2017 SAADA event, even the seeming domestic bliss of the Dhillonn footage is haunted by the unspoken violence of Sharanjit's assimilation from someone whose turban instantly marked him as 'other' to a clean-shaven man dressed in Western-style clothes in later footage. Violence that is merely hinted at in the historic footage rages out of control in CNN headlines running across the bottom of the screen at the end of Alam's piece. We move from romance, to humor, to sorrow, to outrage, all the while questioning linear narratives of political progress and racial reconciliation.

Describing his incorporation of the footage of the Dhillonn children taking their first steps, Alam explained:

> To me, the greater narrative of learning to walk, getting up and falling back down again connected heavily with present moments where the Sikh community has been targeted since 9/11 . . . It's easy for us to say we've progressed so much since the 1950s, but often it feels like we're taking two to three steps forward and then six steps back. And maybe in some places like Norman, Oklahoma, maybe there were aspects that were better [for] immigrants, before people got caught up to this degree of national xenophobia that can now catch fire so quickly on social media and spread.
>
> (Tseng, 2017)

Mallick concurred: 'In some ways, "Lavaan" is exploring this promise of a multicultural and pluralistic America that has not been kept', he said (Tseng, 2017).

In Alam's piece, the quotidian Dhillonn footage takes on a visceral, haunting beauty. Alam described his motivations:

> I wanted to ask of their world questions for my own world. How one feels when you see the image of a child falling down but getting back up over and over again. This poetry that comes through the specifics of the American everyday: guns, Coca Cola, and ice cream. Objects that speak to each and every one of us in related but different ways. Or the hats that Sharanjit's son falls in love with and puts on his father's head over and over again. How paradise-like India looks, the place they left behind but visit again. How much it resembles the yard in which the two girls are swinging, back and forth, wearing traditional Indian kurtis. All of that footage of India comes towards the end of the home videos. There is an internal circularity, a logic to life, travel, the stories we tell ourselves, and I felt that SAADA's footage of the Dhillons already had those essentials in place.
>
> (Z. Alam, interview with the author, 8 April 2017)

In archival terms, I read 'Lavaan' as an activation of the record that hinges on the affect of the viewer. As Kathy Carbone (2017) might describe it, Alam transforms the Dhillonn footage into a 'moving record', that is, a record that moves us as secondary users as it circulates through Alam's activation in the art piece. As the initial record travels through space and time via 'Lavaan', it gets activated and reactivated, contextualised and recontextualised, creating a new record with each viewing, catalysing limitless visceral responses. In considering the Dhillonn footage via 'Lavaan', we get a glimpse of how the archive is both infinite and infinitely affective.

When Alam presented the piece at the April 2017 SAADA event, its emotional impact was palpable. A room full of 100 people, mostly second generation South Asian Americans, stared raptly at the screen, some visibly moved to tears. The room erupted into applause when the piece was over, and audience members engaged Alam in a lively discussion that traced the historic roots of contemporary racism and drew on archival materials in exciting new ways. Alam described the process of making the piece as a 'joy'. He said:

> There's something about giving old tape new life, even after the content is considered 'dead'. Things can always renew themselves through whatever we give them. Working on something new like this reawakened the feeling that searching for something in your art is inseparable from movement in general. It's movement that is complex and alive, always changing as you come into contact again and again with whatever the raw material is that you are working with.
>
> (Alam, at event)

Alam also described how his new score and video piece has taken on 'a life of its own'. He recounted one particularly important reaction to the piece at the SAADA event:

> I got the best kind of feedback I could have asked for on the video [at the event.]. An older Punjabi lady talked to me for a very, very long time after my presentation, and she was saying, 'I kept on tearing up during this video . . . just from being able to recognize so many of those scenes from my own life as a mother, as an immigrant.' For me that was like, OK, that is really all I can ask for. For somebody else to realize that their story is worthwhile, that they can recognize something in it, that it's worth sharing.
>
> (Z. Alam, interview with author, 8 April 2017)

Describing that same encounter in an interview with Public Radio International, Alam recalled, 'It made it that much more emotional. She was crying, and I was starting to tear up too' (Tseng, 2017). Alam attributes this visceral response to the record itself:

> Obviously I had some degree of authorial voice in making the music, and an editorial voice in carving out the video footage into a nine minute form, but I think trying to also step away a little bit and let the stories speak for themselves and just kind of have me be the frame or the backdrop for it is definitely the way I want people to react to the story. I think having South Asians realise that we have been here for a lot longer than a lot of us think, as a community and as a presence, is really really important to the overall idea of knowing where we belong and the fact that we belong here.
>
> (Z. Alam, interview with the author, 8 April 2017)

In this way, art becomes a new way – a visceral, emotional way – to engage users who might not otherwise see how archives are important to their lives. In an interview with Public Radio International, Alam said, 'If you take artists who are trained in making things that are beautiful, and you encourage them to go through the archives and create works they're inspired by, there's no better way to connect to people's emotional worlds, and also connect that back to something grounded in reality that has resonance in the present day.' Through this project and others, SAADA as a community archive explicitly centred the affective impact of its outreach efforts on the community it serves and represents. (On a personal note, moments like the premiere of Alam's piece make the countless hours I have spent volunteering for SAADA worthwhile.)

Lessons for mainstream archives: valuing affect in archival practice

Now that I have demonstrated how community archives value the affective responses of the communities they serve and represent when making appraisal and outreach decisions, I want to turn to making some recommendations for mainstream archives moving forward based on my own experiences with SAADA. I wish to stress again here that the boundaries between community and mainstream archives are not ossified, but rather a continuum of practices and concepts from which all types of memory organisations and institutions can draw. Yet, at the same time, one of the hallmarks of mainstream institutions in the American context is white supremacy; more specifically an inheritance of legacies of misrepresentation and silencing of, as well as inequitable extraction of knowledge and resources from, marginalised communities (Caswell, 2017). By 'white supremacy' I am not solely referring to the people and organisations who explicitly identify as such, for example neo-Nazis and the Klan (though such groups are certainly white supremacist), but a much more pervasive, insidious, often-unnamed system of inequality.

White supremacy, as defined by Frances Lee Ansley, is 'a political, economic, and cultural system in which whites overwhelmingly control power and material resources, conscious and unconscious ideas of white superiority and entitlement are widespread, and relations of white dominance and non-white subordination are daily reenacted across a broad array of institutions and social settings' (Ansley, 1989, 993). As decades of scholarship on critical race theory posit, white supremacy is not an aberration from or extraneous to mainstream American institutions; it is foundational to them, 'baked in' to their policies and practices, both historically and contemporaneously. Of particular importance to archival work, white supremacy ensures that, as Zeus Leonardo asserts, 'the referents of discourse are particulars dressed up as universals, of the white race speaking for the human race' (Leonardo, 2014, p. 139 as quoted in Tarver, 2015, p. 10).

For too long, mainstream archival institutions in the US have represented whiteness and white experiences under the guise of the universal human experience. If mainstream institutions are to stop promulgating such oppressive practices and work towards repairing relationships with marginalised communities, they must disrupt the status quo of archival practice and set new values, concepts and practices in place. Valuing affect, in particular the affective value of materials to marginalised groups, is one such crucial intervention.

First, mainstream archives should consider the affective value of representation in records when making appraisal decisions, that is, factoring in the ways in which records emotionally resonate with marginalised groups. Before acquiring collections, archivists may ask: Does this collection further symbolically annihilate a marginalised group? Or, conversely, does it contribute to a sense of representational belonging? What is the emotional impact of these records on those most commonly left out of the conversation? As archivists from dominant backgrounds might not be able to accurately answer these questions alone, input from marginalised communities may be a crucial part of this shift in appraisal practice (in addition to the obvious ethical imperative to recruit and retain more people of colour in the profession). For example, archivists may form community-based advisory boards to set collection policy and determine priorities for appraisal and acquisition. Such labour must be compensated and publicly acknowledged in order to disrupt legacies (and ongoing practices) of knowledge extraction from marginalised communities. This recommendation diverges significantly from standard appraisal practices that purport to originate from an unmarked 'neutral' position and rely on the logic of documenting crucial functions (as in functional analysis) or evaluating evidential values rather than the emotional impact of materials on users.

Next, as the example of Zain Alam's artistic reuse of the Dhillonn home movies through SAADA's Where We Belong project illustrates, community archives have actively encouraged the activation of records in their care for affective ends. Mainstream repositories can learn strategies for matching records to users based on affect, going well beyond the standard detached reference interview to a deeper probing that acknowledges the emotional dimensions of archival use. In particular, mainstream archives can encourage artistic use, not only through artist-in-residency programs, but by encouraging archivists to get to know the internal motivation of artists using their collections. This begins with archivists not only acknowledging their own affective reactions to records, but also acknowledging such affective reactions to records in their users. 'How does that make you feel?' should be as commonplace a question in archives as 'Would you like to see the next box?' or 'What is the end product of your research?'.

Finally, I recommend that outreach strategies developed by community-based archives be employed by mainstream institutions to break down barriers, repair extractive colonialist legacies and smash narrow conceptions of archival users that prioritise academics over community members. As the reception of Alam's piece – both in person at the event and through dispersed community-led discussions – showed, community archives have harnessed the power of affect to connect people to records, to help them understand their community's history, and to empower them to see their place in the world. Mainstream repositories may do the same through active outreach that both brings materials to marginalised communities and welcomes such communities into the archives. Artists-in-residency programs, public events, private gatherings and social media campaigns are just four of many outreach strategies archives of all types can employ.

Such an expansion of outreach can catalyse a wealth of meaning-making through the activation of records, attracting new user groups and demonstrating the importance of the archives to society writ large, but it will only happen if mainstream archives actively seek to change the status quo. It is time archivists from mainstream institutions stopped being baffled by the racial homogeneity of the reading room and instead investigate the ways in which white supremacy has infiltrated their work and start to dismantle it (Caswell, 2017).

Conclusion: learning from community archives

For too long, mainstream archives have solely considered the affective impact of their work on dominant groups. Such considerations have usually remained unspoken. For example, donor relations efforts in mainstream archives have capitalised on rich white male donors' aggrandised sense of accomplishment and pride attained through the acquisitions of their records, all the while devaluing or ignoring entirely the symbolic annihilation of people of colour and other oppressed people engendered by the same acquisitions and their attendant silences and misrepresentations. It is thus no surprise that mainstream archives have also only been held accountable to the dominant groups whose records they have collected. By valuing the affect of marginalised groups, repositories of any kind shift to whom they are accountable and for what. Mainstream archives can learn from community archives new ways to be accountable to new communities, new modes of practice that repair harm and restore communities broken by injustice rather than further exploiting them, and new ways of enacting and articulating the impact of archival work more broadly.

This article has advocated for adding a sixth principle – valuing the affect of marginalised communities – to the five community archives principles first proposed in 2014 (Caswell, 2014a). In fact, affective dimensions permeate many aspects of the policies and practices of participation, shared stewardship, multiplicity, activism and reflexivity in which community archives are grounded. Yet, the way in which community archives explicitly foreground the emotional impact of materials on the communities they serve and represent warrants an additional principle, particularly when considering how community-based and mainstream archives diverge and how community-based principles can transform mainstream policies and practices.

While arguing that mainstream archives have the difficult but crucial work ahead of unflinchingly confronting those practices that further marginalise racialised communities, this chapter ultimately asserts that both types of institutions – mainstream and community-based – are crucial for ending distorted representations of marginalised groups in the historic record. There is simply enough work to end oppression for everyone to do.

The author would like to thank Samip Mallick, Zain Alam, Bibi Dhillonn, and Jessica Tai, as well as the Pew Center for Arts and Culture for funding SAADA's Where We Belong: Artists in the Archive project.

References

Ansley, F. (1989) Stirring the Ashes: race class and the future of civil rights scholarship, *Cornell Law Review*, **74** (6), 993–1077.

Barriault, M. (2009) Archiving the Queer and Queering the Archives: a case study of the Canadian Lesbian and Gay Archives. In Bastian, J. and Alexander, B. (eds), *Community Archives: the shaping of memory*, Facet Publishing.

Bastian, J. (2003) *Owning Memory: how a Caribbean community lost its archives and found its history*, Libraries Unlimited.

Carbone, K. (2015) Artists in the Archive: an exploratory study of the artist-in-residence program at the City of Portland Archives & Records Center, *Archivaria*, **79**, 27–52.

Carbone, K. (2017) Moving Records: artistic interventions and activisms in the archives, Dissertation, UCLA.

Caswell, M. (2012) *SAADA and the Community Archive Model: what is a community-based archives anyway?*, Tides: South Asian American Digital Archive Blog, www.saadigitalarchive.org/blog/20120418-704.

Caswell, M. (2014a) Toward a Survivor-Centered Approach to Human Rights Archives: lessons from community-based archives, *Archival Science*, **14** (3–4), 307–322.

Caswell, M. (2014b) Inventing New Archival Imaginaries: theoretical foundations for identity-based community archives. In Daniel, D. and Levi, A. (eds), *Identity Palimpsests: ethnic archiving in the U.S. and Canada*, Litwin Books, 35–55.

Caswell, M. and Mallick, S. (2014) Collecting the Easily Missed Stories: digital participatory microhistory and the South Asian American Digital Archive, *Archives and Manuscripts*, **42** (1), 73–86.

Caswell, M., Cifor, M. and Ramirez, H. (2016) 'To Discover Yourself Existing': uncovering the affective impact of community archives, *The American Archivist*, **79** (1), 56–81.

Caswell, M., Migoni, A., Geraci, N. and Cifor, M. (2017) 'To Be Able to Imagine Otherwise': community archives and the importance of representation, *Archives and Records*, **38** (1), 1–20.

Caswell, M. (2017) Teaching to Dismantle White Supremacy in the Archives Classroom, *Library Quarterly*, **87** (3), 222–235.

Cifor, M. (2016) Affecting Archives: introducing affect studies to archival discourse, *Archival Science*, **16** (1), 7–31.

Cifor, M. and Gilliland, A. J. (2016) Affect and the Archive, Archives and their Affects: an introduction to the special issue, *Archival Science*, **16** (1), 1–6.

Cook, T. (2013) Evidence, Memory, Identity, and Community: four shifting archival paradigms, *Archival Science*, **13** (2–3), 95–120.

Daniel, D. (2010) Documenting the Immigrant and Ethnic Experience in American Archives, *American Archivist*, **73** (1), 82–104.

Flinn, A. and Stevens, M. (2009) 'It Is Noh Mistri, Wi Mekin Histri'. Telling Our Own Story: independent and community archives in the UK, challenging and subverting the mainstream. In Bastian, J. and Alexander, B. (eds), *Community Archives: the shaping of memory*, Facet Publishing.

Flinn, A., Stevens, M. and Shepherd, E. (2009) Whose Memories, Whose Archives? Independent Community Archives, Autonomy and the Mainstream, *Archival Science*, **9** (1), 71–86.

Gilliland, A. J. (2014) *Conceptualizing 21st-Century Archives*, Society for American Archivists.

Huvila, I. (2008) Participatory Archive: towards decentralised curation, radical user orientation, and broader contextualisation of records management, *Archival Science*, **8** (1), 15–36.

Kaplan, E. (2000) We Are What We Collect, We Collect What We Are: archives and the construction of identity, *American Archivist*, **63** (1), 126–151.

Krause, M. and Yakel, E. (2007) Interaction in Virtual Archives: The Polar Bear Expedition Digital Collections Next Generation Finding Aid, *American Archivist*, **70** (2), 282–314.

Leonardo, Z. (2004) The color of supremacy: Beyond the discourse of 'white privilege'. *Educational Philosophy and Theory*, **36** (2), 137-152.

Pluralizing the Archival Curriculum Group (2011) Educating for the Archival Multiverse, *American Archivist*, **74** (1), 69–101.

Society of American Archivists (SAA), *Women Archivists' Section (2017)*, The 2017 WArS/SAA Salary Survey: initial results and analysis, www2.archivists.org/sites/all/files/WArS-SAA-Salary-Survey-Report.pdf.

SAADA (2017a) *Where We Belong: Artists in the Archive*, www.saada.org/wherewebelong.

SAADA (2017b) *Where We Belong Kit*, http://saada-online.s3.amazonaws.com/static/projects/wherewebelong/WWB-Kit.pdf.

Sheffield, R. (2015) The Emergence, Development and Survival of Four Lesbian and Gay Archives, Dissertation, University of Toronto.

Shilton, K. and Srinivasan, R. (2007) Participatory Appraisal and Arrangement for Multicultural Archival Collections, *Archivaria*, **63**, 87–101.

Tarver, D. A. (2015) A Latina Critical Race Study of Embodied 'Nice' White Supremacy in Teacher Education and Researcher Preparation, Dissertation, University of Florida.

Tseng, A. (2017) Why this Musician Wants to Understand Xenophobia Today by Remembering the Past, Public Radio International, www.pri.org/stories/2017-08-05/why-musician-wants-understand-xenophobia-today-remembering-past.

Wurl, J. (2005) Ethnicity as Provenance: in search of values and principles for documenting the immigrant experience, *Archival Issues*, **29** (1), 65–76.

Zavala, J., Migoni, A., Cifor, M., Geraci, N. and Caswell, M. (2017) 'A Process Where We're All at the Table': Community archives challenging dominant modes of archival practice, *Archives and Manuscripts*, **45** (3), 1–14.

CHAPTER 3

Community archives and the records continuum

Michael Piggott

Introduction

The aim of this chapter is straightforward – a thought experiment which will bring community archives and the records continuum into contact and then analyse the results. What is revealed about the processes of and thinking behind community archives when the conceptual framework of the records continuum is applied to it? What parallels emerge when we place these two ways of imagining archiving and recordkeeping side by side?

Before proceeding, of course we should ask if such an experiment has ever been done before.

At the University of Dundee, in December 2010, Terry Cook, the keynote speaker, presented one of his classic broad sweep surveys. It canvassed four professional mindsets that have dominated archival discourse during the 20th century: the first three can be summarised as evidence, memory and identity. Having allocated the records continuum model largely to the evidence paradigm, Cook ended by heralding a fourth emerging paradigm of 'community'. In essence, he said that community concerned 'participatory archiving'; it was about 'a democratising of archives suitable for the social ethos, communication patterns, and community requirements of the digital age', an age where 'the activist archivist mentors collaborative evidence- and memory-making'. At different points labelling it a framework, a mindset and praxis, he wrote:

> Community archiving, as concept and reality, evidently makes us think differently about ownership of records, replevin, oral and written traditions, the localism-globalism and margins-centre nexus, multiple viewpoints and multiple realities about recordkeeping, and so much else, including evidence, memory, and

obviously identity, and, depending on our responses, around deeper ethical issues of control, status, power, and neo-colonialism.

(Cook, 2013, 116)

Our comparison will be narrower, but Cook's judgement carries weight and we will return to it at the end of the chapter.

The records continuum

It is time to consider our experiment's two inputs – the constant variables community archives and the records continuum model. Given the former is the focus of this entire volume, it is to the latter that we need to pay particular attention.

Commenting recently on the Netherlands archival profession, Eric Ketelaar noted that it had been professionalised very early. He quoted van der Gouw to the effect that we 'had our bible before our church', with the result that 'for a very long time the profession did not really evolve' (Glaudemans, Jonker and Smit, 2017, 295). All archival communities have distinctive interests, traditions and fault lines, as those who have responded to Ketelaar's challenge to pursue comparative archivistics know.

In Australia, we had our theology (the so-called series system) before our church, and key ideas in it re-emerged soon enough with the records continuum model. According to Gillian Oliver it is one of only five conceptual models and theories relating to the management of records in current environments. The others were the life cycle, recordkeeping informatics, diplomatics and rhetorical genre studies (Oliver, 2017).

Almost 20 years ago, the model was described by Terry Cook as 'the world's most inclusive model for archives' (Cook, 2000, 16) and by Upward himself as no less than 'a fully-fledged paradigm shift in which a worldview is being replaced' (Upward, 2000, 117). In 2015, the Australian Society of Archivists honoured Upward with the award of a Fellowship, stating:

> The Upward name is inseparable from his records continuum model of the mid-1990s, which was immediately recognized as a once-in-a-generation breakthrough. While other colleagues contributed, Frank's pivotal role in developing a unified model of archives and records is undisputed. The multi-layered genius of this model brought together records, archival documents, accountability, digital recordkeeping and evidence, with the cultural and memory dimension of archival endeavour in ever-changing social and technological environments. The continuum model continues to be taught, referenced, explored and tested by scholars internationally – an impressive living legacy.
>
> (ASA, 2015)

A large body of writing has been produced explaining, defending, applying and extending the records continuum model. Though in 1993 there were hints of the model to come (Upward, 1993), the classic articulation remains his two-part essay that launched it upon the archival world in 1996–97 (Upward, 1996, 1997). There he wrote that the model was already proving valuable 'as a way of conceptualising the nature of recordkeeping' (recordkeeping taken to include archiving). For current purposes, while primarily referencing Upward's published writing on the model, we also draw from a selection of work by so-called continuum thinkers. For completeness, we should also note their latest major title, though its 288 pages barely acknowledge 'community archiving' (Upward et al., 2018, 159 and 196).

The model has been called a perspective, a view of reality, a way of thinking and a way of seeing. Initially a response to the challenges of accountability and electronic records, its intent was to provide a unifying theory and, astoundingly, its focus is the entire universe of archives and records, past and present. The Society of American Archivists glossary rightly defines it as a model of archival science. In this respect, its adaptations and readings, and the success or otherwise of its developers and supporters in explaining and defending it, are irrelevant. The truly epic scale of its vision is self-evident – except to those who limit it merely to the status of an alternative to a life cycle model (Yeo, 2015; Duranti, 2015), argue the two are more compatible than at first thought (Shepherd, 2010) or contend the new model has never fully exorcised the old (Brothman, 2006).

The model is based on four assumptions:

- Records are 'inclusive of records of continuing value (=archives)';
- Records are also conceptual constructs, i.e. logical entities regardless of particular physical or digital form;
- Recordkeeping, ideally, needs to be integrated into business and societal processes and purposes;
- Archival science – a science of knowledge, not universal laws – is the foundation for organising knowledge about recordkeeping.

To reiterate, the model is a generalised and fundamental way of seeing archiving and recordkeeping and asserts that these processes operate through time and across space 'in any period of history' (Upward, 1997, 31), meaning that records include aural and visual knowledge found in pre-literate societies (Upward, 1997, 26). Records can be kept 'for a split second or a millennium' (Upward, 1996, 276).

The model attempts a totalising summary stating what recordkeeping and archiving is all about. Expressed using the model's four axes which 'encapsulate major themes in archival science' (Upward, 1996, 277), it amounts to identity, evidentiality, transactionality and recordkeeping. Expressed in a narrative sentence, it says that records (in their classic proto and later manifestations, documents, records, archive and archives) result from actions and support objectives (acts, activities, functions and purposes) of agents (actors, units, organisations and institutions) which produce intended and other effects (traces, evidence, corporate memory and collective memory).

To Australian archivists in the 1990s, the model's components, taken separately, would have simply and unremarkably implied provenance. The real success of the model lay in the categories' relationships and interactions. What connects and fuels them, what transports the analysis of recordkeeping and archiving to any time-and-relative-dimension-in-space is four auxiliary processes: creating, capturing, organising and pluralising. They are tools for analysing recordkeeping and archiving, not stages in the life of a typical record. As Upward wrote (1996, 280), 'The dimensions are not boundaries, the coordinates are not invariably present, and things may happen simultaneously across dimensions . . .'.

Finally, because it is so relevant to the occasional attempts by continuum thinkers to address community and related archiving, the original explanation of the fourth process, pluralising, warrants particular note. It is the arena where 'the document connects with other memory banks' (Upward, 1997, 16), where collective memory (social, cultural or historical) can be developed, recalled and disseminated (Upward, 1996, 281).

Mutual indifference

The key 1990s articulations of the model barely alluded to community archives. In later writing, Upward and like-minded colleagues have noted both community participation in appraisal description and access and indigenous communities' archiving, in particular championing their equal status as co-creators and annotators of (typically government dossier) records rather than as mere subjects of those records. Occasionally one can glean passing references to all sorts of 'communities' by continuum thinkers in their writing on informatics, on complementary continuum models and on the 'archival multiverse'. Occasionally too they have read the model back into straightforward projects supporting communities (e.g. Henningham, Evans and Morgan, 2017). Otherwise, the near invisibility of community archiving has remained (Upward, 2005a; Upward, McKemmish and Reed, 2011; McKemmish, 2017; Upward, 2017) – with at least one exception.

As this chapter was being drafted, three of Upward's colleagues looked directly if briefly at community archives. Arguing that a continuum sensibility helps support social justice and can underpin critical archives studies agendas, Evans, McKemmish and Rolan (2017, 10) dismissed community archives in a single sentence lacking any supporting references to justify their narrow conception of community archiving. While Cook (2013, 116) had conceived of community archiving expansively and called it 'a radical re-imagining' of the archival profession's purpose, they observed that 'extending the collection-oriented, traditional accessioning and appraisal approach to encompass community archives simply replicates the existing archival paradigm (albeit under community control) – in effect, creating more gated islands of information in an otherwise inter-networked world'.

Was the reaction of scholars of community archives any different? Equivalent indifference it would seem, the honourable exception being New Zealand archives consultant Joanna Newman's 2010 thesis and several subsequent publications (e.g. Newman, 2012). One looked in vain for acknowledgement from one of its most prolific champions, Andrew Flinn.

Even Anne Gilliland, someone with an extensive familiarity with the literature of both the continuum model and community archives practice, has seen little need for interaction – surely meaningful not mere indifference. Indeed, neither in a recent magisterial survey of current thinking nor in joint writing with Flinn about community archives nor in work as a co-author with Sue McKemmish supporting participatory archives, has she deployed the continuum model (Gilliland, 2017; Gilliland and Flinn, 2013; Gilliland and McKemmish, 2014). And this is despite continuum thinkers having demonstrated how to map community groups to the model; Barbara Reed for one providing a readily adaptable example (in a case study using a fictitious advocacy community group POD, i.e. People Opposed to Detention) in one of her 2005 Archives and Manuscripts theme issue articles (Reed, 2005a).

That the continuum model has been seen to have no analytical value in understanding perhaps the most common archival practice of the digital age is curious. Unavoidably, it directs some attention to the universalising claims made for the model itself, although explaining why it appears to have so little relevance would require a separate volume assessing the model's merits, contexts, impact, misunderstandings and reception. Additional to early reactions to the continuum model (e.g. Cook, 2000; Harris, 2007), there is now a modest body of theses (Gibbons, 2015; Karabinos, 2015; Koerber, 2017) and commentary (Piggott, 2012; van Bussel, 2017; Karabinos, 2018), while some broadly sympathetic have offered major adaptations (Gibbons, 2015; Rolan, 2017; Frings-Hessami, 2017). The contrast with the extensive community archives literature, including this new volume, is to say the least interesting. A new assessment would examine alternatives and appraisals by supporters and the more neutral. Such a need was perfectly illustrated by Kate Cumming at the beginning of an article on the continuum (2010, 41), where, disarmingly, she admitted under the heading 'Research limitations/implications' that 'The paper is strongly supportive of the continuum approach, and *as such is not an impartial assessment* of the model and of the criticism that has been levelled against it' [emphasis added].

The experiment begins

In applying the continuum model to community archives, we can see activity in each of the dimensions of create, capture and organise. As organisations, community archives document their own business transactions and thereby form an archive. Regardless, that is, of how seriously or vicariously this documenting is undertaken and of how loosely or virtually the organisation operates. But the fourth dimension process of 'pluralising' memory is relevant too, given what it is that community archives do. Indeed, because so many are what Australians call a 'collecting archive', i.e. one that not only creates and manages records of its own business but also, because of the nature of that business, harvests and preserves others' records too, we can locate community archives on all the model's axes and dimensions, including the fourth.

Being so located is of marginal import but useful here because it was this fourth dimension aspect of the model in particular that attracted early negative attention.

The first critical response to the model, as opposed to reactions to what particular readings were seen to emphasis or neglect (Macpherson, 2002; Upward, 2005a) came from renowned Canadian archivist Terry Cook. In a keynote address to an Australian Society of Archivists' conference in August 2000, he shared a sympathetic outsider's observations on the state of debate within the archives professions of the English-speaking world (including Australia), deploring philosophical divisions between what, for convenience, he labelled evidence and memory.

As for the model, Cook praised it in terms much quoted by its supporters, while rarely adding that the praise was qualified (2000, 16–17). He said as drawn it was too easily interpreted as stressing recordkeeping and evidence for accountability at the expense of archiving for societal memory – but this concentration was also mirrored in the literature and in professional rhetoric and work strategies. These were misunderstandings of the model, not inherent conceptual flaws. Then there were further qualifications. To 'the world's most inclusive model for archives' he proposed a fifth dimension to strengthen the focus on collective memory and a separate memory axis. Cook pulled his punches by saying these were enhancements and suggestions offered for consideration; but they still carried force. He added that the work of collecting archives and 'private-sector personal, family, and group records' (and also, we may infer, 'community archives') were under-emphasised (Piggott, 2020).

As if accepting there was something to these arguments, in 2004 records continuum supporters organised a 3-day seminar, 'Archives and Collective Memory: challenges and issues in a pluralised archival role'. Indeed, in a key paper to the seminar, Barbara Reed noted supporters had been 'accused quite publicly of disrespecting or devaluing the cultural dimensions of recordkeeping' and named South African Verne Harris, Australian Paul Macpherson and, remarkably, Cook himself as among the accused (Harris, 2007; Macpherson, 2002; Reed, 2005b, 177). Seven of the seminar papers later published in a 2005 theme issue of *Archives and Manuscripts* ranged widely, Upward and Reed explicitly linking their content to the 'pluralised space' of the continuum's fourth dimension.

But directly and by implication, community archives were acknowledged. Eric Ketelaar explored mapping a 'memory continuum' onto the records continuum model, implying that this was something the existing model under-emphasised. In the process he discussed the concepts of 'communities of records', 'joint heritage' and 'communities of memory' (Ketelaar, 2005). One of Barbara Reed's papers noted the former Australian Society of Archivists' President Baiba Berzins championing, as far back as 1985, a 'network of . . . institutional, personal and community archives throughout Australia' (Reed, 2005b, 186). Little had eventuated however, the dominant pattern being for community archives to prefer institutional custodians, the Estonian Archives and the Australian Lesbian and Gay Archives cited as two of the very few exceptions.

How might the model have been deployed?

Mutual indifference of course need not remain the default attitude. Let me offer two possibilities that community archives supporters might have pursued.

The first, given its focus on communities, is the community informatics work of Upward and colleagues. In his *Encyclopedia of Archival Science* entry, Upward explained that the records continuum model 'has helped promote an informatics approach' (2015, 337) and that three major strands have emerged from colleagues at his university, one being community informatics. Yet there is no necessary logical link and the gains would seem to be limited. Surveying the coverage of the 13 volumes of *The Journal of Community*

Informatics, a journal focused on 'the study and the practice of enabling communities with Information and Communications Technologies', one finds references to neither the records continuum model nor to community archiving.

Even so, community informatics research brought together by Mauro Sarrica and Upward's Monash University colleagues Tom Denison and Larry Stillman in 2014 show where fruitful exchanges might happen. For example, the discussions of community archives scholars about how to define such archives have their parallel in community informatics scholars grappling with the concept of 'community'. More interesting still is the chapter case study dealing with the aftermath of the 2009 earthquake in L'Aquila, Italy. This analysed a grassroots protest of the so-called People of the Wheelbarrows, a community whose members used an array of social media to facilitate and publicise their activism, as well as to document their lives and responses to the earthquake more generally (Farinosi and Treré, 2014).

A second application, full of possibilities, could aid efforts to understand the modern phenomenon of community archiving, in particular the conditions and factors which explain their genesis. Often they centre on the initiative of a single remarkable activist who was already preserving personal papers and other material. During her doctoral research on four Canadian and US lesbian and gay archives, Rebecka Sheffield learnt that New York's Lesbian Herstory Archives 'grew first as a personal collection nurtured and cared for in its founder's own apartment'; indeed, three of the four communities in Sheffield's case studies began via a single individual (Sheffield, 2017, 370; Sheffield, website).

Equivalent Australian examples include the Australian Lesbian and Gay Archives (ALGA) formed in 1978, incorporated in 1983 (initially as Australian Gay Archives, and ALGA in 1991), and which grew from a collection begun in Melbourne in 1977 by the late Graham Carbery (Carbery, 1995; ALGA and Victorian Pride Centre websites). More recent is the Parramatta Female Factory Precinct Memory Project. It started in 2012 as the first Australian member of the International Coalition of Sites of Conscience but had links back to Bonney Djuric's initiative of 2006 setting up 'Parragirls', a contact register and support network for former residents of Parramatta Girls Home (Djuric, 2016).

So, we come to the puzzle of beginnings. Understanding of initiatives such as 'Parragirls' is undoubtedly helped by the insights of psychology and sociology. But what then of the heritage and memorialising elements? To leading continuum thinker Sue McKemmish, in such circumstances a kind of 'de-privatisation' is in play from the beginning (McKemmish, 1996). The personal archive, by its nature documenting and witnessing an individual's place in the world and relationships to and with others and thus already implying a bigger setting, is carried beyond the boundaries of an individual life to be preserved and made accessible via public heritage institutions, publications and biographies, and perhaps supported and fostered by its own dedicated community. 'Evidence of me' becomes, and in a sense already is, 'evidence of us'. In 1996, McKemmish did not mention the pluralising fourth dimension, although she acknowledged the model then being drafted was 'a key reference point' and fifteen years later made the links explicit (McKemmish, 2011).

Common themes – stuff, time and society

To this point, we have noted the mutual indifference of leading scholars of the records continuum and community archives. In stark contrast, there was a quasi-comparison by Terry Cook via his 2010 Dundee conference presentation that rated community archives as just right for the digital age. At the 2016 ICA congress in Seoul, another attempt to consider both was made. The wider archival community is yet to see the published results, although one session participant has reflected that illumination and shared language were at a premium (Flinn, 2018).

During my own consideration of the two approaches, a number of parallels emerged. One was a pattern of assertions that they represent paradigm shifts, in contrast to a certain ambivalence about the term in Cook's 2010 conference presentation. At the very least these are exaggerations as van Bussel noted regarding the continuum's champions (2017, 27). But in both cases there is clearly a misunderstanding of paradigm's intended span. Even so, one of the keenest users, Upward himself, has written that 'high modern society has a history of labeling its ages in an indiscriminate fashion', warning 'Reliable judgments can only be made historically . . .' (1997, 21). Indeed.

Reading the respective bodies of writing, one is also struck by common undercurrents of intellectual anxiety and defensiveness. As if never fully certain of his theory's superiority, Upward has harnessed an ever-increasing array of ideas and alpha intellectuals against which to set his theory. On the other hand, Flinn and followers have worried inordinately over definitions. The contrast between their respective entries on the records continuum and community archiving in the *Encyclopedia of Archival Science* are palpable in this and many other ways. The very first sentence of Flinn's began: 'Despite growing international usage, the term community archives has not been precisely defined or even deemed capable of precise definition'. Upward's began: 'John Keane argues in his book The Life and Death of Democracy that . . .'.

Three further themes, summarised as 'stuff', 'time' and 'society', will detain us a little longer.

Stuff

Defining record and archive has been an enduring professional issue, stimulated in recent years by postmodern insights and the digital preservation imperative. Each of Cook's four paradigm/mindsets noted earlier have seen different characteristics emphasised. Scholars including Duranti, Livelton, Nesmith, Hofman and Yeo have offered views, while recently Ketelaar concluded enough is enough: adherence to canonical terminology means a discipline can never renew itself. Identifying a second 'archival turn' in which things such as a city and the human body can be viewed metaphorically as archive, he wrote: 'Let anything be "as archive" and let everyone be an archivist'. Ultimately, he wrote, what matters is 'how does this particular individual or group perceive and understand an archive' (Ketelaar, 2017, 231, 239).

From his direct contact with community archiving, Flinn reached the same conclusion: 'a person or group's archives are whatever they say they are', including 'documentary materials, material culture, published works and duplicates, oral histories and audio-visual material, ephemera, clothes and works of art' (2011, 165; 2015, 146). Community archives have always practised this philosophy, documenting by gathering then managing all manner of analogue and/or digital 'stuff'. Some is archives as traditionally understood, but community archivists seek and preserve the broadest range of heritage materials. When considered as 'stuff' this eclecticism has a theoretical basis (Boscagli, 2014; Manalansan, 2014). In practice, it is simply a determination to comprehensively document one's history and experience (or locality, ethnicity, identity social cause or event) with meaningful things. Familiar binaries such as original/copy, analogue/digital and archive/library/ museum are simply not seen as important (Gilliland and Flinn, 2013; Bastian, 2017).

The catholic almost chaotic richness of such archiving is well captured by Kirsten Thorpe, an indigenous Australian woman and descendant of the Worimi people of Port Stephens, in describing the collecting focus of an Aboriginal community archives:

> These materials encompass multiple forms and types of records and relate broadly to the local community: the land, its people, language, knowledge and histories. These records might be sourced from multiple places nationally and internationally besides Aboriginal keeping places, including museums, archives, libraries or other private repositories, and local historical societies, and could include business records in community organisations, or records created specifically to be part of the community archive.
>
> (Thorpe, 2017, 903)

Government archives, including files that treated indigenous Australians as subjects, were especially seen as resources in which community members had rights as 'co-creators' to copies or repatriated originals. In addition, the collection embraced 'intangible records', i.e. those transmitted orally by members of the community or passed on through art, dance or storytelling. This 'living archive' component means the archives are 'not only a place for storing or gathering materials, but also a place where information can be contested'(Thorpe, 2017, 903).

Up to a point, the records continuum proponents have been equally broad-minded. In Upward's model, records are logical not physical entities. They arise from social and/or organisational activity or the conduct of affairs; in summary, from 'human activities' (Upward, 1996, 279). Thus:

> The deeply human concern for the establishment of an archive first showed up in cave paintings, dance, song and storytelling as artistic preservation tools for the carriage of survival information through time. Once societies began to trade with each other, recordkeeping concerns were added to the arts of the earliest communities.
>
> (Upward, 2005a, 213)

This carriage of survival information through time happens when records are 'dis-embedded' or captured into a recordkeeping system. They memorialise or evidence that activity. In theory, this allows for non-traditional recordkeeping systems including cultural practices, but in 1990s Australia, even while facing the electronic records challenge, continuum thinkers agonised over nothing more than whether a personal diary was a record. Non-record materials were out-of-scope and those who would not accept the distinctions, for example those practising what they called 'audiovisual archiving', were ridiculed as pursuing 'stuff for stuff's sake' (Hurley, 1996, 13).

For Upward and colleagues, continued focus on this bigger world of 'stuff' has led in two different directions. One basically was an old concept with the new label 'evidentiary texts', which at their core comprise texts that are 'inclusive of records as they exist in multiple cultural contexts (i.e., the societal record), because the term "records" could be read as pertaining only to institutional/bureaucratic forms of recordkeeping' (Gilliland, McKemmish and Lau, 2017, 17). The second result is more predictable: information. Within a decade of the records continuum model being officially announced, there were further models for information, publications, information systems and cultural heritage, all different except for their common dimensions of create-capture-organise-pluralise (Upward, 2000, 2005b; Upward and McKemmish, 2006; Upward and Stillman, 2006). One is tempted to observe that, via 'stuff', community archives got there first.

Time

Archival interest in time is unremarkable. That recordkeeping systems comprise records created, consulted and added to over time (even spans of hundreds of years) is self-evident. They also cover, allude to and/or evidence subjects, events and activities that potentially have even greater reach. Orally transmitted memory records, for example those of Australia's indigenous peoples, may well reference matters of great antiquity, while in cultures where written records replaced memory such as M. T. Clanchy has described, 'time out of mind' stretched to the limits of what could be remembered by a community's oldest living person (Clanchy, 1979). Present day records can also influence the future. Finally, and equally obviously, records can, and often do, document relationships and facilitate business spanning the globe and yet remain, especially with digital records, in a sense nowhere.

Both Upward and Flinn and their respective colleagues and followers have thought about time, although in quite different ways.

From Upward's earliest published mentions of the model, he drew on sociologist Anthony Giddens' ideas, using time and space as a single merged idea. Being a continuum, the model 'is continuous and is a time/space construct, not a life model' (Upward, 1996, 277). He set his understanding of recordkeeping and archiving against the background of modern and now postmodern social systems. With clocks, calendars, maps and now the technology of a globalised hyperconnected world, organised human thinking and operating no longer occurs in a simple fixed temporal and spatial reality. Upward has also been much taken with the idea that records come into being over time, and in many ways as part of recordkeeping systems within the archive, and the collective archives go on changing.

Upward's ideas about time have changed as his thinking in the past 25 years about the meaning of records and information in society has deepened and linked up with wider and wider intellectual frameworks. He has drawn on the works of philosophers and scientists who have contemplated the ultimate meaning of time, including Albert Einstein himself. Poets, too. Inspired by Ketelaar's rhetorical use of T. S. Eliot's poem 'Burnt Norton', he has discerned in it considerable archival relevance. The final line of the second stanza – 'Only through time time is conquered' – apparently carries great significance, while to him and his colleagues, the entire poem is 'a treatise on space-time' no less (Upward et al., 2018, 284; 2013, 48). And now, to the space-time continuum and 'archival time' from the mid-2010s, Upward's two most recent set pieces on the records continuum have added a new phenomenon, space-time eddies (2015, 2017).

To Andrew Flinn and colleagues, time is not nearly so complicated. They have been interested firstly in the broad causal history of community archives.

In the UK, their antecedents are traced to 17th century antiquarianism, to 19th century antiquarian societies and to their 20th century local history successors. In Australia, much younger in European terms, historical societies focused on 'pioneers' and anniversaries of discovery and settlement existed in considerable numbers by the 1930s, then proliferated in the 1960s and 1970s in parallel to trends Flinn identified in his own country, including the rise in popularity of genealogy and oral history (Griffiths, 1996; Sear, 2013). Whether these and other enabling and causal factors explain the re-emergence of a long-standing and widely practised phenomenon in different settings around the world remains to be investigated.

A second interest examines time's impact on the fluctuating and often finite experiences of individual community archives. This has occasionally prompted archivists (and indeed local history librarians and museum curators) into rescue mode and their academic colleagues to explanatory theorising. In his classic *Local History and the Library* over 60 years ago, John Hobbs identified continuity as one of the local library's supreme virtues. Local historical societies 'rise and wane' and they 'often tend to be dominated by individuals or sectional interests' (1962, 17). In introducing *Theories, Practices and Examples for Community and Social Informatics*, Denison, Sarrica and Stillman generalised: 'Communities may have long or short lives depending on their needs' (2014, Introduction).

A third framework argues that, as with social movements more generally, community archives follow a four-stage life cycle of emergence, coalescence, bureaucratisation and decline (Sheffield, 2017, 370–2). These ideas aside, further case studies of different settings around the world will test what combination of internal politics and wider and societal contexts makes sense.

Society

'The archive – all archive – every archive – is figured' wrote three of the editors introducing that seminal text *Refiguring the Archive* (Hamilton et al., 2002, 7). In part, this eloquent and loaded formulation reminds us that archiving and recordkeeping happen 'in society'. They are part of, reflect and facilitate societies' traditions, power relations, social networks and cultures, or, as Tom Nesmith wrote, 'A society is a kind of information gathering and processing phenomenon'. Explaining that conclusion, he might well have been foreshadowing the conclusion to this chapter :

> People make and archive records in social settings for social purposes. They do so with a concept of how their social setting works, where they fit into it, and might change it. Socio-economic conditions, social assumptions, values, ideas,

and aspirations shape and are shaped by their views and recording and archiving behaviour.

(Nesmith, 2006, 352)

Upward, Flinn and their respective followers genuinely do know this, although the need for and manner of their elaborations are different.

Flinn's long set-piece 'Community Historians, Community Archives' illustrates the nature (and limits) of his sociological interest. There is some discussion of the idea of 'communities', including the glue that holds them, which quickly narrows to his real interest, that subset which purposefully document their heritage. He canvasses factors behind their growing numbers, including widespread interest in family history and the impact of social demographic economic and traumatic change, and notes implications for cultural capital, community cohesion and democratisation of heritage. But only one social science source was referenced, Michael Drake's *Time, Family and Community: perspectives on family and community history*, while in later writing with Gilliland acknowledging new social movement theory (Gilliland and Flinn, 2013).

Upward's perspective is inevitably more generalised and theoretical and, famously, has deployed the sociological theories of Anthony Giddens to help explain how social systems function in the world of high modernity. He was not the first archivist to see the potential relevance of Giddens' ideas (or, we might add, Max Weber's) as he himself acknowledged, but he was certainly the most serious in exploring their potential. The records continuum theory and model only make sense knowing this, in particular structuration theory of time-space distanciation and the perpetuation of social relationships through memory traces. For Upward, one key relevant Giddens text was *The Constitution of Society*, which included discussion of the role of recorded information in shaping society. Trying to explain structuration, David Gauntlett said: 'there is a social structure – traditions, institutions, moral codes, and established ways of doing things; but it also means that these can be changed when people start to ignore them, replace them, or reproduce them differently' (2008, 102). Put that way, the dissatisfaction of communities with established archival institutions does indeed come to mind.

Conclusion

In his Dundee keynote, having dealt with the continuum model, Terry Cook concluded that community archiving was an emerging paradigm 'suitable for the social ethos, communication patterns, and community requirements of the digital age' (2013, 116). More recently, Sue McKemmish described the emergence of the records continuum worldview as 'a paradigm shift' and concluded that it was 'particularly relevant to understanding the complexities and pluralities of the archival multiverse in a digital age' (2017, 153). Can they both be right?

The community archives and records continuum 'communities of practice' have largely ignored each other. That they themselves can be conceived of as communities, centred on for example the Community Archives and Heritage Group in the UK and Ireland and the Records Continuum Research Group in Australia, is one of many ironies. That bringing the model to bear upon community archives illustrated possible benefits is another.

During our experiment, several parallel themes were observed, the most important being societal. All concerned seem to understand that the only reliable analytical anchor is social context, whether the archiving specifics are 19th century societies of antiquarians, Giddens' high modernity or 21st century 'chaser communities' documenting storm events, Cleveland citizens recording police violence or Keepers of Ghosts researching fading hoarding advertisements (Czuchnicki, 2012; Blake, 2016; Cianci and Schutt, 2014). And both sides seem to sense that today, hints of an actual paradigm shift may be discernible. We live in liquid times; in a time of archival flux. Ideas such as the singularity, virtual communities, iPhone activism, algivists, big data and hyperobjects barely begin to encapsulate it, let alone the ubiquitous impact of 'Big Tech' and the growing acceptance that even space-time is unravelling. So perhaps rapprochement will replace indifference and we may imagine Upward and Flinn as co-presenters of a TED talk, moderated by Gilliland, in which they explain 21st century community archiving and its underpinning theories and models.

References

Australian Society of Archivists (2015) Fellowship Citation, Frank Upward, https://www.archivists.org.au/documents/item/703.

Australian Lesbian and Gay Archives (ALGA), http://alga.org.au.

Bastian, J. (2017) GLAMS, LAMs and Archival Perspectives. In MacNeil, H. and Eastwood, T. (eds), *Currents of Archival Thinking*, 2nd edn, Libraries Unlimited.

Blake, J. (2016) *#ArchivesForBlackLives: building a community archives of police violence in Cleveland*, https://medium.com/on-archivy/archivesforblacklives-building-a-community-archives-of-police-violence-in-cleveland-93615d777289.

Boscagli, M. (2014) *Stuff Theory: everyday objects, radical materialism*, Bloomsbury.

Brothman, B. (2006) Archives, Life Cycles, and Death Wishes: a helical model of record formation, *Archivaria*, **61** (Spring), 235–69.

Carbery, G. (1995) Australian Lesbian & Gay Archives, *Archives and Manuscripts*, **23** (1), 30–7.

Cianci, L. and Schutt, S. (2014) Keepers of Ghosts: old signs, new media and the age of archival flux, *Archives and Manuscripts*, **42** (1), 19–32.

Clanchy, M. (1979) *From Memory to Written Record: England, 1066–1307*, Harvard University Press.

Community Archives and Heritage Group (UK & Ireland), www.communityarchives.org.uk.

Cook, T. (2000) Beyond the Screen: the records continuum and archival cultural heritage. In Burrows, L. (ed.), *Beyond the Screen: capturing corporate and social memory*, Australian Society of Archivists.

Cook, T. (2013) Evidence, Memory, Identity, and Community: four shifting archival paradigms, *Archival Science*, **13** (2–3), 95–120.

Cumming, K. (2010) Ways of Seeing: contextualising the continuum, *Records Management Journal*, **20** (1), 41–52.

Czuchnicki, C. (2012) History of Storm Chasing, https://www.rmets.org/weather-and-climate/weather/history-storm-chasing.

Denison T., Sarrica, M. and Stillman, L. (eds) (2014) *Theories, Practices and Examples for Community and Social Informatics*, Monash University Publishing.

Djuric, B. (2016) Living Traces – An Archive of Place: Parramatta Girls Home, *Archives and Manuscripts*, **44** (3), 165–70.

Duranti, L. (2015) Records Lifecycle. In Duranti, L. and Franks, P. (eds), *Encyclopedia of Archival Science*, Rowman & Littlefield.

Evans, J., McKemmish, S. and Rolan, G. (2017) Critical Archiving and Recordkeeping Research and Practice in the Continuum, *Journal of Critical Library and Information Studies*, **1** (2), 1–38.

Farinosi, M. and Treré, E. (2014) Social Movements, Social Media and Post-disaster Resilience: towards an integrated system of local protest. In Denison T., Sarrica, M. and Stillman, L. (eds), *Theories, Practices and Examples for Community and Social Informatics*, Monash University Publishing.

Flinn, A. (2011) The Impact of Independent and Community Archives on Professional Archival Thinking and Practice. In Hill, J. (ed.), *The Future of Archives and Recordkeeping: a reader*, Facet Publishing.

Flinn, A. (2015) Community Archives. In Duranti, L. and Franks, P. (eds), *Encyclopedia of Archival Science*, Rowman & Littlefield.

Flinn, A. (2018) Personal communication with author, 15 June 2018.

Frings-Hessami, V. (2017) Looking at the Khmer Rouge Archives Through the Lens of the Records Continuum Model: towards an appropriated archive continuum model, *Information Research*, **22** (4), paper 771, www.informationr.net/ir/22-4/paper771.html.

Gauntlett, D. (2008) *Media, Gender and Identity: An Introduction*, Routledge.

Gibbons, L. (2015) Culture in the continuum: YouTube, small stories and memory-making, PhD thesis, Monash University.

Gilliland, A. J. (2017) Archival and Recordkeeping Traditions in the Multiverse and their Importance for Researching Situations and Situating Research. In Gilliland, A. J., McKemmish, S. and Lau, A. J. (eds), *Research in the Archival Multiverse,* Monash University Publishing.

Gilliland, A. J. and Flinn, A. (2013) Community Archives: what are we really talking about? Keynote presented at CIRN Prato Community Informatics Conference, 2013, https://www.monash.edu/_data/assets/pdf_file/0007/920626/ gilliland_flinn_keynote.pdf.

Gilliland, A. J. and McKemmish, S. (2014) The Role of Participatory Archives in Furthering Human Rights, Reconciliation and Recovery, *Atlanti: Review for Modern Archival Theory and Practice,* **24**, 78–88.

Gilliland, A. J., McKemmish, S. and Lau, A. J. (eds) (2017) *Research in the Archival Multiverse,* Monash University Publishing.

Glaudemans, A., Jonker, R. and Smit, F. (2017) Beyond the Traditional Boundaries of Archival Theory: an interview with Eric Ketelaar. In Smit, F., Glaudemans, A. and Jonker, R. (eds), *Archives in Liquid Times,* Stichting Archiefpublicaties.

Griffiths, T. (1996) *Hunters and Collectors: the antiquarian imagination in Australia,* Cambridge University Press.

Hamilton, C., Harris, V. and Reid, G. (2002) Introduction. In Hamilton, C., Harris, V., Taylor, J., Pickover, M., Reid, G. and Saleh, R. (eds), *Refiguring the Archive,* Kluwer Academic Publishers.

Harris, V. (2005) Record-keeping and Records Continuum Thinkers: examining a seminal Australian text (Archives: Recordkeeping in Society), *Archives and Manuscripts,* **33** (2), 160–70.

Harris, V. (2007) Law, Evidence and Electronic Records: a strategic perspective from the global periphery. In Harris, V., *Archives and Justice: a South African perspective,* Society of American Archivists.

Henningham, N., Evans, J. and Morgan, H. (2017) The Australian Women's Archives Project: creating and co-curating community feminist archives in a post-custodial age, *Australian Feminist Studies,* **32** (91–2), 91–107.

Hobbs, J. (1962) *Local History and the Library,* Andre Deutsch.

Hurley, C. (1996) Beating the French, *Archives and Manuscripts,* **24** (1), 12–18.

Karabinos, M. (2015) The Shadow Continuum: testing the records continuum model through the Djogdja Documenten and the migrated archives, PhD thesis, Leiden University.

Karabinos, M. (2018) In the Shadow of the Continuum: testing the records continuum model through the Foreign and Commonwealth Office 'Migrated Archives', *Archival Science,* **18** (3), 207–224.

Ketelaar, E. (2005) Sharing: collected memories in communities of records, *Archives and Manuscripts*, **33** (1), 44–61.

Ketelaar, E. (2017) Archival Turns and Returns: Studies of the archive. In Gilliland, A. J., McKemmish, S. and Lau, A. J. (eds), *Research in the Archival Multiverse*, Monash University Publishing.

Koerber, M. (2017) A Critique of the Records Continuum Model. Minor thesis for the Master's of Information Management (Archives and Records Management), University of South Australia.

Macpherson, P. (2002) Theory, Standards and Implicit Assumptions: public access to post-current government records, *Archives and Manuscripts*, **30** (1), 6–17.

Manalansan, M. (2014) The 'Stuff' of Archives: mess, migration and queer lives, *Radical History Review*, **120**, 94–107.

McKemmish, S. (1996) Evidence of Me … , *Archives and Manuscripts*, **24** (1), 28–45.

McKemmish, S. (2011) Evidence of Me … in a Digital World. In Lee, C. (ed.), *I, Digital: personal collections in the digital era*, Society of American Archivists.

McKemmish, S. (2017) Recordkeeping in the Continuum: an Australian tradition. In Gilliland, A. J., McKemmish, S. and Lau, A. J. (eds), *Research in the Archival Multiverse*, Monash University Publishing.

Nesmith, T. (2005) Book review of Archives: Recordkeeping in Society, *Archives and Manuscripts*, **33** (2), 172–7.

Nesmith, T. (2006) The Concept of Societal Provenance and Records of Nineteenth-Century Aboriginal-European Relations in Western Canada: implications for archival theory and practice, *Archival Science*, **6** (3–4), 351–60.

Nesmith, T. (2008) Re-exploring the Continuum, Rediscovering Archives, *Archives and Manuscripts*, **36** (2), 34–53.

Newman, J. (2012) Sustaining Community Archives, *APLIS*, **25** (1), 37–45.

Oliver, G. (2017) Managing Records in Current Recordkeeping Environments. In MacNeil, H. and Eastwood, T. (eds), *Currents of Archival Thinking*, Libraries Unlimited.

Piggott, M. (2012) Two Cheers for the Records Continuum. In Piggott, M., *Archives and Societal Provenance: Australian essays*, Chandos.

Piggott, M. (2020) Cook's Australian Voyages: Towards the Continuum's Fourth Dimension. In Nesmith, T., Schwartz, J. and Bak, G. (eds), *'All Shook Up'. The Archival Legacy of Terry Cook*, Forthcoming.

Records Continuum Research Group, https://www.monash.edu/it/our-research/research-centres-and-labs/rcrg.

Reed, B. (2005a) Reading the Records Continuum: interpretations and explorations, *Archives and Manuscripts*, **33** (1), 18–43.

Reed, B. (2005b) Beyond Perceived Boundaries: imagining the potential of pluralized recordkeeping, *Archives and Manuscripts*, **33** (1), 176–98.

Rolan, G. (2017) Agency in the Archive: a model for participatory recordkeeping,

Archival Science, **17** (3), 195–225.

Sear, M. (2013) History in Communities. In Clark, A. and Ashton, P. (eds), *Australian History Now*, NewSouth.

Sheffield, R. (2017) Community Archives. In MacNeil, H. and Eastwood, T. (eds), *Currents of Archival Thinking*, 2nd edn, Libraries Unlimited.

Sheffield, R., www.rebeckasheffield.com/new-page-1/.

Shepherd, E. (2010) Archival Science. In Bates, B. and Maack, M. (eds), *Encyclopedia of Library and Information Science*, CRC Press.

Thorpe, K. (2017) Aboriginal Community Archives: a case study in ethical community research. In Gilliland, A. J., McKemmish, S. and Lau, A. J. (eds), *Research in the Archival Multiverse*, Monash University Publishing.

Upward, F. (1993) Institutionalizing the Archival Document – Some Theoretical Perspectives on Terry Eastwood's Challenge. In McKemmish, S. and Upward, F. (eds), *Archival Documents: providing accountability through recordkeeping*, Ancora Press.

Upward, F. (1996) Structuring the Records Continuum. Part One: post-custodial principles and properties, *Archives and Manuscripts*, **24** (2), 268–85.

Upward, F. (1997) Structuring the Records Continuum. Part Two: structuration theory and recordkeeping, *Archives and Manuscripts*, **25** (1), 10–35.

Upward, F. (2000) Modelling the Continuum as Paradigm Shift in Recordkeeping and Archiving Processes, and Beyond – A Personal Reflection, *Records Management Journal*, **10** (3), 115–39.

Upward, F. (2005a) The Records Continuum. In McKemmish, S., Piggott, M., Reed, B. and Upward, F. (eds), *Archives: recordkeeping in society*, Centre for Information Studies, Charles Sturt University.

Upward, F. (2005b) Continuum Mechanics and Memory Banks: (1) multi-polarity, *Archives and Manuscripts*, **33** (1), 84–109.

Upward, F. (2005c) Continuum Mechanics and Memory Banks: (2) the making of culture, *Archives and Manuscripts*, **33** (2), 18–51.

Upward F. (2015) Records Continuum. In Duranti, L. and Franks, P. (eds), *Encyclopedia of Archival Science*, Rowman & Littlefield.

Upward, F. (2017) The Archival Multiverse and Eddies in the Spacetime Continuum. In Gilliland, A. J., McKemmish, S. and Lau, A. J. (eds), *Research in the Archival Multiverse*, Monash University Publishing.

Upward, F. and McKemmish, S. (2006) Teaching Recordkeeping and Archiving Continuum Style, *Archival Science*, **6** (2), 219–230.

Upward, F., McKemmish, S. and Reed, B. (2011) Archivists and Changing Social and Information Spaces: a continuum approach to recordkeeping and archiving in online cultures, *Archivaria*, **72** (Fall), 197–237.

Upward, F., Oliver, G., Reed, B. and Evans, J. (2013) Recordkeeping Informatics: re-figuring a discipline in crisis with a single minded approach, *Records Management*

Journal, **23** (1), 37–50.

Upward, F. and Stillman, L. (2006),
    http://webstylus.net/wp-content/uploads/2009/12/upwardfinal.pdf.

Upward, F., Reed, B., Oliver, G. and Evans, J. (2018) *Recordkeeping Informatics for a Networked Age*, Monash University Publishing.

van Bussel, G.-J. (2017) The Theoretical Framework for the 'Archive-As-Is'. An Organisation Oriented View on Archives. In Smit, F., Glaudemans, A. and Jonker, R. (eds), *Archives in Liquid Times*, Stichting Archiefpublicaties.

Victorian Pride Centre, https://pridecentre.org.au.

Yeo, G. (2015) Record(s). In Duranti, L. and Franks, P. (eds), *Encyclopedia of Archival Science*, Rowman & Littlefield.

PART 2

Case Studies

CHAPTER 4

Tuku mana taonga, tuku mana tāngata
Archiving for indigenous language and cultural revitalisation: cross sectoral case studies from Aotearoa, New Zealand

Claire Hall and Honiana Love

Introduction

The starting point of this chapter is the contested history of a small South Pacific nation where state institutions hold, and administer, significant archival collections belonging to indigenous Māori. Many of these records were appropriated through processes of colonisation: war, theft and the dispossession of land, language and culture.

Pre-colonisation, Aotearoa New Zealand's indigenous Māori exercised sophisticated ways of storing and disseminating knowledge: oration, song, performance and crafts. The arts of remembering and passing on traditional knowledge are highly valued. Māori knowledge focuses on connection between people and place, voyaging stories and ancestors, creation and gods. Traditionally, transmission takes place within an information hierarchy carefully established to allow the receiver simultaneously to attain both the *content* and the *context* of what is being shared. Each fragment of traditional knowledge – a story or song, a piece of writing – is layered with clues and codes guiding correct sharing and usage.

One of the notable impacts of colonisation in this country is the number of taonga Māori (ancestral treasures, tangible and intangible) historically coveted by tau iwi (non-Māori) collectors and 'gifted' to national and international collecting institutions. Historical donation or deposit by traditional owners – with or without stipulated succession – has likewise rendered Māori archives inaccessible to intergenerational successors. At worst, those with ancestral ties may be granted the same access right as tau iwi (non-Māori) researchers walking in off the street.

While acknowledging the primacy of these treasures and their status as ancestors, this article focuses on the traditional indigenous knowledge they hold and how it is presented, and represented, in two comparative modes of contemporary archiving practice in Aotearoa New Zealand.

The story moves now to Taranaki, a region on the west coast of New Zealand's North Island. It is named for the tupuna (ancestral) mountain of the region's tribes. In 2008, we were asked to establish a pan-tribal community archive of Taranaki mātauranga (traditional knowledge) for language and cultural revitalisation.

In 2012, we wrote:

> Four years into developing Te Pūtē Routiriata o Taranaki (the Taranaki Māori archive) we have more questions than answers, but we are at least confident that we now have the questions that will elicit the right answers – not only for Taranaki Māori communities, but possibly for other iwi (tribes) and hapū (subtribes) as well.
>
> (Hall and Love, 2012)

Over the past decade, the community archive has grown from a prototype database and small physical collection into a bricks-and-mortar community archive with a training and outreach programme. Its digital archive has migrated to the indigenous knowledge management platform *Mukurtu* (http:// mukurtu.org), with significant growth in physical and digital holdings.

At the time of writing, Claire remains involved in the archive's day-to-day operations, while Honiana has moved into a leadership role with New Zealand's archive of television, film and sound, Ngā Taonga Sound and Vision. We continue to confer and collaborate over issues of indigenous knowledge management, particularly as they relate to kaitiakitanga (guardianship) of Taranaki taonga tuku iho – tangible and intangible cultural heritage traditionally owned by the region's tribes.

This chapter examines some of the intersecting spaces we inhabit in our respective roles: grey areas between community archiving and institutional practice, where conversations about the nuances of traditional ownership, sovereign rights, representation and repatriation are gaining momentum. Rather than advocating one 'pure' approach over another, we (pragmatically) posit 'comfortable cohabitation' as a fulcrum on which decisions relating to Māori archives may swing one way or another; for or against this country's 1840 Treaty of Waitangi (https://nzhistory.govt.nz/ politics/treaty-of-waitangi) obligation to uphold Māori indigenous and sovereign rights to their cultural heritage.

Fast forward 178 years to an era characterised by the settlement of redress claims and vigorous Māori cultural revitalisation efforts, political trends that collide head-on with a mainstream hard push for open data. This latter inevitably scoops up mātauranga Māori in Crown and state archival collections. There is no going back to a traditional model for sharing knowledge. But Treaty of Waitangi obligations are an onus on institutions, archivists and record keepers of all stripes to initiate conversations about how to return decision-making power to traditional owners who have typically had very little say in institutional collecting.

In the absence of Māori leadership, information management principles are routinely imposed over traditional methods of transmission and dissemination. Information is routinely digitised for free and for wide access and sharing, without proper consultation. The ease with which media enters public domain media is at odds with the protective information hierarchies traditionally underpinning indigenous historical knowledge.

Details of depositors – as opposed to traditional owners – are routinely recorded as core information by institutional archives. The circumstances by which the information came to be recorded, stored and transmitted is considered peripheral, rather than an integral part of the record. Similarly, the paths the informants took to gain particular knowledge most often goes unrecorded. In our day-to-day practice as archivists, we routinely see and feel the deleterious impact this practice continues to have on both historical record and the mana kaitiaki (inherited guardianship and ownership rights) of alienated traditional owners. An important part of decolonising archival practice in this country is ensuring that the correct – and correctly sourced – contextual information sits on record.

Te Pūtē Routiriata o Taranaki, and other Māori archives in Aotearoa, are a direct challenge to contested collecting and handling practices. Awareness is also growing within mainstream archives of an obligation under Article 2 of this country's Treaty of Waitangi to reconnect Māori with their ancestral knowledge and appropriately represent a Māori world view in collection records. (Article 2 of the Treaty of Waitangi guarantees Māori 'tino rangatiratanga' or the unqualified exercise of their chieftainship over their lands, villages and all their property and treasures.) This requires not only a will to do so, but capture, storage, access and dissemination methods of which knowledge owners approve.

This chapter updates the authors' observations of Māori archiving in Aotearoa New Zealand in recent years. It reflects ten years of progressive practice from two perspectives, presenting a few experiential case studies into meta-handling and indigenous context for a range of traditional knowledge. These prompt consideration of some of the different scenarios relevant to Māori knowledge within tribal and institutional archives.

Case one: repatriating the Taranaki letters

More than 30 years ago, a group of prominent Taranaki Māori leaders and kaumatua (elders) formed Te Reo o Taranaki, a charitable trust mandated to consolidate efforts to revitalise the region's distinctive dialect of te reo, the Māori language:

> The impetus was from our elders, the intent was for you who are learning, you who are sustaining our paepae (orator's bench), you who nurture our children, you who provide livelihood for our homes and our families where our reo must endure . . . persist, to be passed onto future generations.
>
> (Hond and Sundgren, 2003)

In 2005, archiving was identified as crucial in a tactical plan to fill the void of Taranaki's muru raupatu: the documented historic land confiscation and dispossession, with resultant loss of language and culture (Waitangi Tribunal, 1996). In Aotearoa, language revitalisation is part of an effort to counter the ongoing impact of this country's colonisation by Britain in the mid-1800s.

Five generations on, with the number of native or highly proficient speakers of Taranaki dialect perilous, the need to find exemplars of traditional language use for revitalisation was critical. Inevitably, the search for recorded sources turned to Crown and state institutions holding Taranaki records and archives.

One such collection of correspondence was stolen by colonial soldiers sacking and razing papakāinga (communal home base) during a phase of history dubbed the Taranaki land wars. After being screened for military intelligence, these plundered letters were first the booty of a collector affiliated with New Zealand's Polynesian Society (www. thepolynesiansociety.org), ultimately deposited on long-term loan with New Zealand's National Library.

Working with the library's Māori librarians, Te Reo o Taranaki helped navigate a process of digital repatriation, reconnecting traditional owners with the letters' mauri and mātauranga – intangible heritage and intrinsic Māori knowledge. Until this point, the letters' customary owners – descendants of the original scribes – have had no say in how these records are cared for, arranged, described or accessed. The impetus to reconnect these records with customary owners came by happenstance: at a public talk a descendent of one of the writers learned of the library's intention to digitise and publish the letters online and appealed for a different process (Hall, 2017; Hall, Love and Tikao, 2017). This is an example of how the ease of capturing and sharing media sits at odds with the protective information hierarchy that once conveyed indigenous knowledge. It also reveals the very real risk institutions face of perpetuating historic injustice by ill-considering the difference between possession and guardianship from a traditional knowledge perspective.

Lynette Russell writes that the value of confronting the 'hidden histories' of colonised indigenous records far exceeds the prima facie benefit of augmented institutional record:

> ... indigenous knowledge is ... local knowledge ... that is unique to a given culture or society. It contrasts with the international knowledge system generated by universities, research institutions, and private firms. It is the basis for local-level decision making in agriculture, health care, food preparation, education, natural-resource management, and a host of other activities in rural communities.
>
> (Russell, 2005, 3)

In the case of the Taranaki letters, the local context is dialect revitalisation. Digital surrogates of letters were made available to local tribes through the community archive. A sample set of around a third of the collection was rearranged and (re)described to reflect Taranaki tribal history and how their content might bear relevance to language revitalisation. This selection was transcribed and imported into a *Mukurtu* database, a content management platform chosen for its ability to reflect nuanced cultural protocols in sharing and access rules, described here by co-developer Kim Christen:

> Within Mukurtu CMS, customizable cultural and sharing protocols allow for finegrain management of access within the archive. Protocols may be based on family groups, clans, ritual societies, gender, age, seasonal activities, etc. ... [and] are flexible, adaptable and can be changed at any time. The salient point is that the communities themselves decide together how best to share and circulate their cultural materials. For example, if a tribe has traditional access parameters around the viewing of sacred materials limited only to elders, or if some songs should only be heard in specific seasons ... they can use these protocols to determine access within the database itself.
>
> (Christen, 2015, 5)

Decision making authority for what happens next – at a community level – now sits with the two tribes involved in the pilot. While the collection has been withheld from online publication, it remains available to the general public – at the discretion of a librarian rather than the traditional owners – in the library's reading room.

This project is an example of an institution and a pan-tribal community archive working together to redress balance in one case of dispossessed historical artefacts. In context, this is an isolated project and not the rule for the significant tranche of Māori content in institutional care. This raises questions around the accuracy of historical record and documented provenance, not to mention the intrinsic cultural and intellectual property rights of traditional knowledge in public domain.

Russell contends that the concept of public domain is one of two critical issues that must be confronted in conversations around indigenous knowledge archiving. The second is 'incommensurable ontologies', or the irreconcilable differences between western and traditional modes of valuing, organising and applying traditional knowledge (Russell, 2005). Christen also challenges mainstream concepts of public domain and information freedom and the way these are routinely imposed upon indigenous knowledge. She notes that her use of the term indigenous is intentionally inclusive and not designed to restrict people's nuanced self-definitions of cultural identity. Christen describes 'the contours of information circulation … across cultures' as existing within 'messy spaces where different notions of collaboration, collection and curation intersect' (Christen, 2012, 2874).

These two perspectives reflect aspects of 'bringing home' the Taranaki letters, a fluid process that has taken more than five years to evolve. Through a filter of efficient archiving, the pilot might well be deemed improvident. Through a filter of indigenous knowledge management, the fluid process is, in and of itself, the very point of this collaborative exercise. And through a filter of history, five years invested in repatriation and reconciliation is a mere blip on a timeline defined by colonisation and spanning nearly 160 years.

Case two: researching Taranaki's seaweed piupiu

This case demonstrates the difference in transmission and attribution methods for kōrero tuku iho (intergenerational knowledge) in an ao Māori context, versus institutional record-keeping practices. It relates to a piece of oral history about a raranga (weaving) practice attributed to a south Taranaki kuia (female elder) and passed on to one of her mokopuna (descendents) by way of her father. This scenario represents the passage of mātauranga (traditional knowledge) across four generations of one family, its ultimate recipient intent on using this knowledge to revive her great-grandmother's weaving techniques (Waikerepuru, 2017).

The story relates to a distinctive tīpare (headband) commonly worn by her father and renowned Taranaki elder Te Huirangi Waikerepuru: orator, academic and language revitalisation campaigner.

Waikerepuru told his daughter Ria Waikerepuru that the tīpare (headband) was woven for him in his boyhood by his kuia (female elder) Hariata Tāmaka. The piece, he says, was originally the waistband of a distinctive seaweed piupiu, a waist to knee garment traditionally woven in flax. The embroidered taniko (a traditional finger-weaving pattern with an embroidered appearance) waistband is all that physically remains of the piupiu; replicating its original form is a means of keeping family memory and cultural identity strong for future generations (Waikerepuru, 2017).

In the context of understanding holistic Māori wellbeing, Rebecca Wirihana and Cheryll Smith write that Māori relationships with ancestors demonstrate the significance of deep interconnections to a Māori world view and strong, positive identity. They emphasise the importance of creation stories maintained by whakapapa kōrero, traditional knowledge passed from generation to generation, traditionally through oral transmission:

> Whakapapa knowledge and the practices associated with wellbeing were sustained by the intergenerational transfer of knowledge, this meant that wellbeing relied on a firm grounding in cultural knowledge.
>
> (Wirihana and Smith, 2014, 204)

The Waikerepuru family case reflects this. It is also an enactment of inherited kaitiakitanga (customary guardianship), a responsibility often misunderstood by non-indigenous practitioners and institutions (Smith et al., 2016).

Ria Waikerepuru turned to her Taranaki weaving contemporaries for corroborating stories of a seaweed weaving tradition back home. With nothing solid forthcoming, research eventually led her to institutional sources. One turned up a 1910 photograph of a poi group (where songs are performed, usually by women, in which the poi – a swinging ball on the end of a string – is swung in various movements to accompany singing) wearing what appears to be seaweed piupiu.

At the time of Ria's original research, the National Library catalogue description read:

> Poi dancers, circa 1910. Shows a group of Māori women wearing piupiu and holding poi. A man in the background holds an accordion. Possibly taken at Parihaka.
>
> (Waikerepuru, 2017)

Parihaka is a small coastal Taranaki community renowned as a centre of non-violent resistance to European occupation of confiscated land in the region. The detail 'possibly taken at Parihaka' was the first tangible match in her search for corroboration of her father's story. She recalls kuia Hariata being from Taiporohēnui, a papakāinga (collective homestead) in south Taranaki, and stories told of her travelling to Parihaka with Ria's father, the young Huirangi.

Figure 4.1. *Poi dancers. Ref: PA1-o-316-100. Alexander Turnbull Library, Wellington, New Zealand* (https://natlib.govt.nz/records/22498138)

Curious about where the information referenced in the library record came from, she called a librarian. Ria was advised that there was no recorded source or context for the 'possibly taken at Parihaka' description; the librarian who added this information no longer worked there. Following a brief discussion, the record's description was augmented to read:

> Source of descriptive information – Information relating to Parihaka is from an unidentified source.

Ria notes her own conversation with the librarian about the seaweed piupiu was also added to the item's permanent record – without consultation or contextualisation. Her identity and authority is noted only as a 'library client':

> Seaweed piupiu identified by Library client who also provided information regarding Matatua and Whakatane district.

This statement also bears reference to Ria's observation that one of the women in the photograph wears a shoulder sash emblazoned with the word *Mataatua*. She casually observed a possible reference to a migration canoe which landed in the Whakatane region – the geographically opposite coast of the north island to Taranaki.

Smith et al. warn of the risk of 'mayhem at play, as the academic work around indigenous knowledge mātauranga Māori becom(es) institutionalised away from its indigenous communities and contexts, where it began and where it still forms identities, ways of living and being' (2016, 31). This case study demonstrates how the librarians' desire to augment a vague institutional collection record 'oversimplified the way mātauranga Māori is defined in relation to western knowledge (2016, 133). The receiver failed to attain both the *content* and the *context* of what was being shared. Nor did they consider the implications of rendering a casual conversation with a 'library client' to permanent record. This is significant as in a mātauranga Māori context, 'the storyteller may be as important as the story and can be a key authority of knowledge – as well as a transgressor of knowledge' (2016, 138).

Case three: Working with kaitiaki at Ngā Taonga Sound and Vision

This case study explores some of the practical realities of Ngā Taonga Sound and Vision acting as kaipupuri (keepers of the record) working with kaitiaki (cultural and spiritual guardians) to facilitate decision-making for the reuse of traditional knowledge. It touches on how relationships between Ngā Taonga and Māori source communities have evolved and the implications of a Waitangi Tribunal investigation into the issue of protection rights for traditional knowledge.

In the 1970s and 80s, Māori filmmakers, led by pioneers such as Barry Barclay and Merata Mita, began capturing on film the stories and traditions of knowledge holders from iwi and hapū throughout Aotearoa. From the outset it was considered essential that these records be shared in ways that were acceptable to knowledge holders. Access and reuse were discussed and agreed as part of the creation and capture process. The Tangata Whenua series, produced by Pacific Films and directed by Barry Barclay, is an early example of the power of that collaborative process.

One of the episodes, shot in Taranaki, was taken back to kaitiaki before going to air. On being shown the final version, people felt the story it told did not appropriately reflect their community and deemed it unsuitable for broadcast. That right of refusal was honoured by filmmakers and producers. Other episodes from around Aotearoa did air – with permission – and are today considered taonga (treasures) for the knowledge shared by the many elders interviewed.

Relationships created between holders of the record and source communities have endured, even as the record passed from programme producers into the care of the New Zealand Film Archive (later to become Ngā Taonga Sound and Vision). This means that despite the Tangata Whenua footage having no official or legal protection, the original agreement between filmmakers and storytellers has been honoured. A positive outcome – yet this case highlights how easily the original agreement could be lost from institutional memory or put aside as having no legal standing.

The Film Archive took the kaitiaki/kaipupuri model developed by these filmmakers and applied it across its entire taonga Māori collection. This involved retrospectively negotiating and signing memoranda of understanding with multiple kaitiaki for legacy collections containing traditional knowledge, the majority of which were captured and donated without discussions around future reuse. This work continues proactively as Ngā Taonga collections grow.

There are complexities in managing these relationships, in particular the large resource commitment they require from both institution and kaitiaki. This has been possible at Ngā Taonga because the archive is well practiced in managing multiple rights: copyright, ownership and the administration of contractual obligations to depositors are all part of the institution's business as usual rights framework.

The key to success for Ngā Taonga, as holders of the record, has been a commitment to step out of the conversation and make space for kaitiaki to speak on behalf of the record. This often means remaining committed to the decision of kaitiaki, even when that decision may compromise archival standards. A recent example was a request to show material not yet fully preserved. For the kaitiaki, the images were so important that quality was a secondary consideration. A compromise was reached and the archive supplied a viewing copy with the agreement that once preservation was complete a better quality copy would be made available.

While organisations can pass back some of the decision-making process, digitisation and online access means there is no going back to a traditional model for sharing knowledge. By way of balance, Ngā Taonga is exploring ways of building a traditional knowledge sharing model into archival description practices. This is particularly relevant to processes around the access and access restrictions. Kaitiaki-imposed restrictions can be a difficult concept for a non-Māori archive to grapple with, but one that is critical if mainstream archives are to shift towards bicultural practice and allow traditional owners to provide both content and context to safely guide record keepers and administrators.

Kaitiaki are rarely resourced to respond to the many requests for their time and expertise. The complexity of ensuring contextual information sits on record, along with appropriate access protocols for the multiplicity of people who may wish to access information (different age groups, genders, ethnicities and beliefs) is time-consuming, sometimes overwhelming. For a requester, following ethical practice in relation to indigenous records means the process may take considerably longer and be more complex – and frustrating – than expected. These are issues record keepers must be equipped for and open to navigating day-to-day for this model to work.

At present there are no industry or legislated standards for applying a bicultural model within mainstream archives. The idea of formalising protection of rights for traditional knowledge was the focus of a significant chapter in the 2011 Waitangi Tribunal report, *Ko Aotearoa Tēnei: A Report into Claims Concerning New Zealand Law and Policy Affecting Māori Culture and Identity* [Wai 262].

> . . . the Wai 262 claim is really a claim about mātauranga Māori – that is, the unique Māori way of viewing the world, encompassing both traditional knowledge and culture. The claimants, in other words, are seeking to preserve their culture and identity, and the relationships that culture and identity derive from.
>
> (Waitangi Tribunal, 2011, 30–31)

In its report, the Tribunal does not suggest that full authority or control over Māori culture should rest with Māori. Instead, it recommends creating a series of remedies based on the precise level of protection indicated by kaitiaki in relation to historical claims.

Chapter six of the report deals specifically with archives and libraries. It reflects on how kaitiaki can help shape the development of processes for working with their cultural heritage and how Crown agencies can support and develop the role of tribal guardians as kaitiaki of mātauranga Māori/ traditional knowledge held by Crown collections:

> The claimants objected to the fact that their mātauranga in these repositories as generally open to anyone to access, without prior kaitiaki consent. They were particularly concerned that some of their mātauranga that could be accessed was sensitive in nature. They wanted to be treated by the Crown archives and libraries as more than just consultees, and to in fact have real decision-making power. Some even wanted government-held documents containing their mātauranga to be returned to them.
>
> (Waitangi Tribunal, 2011, 527)

The Tribunal goes beyond just providing (albeit very useful) guidance to an organisation like Ngā Taonga. It recommends mechanisms be put in place to ensure kaitiaki play a lead role in setting legal and policy frameworks around decision-making:

> Kaitiakitanga is the obligation, arising from the kin relationship, to nurture or care for a person or thing … kaitiaki can be spiritual guardians existing in non-human form … but people can (indeed, must) also be kaitiaki. … Mana (authority) and kaitiakitanga go together as right and responsibility, and that kaitiaki responsibility can be understood not only as cultural principle but as a system of law.
>
> (Waitangi Tribunal, 2011, 23)

Three basic levels of protection are presented as applicable to kaitiaki relationships, creating a sort of spectrum of representation by which compliance might be measured. These range from full decision-making authority in the hands of the kaitiaki, to partnership with the Crown (not just Māori input, but shared decision-making), to institutional influence over decisions that affect the kaitiaki relationship.

The report also touched on the issue of commercial use of taonga works and the need for new principles to be developed to guide compulsory kaitiaki involvement. It recommends an expert commission be established to consider and make decisions about use objections, provide information and guidance to those who may wish to use taonga works, and maintain a register of specific cultural works so that kaitiaki can be easily identified and consulted.

Seven years on from the release of the Wai 262 report, the Crown has not signaled any substantial move towards implementing any of its findings. This leaves it up to record holders to create their own systems and relies on the goodwill of both organisations and kaitiaki. The value of trust-based relationships is therefore paramount. At Ngā Taonga, these relationships are the key to obtaining information from source communities about the taonga we hold. This is information that the organisation might never otherwise have been able to source about collection items: places, people, events and practices that deeply enrich the record for anyone searching. Such contextual information makes collection records and descriptions more meaningful, and ultimately more accessible. A vital yet often undervalued outcome in a sector where day-to-day operational resources are hard-won and projects highly contestable.

Kapohia ngā taonga – connecting past and present

A desire for data sovereignty – authoritative storage, access and dissemination rights – is driving growth in tribal knowledge banks in Aotearoa. The pan-tribal Taranaki archive is one model of practice; many tribes and sub-tribes are establishing or extending independent archives in the wake of Treaty of Waitangi claim settlements.

The Ngāi Tahu archive is another example of successful practice in Aotearoa. This iwi from the south has spent eight years on an archiving and cultural mapping project, recording and databasing 5,000 Māori place names (http://ngaitahu.iwi.nz/our_stories/cultural-mapping-unlocks-ngai-tahu-history/). Launched in 2018, the Ngāi Tahu atlas is an inspirational model for managing and accessing history for iwi, hapū and whānau (tribe, sub-tribe and family) development. For digital archiving, Ngāi Tahu has created a bespoke platform with a sophisticated, tribally specific knowledge management platform and localised data storage. The Taranaki database, by comparison, is constructed around open source software and relies on an overseas company for development and technical maintenance. While the Mukurtu software itself proved a good fit for purpose – relatively easy and inexpensive to set up, populate and update inhouse – the finished Taranaki database sits in limbo as the organisation contends with a dishonoured service level agreement and virtual abandonment by developers no longer invested in this line of work.

Both the Taranaki and Ngāi Tahu digital archives are examples of information being organised within a Māori-worldview and iwi retaining control of the knowledge management process. The Te Reo o Taranaki experience highlights the 'last mile' problem created by a need to outsource hosting and data storage in a non-Māori market. While a bespoke development and localised data storage alternative are an ideal, it is an expensive proposition for small start-ups.

Iwi archives and databases can more deeply reflect tikanga (traditional cultural practice) in the stewardship of Māori heritage. Digital repatriation offers communities a chance to reconnect and re-contextualise their own records from public repositories, with the potential to decolonise arrangement, description and modes of access. Tribal archiving creates enormous potential for augmented institutional relationships with Māori; co-collaboration requires a flexibility of approach and a commitment to a genuine relationship that only stands to enhance communication.

As with institutions, flax-roots community archives must create their own policies, protocols and information management systems – albeit from a very different standpoint. While liberating, going it alone remains a major challenge for communities; ongoing operational resourcing is a major issue for small tribal archives like Te Pūtē Routiriata o Taranaki. For a long time yet, improving approaches to the care and handling of Māori archives will require a dual approach: localised efforts augmenting and extending institutional practice around kaitiakitanga.

Conclusion

These case studies examine some of the nuances of archival practice related to traditional knowledge records in Aotearoa, from institutional to localised community perspectives. It demonstrates some of the strengths and sensitivities of both models and suggests opportunities for institutional collaboration with indigenous communities as a vital first step towards change.

No one-size-fits-all approach will work for indigenous archiving in this country. Nor can the spaces between institutional and alternative practice be considered on a neat continuum. Relationship-based, collaborative practice is difficult to define; what works in one case won't necessarily work in another, as these examples illustrate. Indigenous archiving in this country is an emerging field that operates in a space of ambiguity and change. So is the nature of a colonised country in which the mainstream remains resistant to conversations about restoring indigenous sovereignty. The nation's response to the pivotal Wai 262 report is a point in case.

Rather than striving for a one-size-fits-all solution, practitioners of all stripes must defer to source communities if rangatiratanga is truly desired. Te Paerangi National Services (www.tepapa.govt.nz/learn/for-museums-and-galleries/help-and-support-for-museums-and-galleries) is an example of how institutional outreach can bolster capacity and expertise in a culturally responsive way. The growing emphasis on context and collaborative management of Ngā Taonga collections, including developing Māori language cataloguing standards, is another model of dynamic practice, as is the profiled National Library partnership around the Taranaki letters. While positive, each of these examples illustrate the ad-hoc nature of change and how it still falls to small groups or leading individuals to challenge mainstream norms.

It is unrealistic to expect archivists themselves to change the entrenched practices of organisations which, in the absence of traditional knowledge holders, have imposed information management principles over traditional modes of transmission and guardianship. But individuals can be thought leaders and this is the challenge we extend to archivists working with Māori collections.

These case studies demonstrate the scope of influence two practitioners committed to different ways of working have been able to have across the sector in recent years. The key to success for Ngā Taonga, as holders of the record, has been a commitment to step out of the conversation and make space for kaitiaki to speak on behalf of the record. Te Reo o Taranaki has taken a role in facilitating discussions with kaitiaki, consolidating localised archiving efforts and bolstering the hands-on skills of community archivists and tribal stewards.

Rather than advocating one method over another, we encourage our peers and bosses to commit to exploring the grey, undefined – and largely undefinable – space that sits between indigenous and institutional practice. We consider this a formative space where Māori-led methods and modes of knowledge management can come to the fore, a crossway between classical archiving and traditional approaches to the care and handling of Māori collections. This space can also be an incubator for conversations about the conscious decolonisation of archival practice in Aotearoa New Zealand.

References

Christen, K. (2012) Does Information Really Want to be Free? Indigenous Knowledge Systems and the Question of Openness, *International Journal of Communication*, **6**, 2870–2893.

Christen, K. (2015) Tribal Archives, Traditional Knowledge, and Local Contexts: why the 's' matters, *Journal of Western Archives*, **6** (1), Article 3.

Hall, C. (2017) Mukurtu for Mātauranga Māori: a case study in indigenous archiving for Reo and Tikanga revitalisation (189). *He Whare Hangarau: Māori Language, culture & technology,* Kirikiriroa / Hamilton, Aotearoa / New Zealand: Te Pua Wānanga ki te Ao, Te Whare Wānanga o Waikato.

Hall, C. and Love, H. (2012) Ka Puta, Ka Ora, *Archifacts Journal*, Archives and Records Association of Aotearoa New Zealand, 25–34.

Hond, R. and Sundgren, H. (2003) *Taranaki Reo Revitalisation Strategy (2005–2015)*, Te Reo o Taranaki Trust.

Ministry for Culture and Heritage, *Treaty of Waitangi*, https://nzhistory.govt.nz/politics/treaty/read-the-Treaty/differences-between-the-texts.

New Zealand, Waitangi Tribunal (1996) *The Taranaki Report: kaupapa tuatahi* (Wai 143).

New Zealand, Waitangi Tribunal (2011) *Indigenous Flora and Fauna and Cultural Intellectual Property* (Wai 262). Report summary (Waitangi Tribunal report), Wellington, N.Z.: The Tribunal.

Russell, L. (2005) Indigenous Knowledge and Archives: accessing hidden history and understandings, *Australian Academic and Research Libraries*, **36** (2), 161–171.

Smith, L., Maxwell, T., Puke, H. and Temara, P. (2016) Indigenous Knowledge, Methodology and Mayhem: what is the role of methodology in producing indigenous insights? A discussion from Matauranga Maori, *Knowledge Cultures*, **4** (3), 131.

Wirihana, R. and Smith, C. (2014) Historical Trauma, Healing and Well-being in Māori Communities, *MAI Journal* (Online), **3** (3), 197–210.

Interviews

Interview with Ria Waikerepuru, December 2017. Recorded by Claire Hall for Te Reo o Taranaki Trust.

Presentations and conference papers

Hall, C., Love, H. and Tikao, A. (2017) Whakahoki ki te kāinga: the long (digital) road home for Taranaki's Atkinson Letters, National Digital Forum keynote, November 2017, www.youtube.com/watch?v=kSyU5SXjs0c&t=19s.

Websites

www.jps.auckland.ac.nz
https://mukurtu.org
https://natlib.govt.nz
https://ngaitahu.iwi.nz
https://ngataonga.org.nz
https://nzhistory.govt.nz
https://teara.govt.nz
https://www.tepapa.govt.nz
https://tereootaranaki.org

Self-documentation of Thai communities: reflective thoughts on the Western concept of community archives

Kanokporn Nasomtrug Simionica

Introduction

Over the past decades, the concept of 'community archives' has moved from a primarily Western narrative into a global discussion. Specifically, the concept has gained traction through scholars in the post-colonial era who began to encourage the archival profession to reconsider the role of archival professionals and think beyond public archival legacies to embrace the stories and heritage of ordinary people, including groups marginalised by their social qualities such as ethnicity, sexuality, religion and gender in the light of decolonisation and social justice.

This chapter, drawn from my doctoral research, explores issues of community archives as they relate to communities in Thailand. Through examples of five different Thai community archives, based on research findings specific to the case studies of Northeast (Isan) communities, I explore narratives of Thai communities in dealing with safeguarding their heritage.

For the purpose of this chapter, community archives are defined as a collection of tangible heritage or an action of self-dedication to preserve the intangible heritage of a community of which community engagement amongst its members in such processes is the most important feature.

Community archives in Thailand

The motivation for the establishment of any Thai community archives is made up of many individuals and it was not possible for me to interview all community members. The motivations of the community as a whole were explored through observation of their participation in communal events, whilst recognising that outward action may be poor evidence for inner motivation. Nevertheless, levels of participation can be seen as indicators of community buy-in to the leaders' objectives.

Heritage encompasses both tangible and intangible elements and the motivations for preserving each can potentially be different, although the analysis below suggests that the two are so interwoven that separation is unhelpful. Nevertheless, individual motivations are likely to have an influence on the tangible heritage, whilst community motivation appears to be more beneficial to the intangible aspects. These different kinds of motivation in relation to both heritage domains are further described in this chapter.

The following examples of Thai community archives informed my research conclusions. The focus of discussion about community archives in Thailand will only be based on communities within the Northeast or Isan region, where the great majority of people are of Lao ethnicity, and should not be taken as representative of all Thai community archives.

Model 1: Mancha Khiri Cultural Home

Mancha Khiri Cultural Home is located in Mancha Khiri district, Khon Kaen province. The Mancha Khiri Cultural Home is in the district town centre and it was established by Mr Surasak, an individual collector and retired primary teacher. A native to the community, he was respected by members of the community as an expert in local history. He had also played a significant role in the development and promotion of textiles using techniques unique to the region. Thereafter he began to merge his inherited traditional-styled houses, which he transformed into a private museum and repository of his collections. The collections held by him consisted of some photographs passed on from his family, equipment and tools donated or acquired from the villagers of the communities he had visited around the areas of Mancha Khiri district, palm leaf manuscripts and excavated pottery rescued from the temple believed to be one of the earliest occupied sites in the district, textiles collected from villagers and recently produced based on his designs, and other items.

Mancha Khiri Cultural Home was selected as one of the case studies mainly because it was managed by an individual collector, even though this criterion for selection was unlikely to correspond with the 'community archive' definition (according to which the focus should be on community engagement).

Model 2: Tha Muang community

Tha Muang is a village community located in Roi-et province. Geographically, the Tha Muang community is located close to Roi-et city centre and is adjacent to the main university of the province. These related geographic factors influenced Tha Muang's development into a so-called 'hybrid community' since it maintained traditional practices, while attempting to re-create new customs to strengthen community co-operation. Therefore, the Tha Muang community became an ideal archival model for an investigation of a community's strategies on maintaining community heritage.

The use of the term 'hybrid community' may be found mostly in the field of communication, particularly in reference to the interaction of people through both online and offline mediums, such as the definition suggested by Gaved and Mulholland (2005). Nevertheless, the use of this term for the Tha Muang community in the context of this chapter is more related to the concept of 'hybridity' discussed in anthropology, sociology and history disciplines, which involves cultural hybridity (Ackermann, 2012), in which the Tha Muang community may be expressed in terms of segregation and adaptation.

Model 3: Dan Sai community

The Dan Sai community mostly refers to the central town of Dan Sai district in Loei province. This particular community is a good example to represent other similar Thai communities where both aspects of heritage – tangible and intangible – were amalgamated in the community's traditional practice. The *tangible* aspect was initially concentrated on the Phi Ta Khon collections displayed at the Phi Ta Khon museum located inside the community's central temple, Wat Phon Chai. This is the main temple for religious events of the Dan Sai community. (Phi Ta Khon is a so-called community symbol of Dan Sai district. It represents a puppet decorated with a colourful mask and costume to be worn by a person and a group of Phi Ta Khon puppets who would dance along with the procession during the Bun Luang Ceremony.)

The *intangible* heritage was the spiritual events supported by members of the community throughout the year, specifically the Bun Luang ceremony and the celebration of Phi Ta Khon, which had been the main annual festival for more than 450 years. The iconic Phi Ta Khon ghost dancing of the Dan Sai community takes place on the second day of the festival along with the Bun Phra Wet procession and it is a famous tourist attraction for the district.

The Bun Luang Festival itself is quite complex and consists of four different ceremonies within three days. Whilst it is not possible to provide further details of each ceremony due to the limited space of this chapter, each ceremony is mostly associated with Buddhist religious and spiritual beliefs. For example, the procession on the second day of the festival celebrates the

Buddha's ultimate generosity in previous life as told in the Vessantara Jataka. Another ceremony that takes place after the procession is called Bun Bang Fai, or Rocket Festival, which traditionally was held to ask for sufficient rainwater for rice farming and is associated with the myth of an indigenous deity, Phaya Thaen, who could control the rain.

Model 4: Surin City Gallery

Surin City Gallery is identified as a gallery even though the work by its staff is more closely akin to that of local historians. Members of the former local historian club, including Ms Pattanan and Mr Assadang, wanted to continue their aims, therefore they became the founders of the Surin City Gallery. They later hired Ms Fone to support administrative tasks, as well as to be a regular researcher for the organisation. The organisation was formed in partnership with two other organisations: the Rajamangala University of Technology Isan (which owns the building that hosts the gallery) and Surin City Council (the main funding body for the gallery).

The collections of the Gallery are mainly photographs collected from communities in Surin province, which are primarily ethnically Cambodian, and are based on their historical interest, for example local craft skills such as textiles and silverwares. The Gallery team conducts oral history research by using the old photographs they receive as a tool for an oral interview with the people appearing in the photographs. They then write the local history and produce publications to disseminate their research results. They also provide outreach activities for the communities, such as mobile photograph exhibitions to schools or temples, as well as providing training on local research for students of the Rajamangala University of Technology Isan.

The Surin City Gallery was a community archive model that seemed to have the activist characteristics associated with the community archives discussed in Western literature, particularly in terms of its background driven by marginalisation. The Gallery's staff aimed to raise their voices via their publications based on oral history research, even though the Gallery's staff were not from the communities that the oral histories represented.

Western provenance and the Thai community archives

Issues concerning 'provenance' discussed by scholars from the Western world can relate to a variety of areas, including appraisal, (post-)custody, description, ownership and identity. The reason for this variety is possibly that the concept of provenance – identified as the ultimate principle of archival science and which discloses the origin of the archival materials, especially referring to the record creators – involves different kinds of factors that will help to identify and authenticate the content and context of a preserved record (Barr, 1987; Bastian, 2003–4; Cook, 1993; Harris, 2002; Hurley, 2005; Ketelaar, 2008; Millar, 2002; Nesmith, 1999; Niu, 2013; Wurl, 2005). Therefore 'provenance' usually relates to the appraisal and description aspects of archival practice.

The re-conceptualisation of 'provenance' in scholarly debates from the 1990s onwards has identified that archival provenance may concern both physical and societal aspects of the records. My research highlights situations in Thai communities that are different from those described by Western scholars in terms of heritage activities related to provenance concerns. For instance, the relationship between community-based archives and mainstream archives is blurred. The initial findings suggest no evidence of interaction between such institutions, while other external organisations, such as university academics, appear to play more important roles than traditional archival professions. The lack of any interface between community collections and traditional repositories meant that none of the communities defined their holdings as an archive, meaning that discussion of 'archival' issues was needed in order to negotiate the lack of a shared vocabulary.

Other relevant issues of provenance discussed in Western literature, such as identity concerns, history and heritage value and information relating to archival practices, could not be easily investigated solely through analysis of the interview data, but could be analysed only through observation, especially in relation to aspects of intangible heritage. However, the concept of 'ethnic provenance' was apparently unconsciously adapted by key individuals from all the case studies when they came to choosing a term for selection of the materials or themes to be included in the repository for which they were responsible or in the community's cultural space. By unconsciously adapting the concept of 'ethnic provenance', the key individuals of the communities gained more opportunities to preserve both tangible and intangible heritage, both of which are significantly related to and support one another to potentially provide an element of sustainable community-based heritage projects in the future.

In terms of provenance, it is clear that 'ethnic provenance' became the unconscious shared practice adopted by key individuals in all case studies. Moreover, the findings show that the individuals' perception of their practice is significantly influenced by motive factors, including the feeling of cultural change and loss by the key individuals and the spiritual motivation that supports a community's cultural and traditional practices. Having adopted 'ethnic provenance', this practice allows community archives in a Thai context a noteworthy intertwining of tangible and intangible heritage in which separation of the two aspects, in terms of consideration of provenance, would make no sense. This is because both aspects are fulfilling one another, such as the recognisable example of Isan textiles shown by the cases of the Tha Muang community and Mancha Khiri Cultural Home. Moreover, the findings also suggest that the key leaders from the Mancha Khiri Cultural Home, the Tha Muang community and the Dan Sai community case studies play an important role in intangible heritage through demonstration of its mobility and adaptability in relation to the tangible heritage (textiles, palm leaf manuscripts and ceremonies). Even though 'ethnic provenance' seems to be useful for the Thai communities to safeguard their heritage, the findings also imply the risk to intellectual rights if owners of the items collected by the key individuals happen to ask for the items back in the future, since their original sources did not appear to be systematically and consistently recorded for long-term use.

In addition to the 'ethnic provenance', which is the unconscious manner used to safeguard the Isan identities applied by key individuals from all case studies, the findings also indicate that the sub-groups' identities are no less significant. Their identities can sometimes be abused or misrepresented by the more powerful group or the outsiders if the participation of all stakeholders – especially members of such communities – does not occur in the processes of heritage documentation, such as in the example of the Phi Ta Khon museum at Dan Sai community.

In relation to the above discussion regarding 'ethnic provenance' and participation of all stakeholders in the processes of a community's heritage documentation, the findings reveal that trust is also an essential element in maintaining Thai heritage, as has been presented in all case studies throughout the chapter. In particular, the case of Surin City Gallery has well demonstrated a high level of trust for the organisation. While the Surin City Gallery team's working space is situated outside of the represented communities, it solely manages the photograph collections and abides by ethical agreements between the Surin City Gallery team and the owners of the photographs, who are members of the communities.

Lastly, in respect of preserving their heritage, Thai communities prefer physical space over digital space, as it seems that support for a digital infrastructure is not yet in place.

Sustainability of the Thai community archives

A community-centric framework for approaching archives and recordkeeping by Anne Gilliland (Gilliland, 2014) includes criteria that could maintain sustainability of community archives in general. Sustainability has been defined as 'the concept of maintaining at a proper level over time, and of responsibility to do so for future generations' (Newman, 2011).

In the Isan communities, relevant themes to sustainability that emerged from the interviews included: income sources; maintenance costs; staffing; heritage valuing; attitude towards the future of the community-based heritage organisations; attitude towards the future of heritage preservation/traditional practices; attitude towards temporal changes of heritage project/activity leaders; planning for substituted staff; knowledge transferring and education of traditions to younger generations; and signs of risk identification/risk management. The findings show both similarities to and differences from the issues identified by Western commentators, as well as problems with applying Western frameworks to the situation in Thailand.

The research data results show that each case study has strengths and weaknesses in relation to sustainability issues. The issue of funding was relevant in all cases: some may have seen it as a challenge whilst others had community support to mitigate the concern of community members. All cases had challenges relating to maintenance issues, including lack of planning and staffing. As for the strength aspects, the interwoven relationship of tangible and intangible heritage seemed promising for the future of community heritage, such as in the case of the Dan Sai community where both museums use the tangible heritage to represent the intangible heritage of the community tradition. While collaboration with internal and external bodies could possibly help the communities with the funding and content for the community archives, this would be beneficial for the communities only if the agenda is based on mutual agreement of all stakeholders. Furthermore, leadership appeared to be significant for sustainability for some communities.

Whether community archives in a Thai context would be sustainable or not notably depends on the motivations for their establishment and existence; therefore, each case presents different strengths and weaknesses in relation to sustainability concerns. Nevertheless, the findings suggest one main factor that is shared amongst all case studies: the high dependency on key individuals. It is also necessary to note that the dependency on leadership is most noticeable from communities with characteristics of strong support for religious and spiritual institutes, as exemplified by the Tha Muang and Dan Sai communities, whereas Mancha Khiri Cultural Home and Surin City Gallery have a different context, thus their level of leadership dependency is lower.

These four case studies share another aspect that is relevant to leadership dependency, namely, trust in the key individuals, be they the religious and spiritual leaders (Tha Muang and Dan Sai communities), individual collectors (Mancha Khiri Cultural Home) or the organisation representing the community (the Surin City Gallery). 'Trust' influences sustainability of the community archives as trust or faith in key individuals could change, risking a community discontinuing its support for the heritage initiatives established by those key individuals.

Another issue with sustainability relates to funding. Each case study presents both strengths and weaknesses in this area. The individual collector, Mr Surasak, seems the least sustainable due to lack of financial support from other sources besides his own budget for maintaining the collections. On the other hand, Chao Poh Guan's collection is likely to be in a better situation due to strong support from the Dan Sai community members because of his prestige in the leading spiritual roles. Another community-based archive in the Dan Sai community, the Phi Ta Khon museum, reveals very different results for the risk of long-term maintenance of the museum and this is mainly because of the conflict of interest amongst the stakeholders from the beginning. The last-mentioned case study, Surin City Gallery, is in a very different situation from the others in terms of financial support due to the context of its establishment. Nevertheless, other factors, especially the conflict of interest, have significant impacts on long-term maintenance issues and consequently caused its termination. Moreover, maintenance issues, including lack of planning and staff, remain challenges shared by all the case studies.

Again, the intertwining relationship between tangible and intangible heritage is clearly presented in this section to imply that intangible heritage is likely to be more sustainable than tangible heritage. For example, the ceremonies could be re-created or re-invented, such as in the case of the monk Somsit's collections at Tha Muang community, whereas old-fashioned tools and equipment could deteriorate over time without constant maintenance, such as in the case of Mr Chalad's collections at his former school, also located in the Tha Muang community. Having said that, the two aspects of heritage are entwined and this seems to be advantageous for the Thai communities as long as the intangible heritage is carried on by members of the communities since the tangible heritage can be preserved at the same time. This can be illustrated by the knowledge of textile making transferred from the Isan ancestors and which is still used by Isan people for different purposes, including clothes to wear for traditional and invented traditions and for wrapping palm leaf manuscripts, as seen in the case of the Mancha Khiri Cultural Home and Tha Muang communities. Moreover, in the case of the Dan Sai community, tangible heritage, including items used for decoration during the Bun Luang and the Phi Ta Khon tradition, is also part of the overall ceremonies (intangible heritage) preserved by Dan Sai community members. Although not as noticeable as in other cases, for the Surin City Gallery this type of relationship is implied by the work that the gallery team pursue; that is, to use the photographs collected from communities for publications based on stories associated with the photographs to raise the voices of those marginal communities.

The area of collaboration with external bodies has shown to be beneficial for the case study communities, especially when the initiatives are defined by the communities and they can negotiate the most advantageous results for themselves (such as the collaboration of university teams with the Tha Muang community and a university researcher with Chao Poh Guan of the Dan Sai community).

The Surin City Gallery case happens to be a lesson learned about the unsustainability of community archives in Thailand: the risks that began during the motivation phase and which resulted in long-term maintenance issues meant that the project was eventually closed down. Nevertheless, personal connections were very important and useful for the Surin City Gallery team to complete their work, including connections with other government organisations in the cultural sector, such as when they learned about the practice of keeping a record of service requests to prevent the copyright issues previously encountered. It is implied that if the Surin City Gallery was situated in a space belonging to the communities with which they have a connection, its position might have been different.

The last case is Mancha Khiri Cultural Home, owned and solely managed by the individual collector, Mr Surasak, which reveals how his connection with other organisations is more for advocacy. As a result, his collections gained fewer benefits from collaboration with external bodies, unlike the case of the spiritual leader Chao Poh Guan's private archive of the Dan Sai community. In general, the findings have demonstrated that sustainability depends on the mutual agreement of all stakeholders and that leadership is significant for some communities.

Learning from both: Western concepts and Thai practices
Provenance

Thai communities were less focused on the issues of unique creation/ownership implied by concepts of authorship and provenance found in Western discourse. Explanation for this could be associated with traditional Thai communities' basis in oral culture more than in textual communication. Evidence of written records was rarely found within the Thai communities. Although knowledge passed from oral tradition could later be recorded, mainly in the form of the palm leaf manuscripts created by the monks or literate men living in a community, this content did not belong to a specific author, but instead belonged to any members who shared the same belief, faith or practice. Most written records found in the communities in the case studies were palm leaf manuscripts whose content included Buddhist texts, medicine, sermons, folklore and music, etc. Such content belonged to people who shared a common belief, which in this case could refer to Isan people as the Isan ethnic group shared the same culture and traditions.

These manuscripts found in communities were not taken as any one person's heritage but as the community's heritage and were mainly kept in the community temples. The community members were more interested in the content than in the creators of those manuscripts, since it was likely to be impossible to search for an owner of such inherited content. Therefore, inherited knowledge within Isan communities was representative not only of members of a specific community, but could also represent the Isan ethnicity in the region that shared similar traditions and culture – this could be referred to as an 'ethnic provenance' (Wurl, 2005). This concept, identified by Joel Wurl, seems very pertinent to the archives of the Isan community, where, as discussed above, place of settlement seems less significant to their identity than the imagined community of Isan ethnicity and shared memories of ancestral migration.

The concept of ethnic provenance seems relevant to understanding the study findings, such as for the monk Somsit of the Tha Muang community whose case demonstrates the ethnic provenance practice quite clearly. The monk was the abbot of the Tha Muang community forest temple and he had a particular interest in local culture, including keen skills in palm leaf manuscript literacy. In addition to his regular habit of inscribing new palm leaf manuscripts, both to conserve the skills and to preserve the content by copying it to the new manuscripts, he also collected them and other local artefacts such as carved wooden sculptures. He consulted the manuscripts collected from Laos as well as exchanged knowledge of the ceremony with the Lao people and collected items used for the ceremony he found in Laos, bringing them back to teach Tha Muong community villagers to recreate the ceremony. In this sense, the monk had collected the archival items (palm leaf manuscripts) that represented Isan ethnicity as well as his community at the same time. The findings suggest that his practice of collecting items from Laos showed that he recognised the similarities in both cultures, his Isan ethnicity and Laos origin, especially in terms of a shared culture in terms of the religion and local belief in Buddhist lifestyles.

A similar example may be found in the case of Mancha Khiri Cultural Home. The individual collector, Mr Surasak, was interested in local textiles, as mentioned earlier, and he was keen to collect these textiles from anywhere he visited, especially local villages within the Mancha Khiri district. He broke the local taboo on preserving deceased people's textiles because he did not want to lose the textiles during cremation. His practice showed that he did not limit his collecting activities to his own town, but looked for items from people of Isan ethnicity from further afield because they shared the same culture.

It can be seen from this study that ethnic provenance plays a significant part in heritage documentation in Thai communities, especially in the Isan region where there is diversity of ethnicity and the majority share similar cultures across the border with Lao People's Democratic Republic and Cambodia. Therefore, to draw the line of cultural and traditional origin is nearly an impossibility, although recognition of where and how the materials have been collected and collated may help to distinguish one community from another for the purpose of intellectual ownership.

Tangible and intangible heritage

Few Western scholars consider intangible heritage to be part of archival practices. The one notable exception is Jeanette Bastian, as she proposed in her article on observing the 'Play mas' carnival (Bastian, 2009). My research, however, suggests that tangible and intangible heritage have such strong connections that it is impossible to identify a single aspect of tangible or intangible heritage when it comes to the terms of archival practices. My research showed significant links between the two aspects of heritage. For instance, the use of textiles in Isan culture demonstrated the intersection of tangible and intangible aspects fairly well, as could be seen in the case of Mr Surasak of the Mancha Khiri Cultural Home.

Inspired by his childhood spent with his grandmother, as well as the knowledge and awareness he gained about the value of local textiles from a renowned scholar in the field of textile preservation, Mr Surasak began to collect and preserve textiles – especially silk sarongs – from villages within or near his hometown, Mancha Khiri district. He regarded these both as representing local identity generally in terms of their designs and also as having specific representative properties in relation to the deceased owners of particular examples. He personally liked the designs of silk textiles and, with his skills relating to fabric patterns, he developed new designs for silk textiles based on his knowledge of traditional designs observed from the local textiles, including those kept in his collections. He collaborated with local tailors to produce fine designs, some of which were given awards and shown at the Mancha Khiri Cultural Home. This example shows that the tangible heritage (local silk textiles) was an archival material of the communities that Mr Surasak represented and was produced by members of those communities. The textiles generated the intangible heritage in relation to the knowledge transferred from Mr Surasak's grandmother to his generation and the next generations via the newly invented designs based on traditional knowledge. The designs became further archival materials of the communities. This example maps to the 'cultivating archives' suggested by Eric Ketelaar (2012).

Similarly, the case of the Tha Muang community also shows a strong connection between the two aspects. This is identified by the example of the invented ceremony initiated by the monk Somsit, abbot of the forest temple. It was clear that although he might have collected palm leaf manuscripts because of his own interest in traditional literacy with the intention of preserving them so far as possible, evidence from the findings also showed that he intended to sustain the intangible heritage based on knowledge gained from the tangible heritage. In other words, he, as one of the few members of the Tha Muang community able to read the palm leaf manuscripts, had transferred knowledge from the manuscripts in relation to the third month ceremony that he invented based on an analysis of data obtained from the collected manuscripts from different locations. Moreover, that specific ceremony required the co-operation of the community members to produce the many items required to fulfil the ceremony. It was confirmed that the community showed their 'buy-in' (acceptance) of the new tradition by their active participation because they had faith in the monk as their religious leader. From this example of the Tha Muang community, it can be seen how tangible and intangible heritage had a productive relationship in preserving and informing an ongoing tradition.

Comparable to the Tha Muang community, the procedures of the Bun Luang and Phi Ta Khon Festival of the Dan Sai community revealed similar results. This particular festival consists of four small, inter-related ceremonies, each of which represents beliefs or customs that the Dan Sai community had long practised and preserved since their ancestral period. For this particular festival, the tangible aspect would be the items for decoration that form part of the ceremonies both for religious and spiritual purposes, as well as the Phi Ta Khon feature itself (and which are represented in the temple museum). The intangible aspect would include the ceremonial processes of all sub-ceremonies as part of the main festival, including performance styles, designs of costume and masks of the Phi Ta Khon feature. The procedures of the preparation and the overall three-day festival were also part of the intangible heritage from a traditional and cultural point of view. The key informants of this case study, namely Chao Poh Guan, the spiritual leader, and the monk Siri Rattana Methee, the abbot of Wat Phon Chai, were the main figures preserving these two aspects of community heritage through their own actions. First, Chao Poh Guan was part of the community archival process via his responsibility as the spiritual leader to encompass essential elements of tangible and intangible heritage and to maintain the local community tradition and culture. Second, the monk Siri Rattana Methee had an ongoing project of collecting relevant photographs of the annual festival, which perhaps could be seen as community self-documentation in order to fill a gap in a more (if not entirely) mainstream organisation for the missing information at the exhibition displayed at the Phi Ta Khon museum. This is also an example of the intersection between tangible and intangible – the intangible is documented in tangible form.

In the case of the Surin City Gallery, the relationship between the two aspects of heritage was not as clear as in the other case studies since the communities were represented through the point of view of the Surin City Gallery's team. Nevertheless, the study showed that photographs and oral histories collected, preserved and disseminated by the Surin City Gallery had increased the opportunity for the hidden voices of the communities to be widely heard by the population of Surin province through the gallery publications and activities that engaged with the local communities. These included the research conducted with silversmiths as part of a project funded by the Surin city council (and for which the Surin City Gallery team were the researchers) to provide content for the organisation's annual report.

In Thai community archives, tangible and intangible heritage are intertwined. Both form important elements in the memory and identity that the community sees as valuable to preserve and pass on to future generations.

Conclusion

The previous section shows that there are sufficient commonalities between the Western literature and the research findings for each to inform the other. The findings from the four case studies have offered some alternative perspectives that can further develop the mainstream professionals' understanding of the range, variety and meaning of archival practices in a community context. It is possible to understand the Thai studies as 'community archives', but care should be taken not to assume that they share all the same features as Western examples of the genre. Particular resonances in literature dealing with less 'Westernised' examples (such as Bastian's archives as place and space; Bastian, 2003–4) have been suggested by the Western scholarship; nevertheless, it should be re-emphasised that care should be taken not to create an artificial binary of 'Western' and 'non-Western' community archives.

The majority of community archives discussed in the Western literature seemed to be mainly driven by the uneasy situation between the conventional and community archives, especially due to the latter feeling underrepresented within the mainstream archival collections. Therefore, the relationship between community archives and mainstream organisations in the Western context seems to be fairly inter-related, even when the former are fiercely independent. The Western literature has enabled this research to identify the findings in the context of Thailand as having 'archival' characteristics. However, in Thailand, questions of whether a community archive is a 'proper' archive are irrelevant because the two types of institution are not seen by either as being related. This might be seen as a drawback if any community archive could not maintain the streaming funds allocated by the funding bodies; for example, the Surin City Gallery had to shut itself down partly because of the insufficient and unreliable funds allocated by the Surin city council.

Additionally, as this study has shown, intangible heritage is very important for Thai communities due to influences of oral tradition and religious and spiritual belief; therefore, associated ceremonies and rituals have been invented by members of the communities and passed on from generation to generation. In the light of this significant finding, Western community archive literature and activities related to intangible heritage should perhaps also recognise both the tangible and intangible heritage of local communities to include folksong, crafting, dance and performance, and the centrality of memory (especially orality) to most community archive endeavours.

The findings of this study also imply the importance of physical space to community archives in Thailand, including the traditionally set-up space – i.e. the temple and spiritual leader's vicinity – and the up-to-the-minute set-up space called a 'learning centre', which is usually built in common spaces used by community members. Taking into consideration the Thai case studies, physical space could be as significant as communities in a Thai context, especially for women's, LGBT and ethnic minority archives.

If sustainability is to be measured by the durability of any heritage activities, it is possible to conclude that the intangible heritage of the Thai community context seemed more promising than the tangible aspect. This was because, despite the agenda of modernisation, the communities have retained faith in their traditional and cultural beliefs and practices, such as in the case of the annual Bun Luang and Phi Ta Khon festival of the Dan Sai community, which is claimed to have existed for more than 450 years. Moreover, the system of donation, such as that of the Tha Muang community for having a village foundation, was an example of independence from any external funding bodies or being much less dependent on them if there were any, i.e. the local government funds.

Furthermore, the intangible heritage had the characteristic of flexibility, making it adaptable through time. This corresponds with the definition of a community as an 'imagined community' (Anderson, 2006) in which community members share memory and a sense of belonging and create the community in which they want to live together. This also supports the existence of the intangible heritage of communities since community archives would be flexible in time and space. The tangible, on the other hand, seems less likely to be sustainable in the long term in Thai communities, unlike the attempt to safeguard records that was mainly found in the Western literature. The old-fashioned equipment and tools were mainly kept but then abandoned after the project leaders could no longer handle the collections, such as in the case of Mr Chalad of the Tha Muang community. None of the communities visited had succeeded in establishing a learning centre or local museum to exhibit the tangible artefacts of old-fashioned tools and equipment. The main project leaders continued to insist on the heritage value of the collections, yet it seemed that improvement of collection management and financial support were needed to maintain the collections for the benefit of future generations.

In order to support the Thai communities in fulfilling the heritage management gap, the analysis of this study suggests that it might be useful to adapt the 'provenance' model, the main archival principle of the Western world, with self-documentation of the Thai communities. Recent recommended models of provenance by Western scholars such as 'participatory provenance', 'societal provenance' and 'ethnic provenance' could be useful for Thai communities dealing with heritage documentation since these areas of provenance embrace social dimensions for ensuring the cohesion of society (Nesmith, 2006; Rydz, 2010; Wurl, 2005). These wider definitions of provenance are useful for understanding what is going on in Thai community archives – what the materials mean to the community. However, there is also the issue that Western experience suggests there may be a problem with ownership and rights in records if items are collected indiscriminately from groups who might define themselves as separate communities and might one day want the records back, or if the community wants to digitise the records but does not know whether they have the right to do so. Provenance is the theoretical concept that could be applicable in a Thai context to prevent and protect local intellect and identity; for instance, descriptions of creators should be recorded clearly for future reference. In terms of 'ethnic provenance', which was evidenced as being widely applied by the Isan communities (such as by Mr Surasak and the abbot Somsit for preserving Isan local identity), recording the origin as well as the tradition invented would be useful for future research in their own communities and in the Laos communities where the cross-cultural interaction happened.

Although there may or may not be a conflict of culture in the future, this practice of provenance recording would be useful for future research in terms of cultural studies on Isan and Laos traditions.

Thai communities could perhaps learn from the Western archival practices for management of volunteers and the value of archival professions for maintaining archival materials as well as documenting community heritage by applying archival principles for more sustainable conditions for the community archives. The case studies showed that the Thai communities had already collaborated with the external bodies who could provide advice on the preservation of community heritage, but there was evidence of a lack of concern for the provenance principle, which could potentially be useful for safeguarding the communities' heritage ownership. Moreover, it seemed that Thai communities mainly relied on donations for funding to run their heritage activities, which means that they could be considered to be sustainable in their own right as long as there is a commitment from the key individuals or members of the communities, such as in the case of the Tha Muang community foundation.

Note

The original research was undertaken as part of a PhD at the University of Liverpool under the supervision of Dr Alexandrina Buchanan. The completion of the thesis was greatly achieved by the helpful input of Dr Andrew Flinn, as thesis examiner. In developing this chapter, the author received kind advice from Professor Jeannette Bastian, co-editor of this book. Dr Bonnie Brereton, a good friend of the author, provided useful comments on the drafted chapter.

References

Ackermann, A. (2012) Cultural Hybridity: between metaphor and empiricism. In P. W. Stockhammer (ed.), *Conceptualizing Cultural Hybridization: a transdisciplinary approach* [electronic book], Springer, 5–25.

Anderson, B. (2006) *Imagined Communities: reflections on the origin and spread of nationalism*, Verso.

Barr, D. (1987) The Fonds Concept in the Working Group on Archival Descriptive Standards Report, *Archivaria*, **25**, 163–170.

Bastian, J. A. (2003–2004) In a 'House of Memory': discovering the provenance of place, *Archival Issues*, **28** (1), 9–19.

Bastian, J. A. (2009) 'Play Mas': carnival in the archives and the archives in carnival: records and community identity in the US Virgin Islands, *Archival Science*, **9** (1), 113–125.

Cook, T. (1993) The Concept of the Archival Fonds in the Post-custodial Era: theory, problems and solutions, *Archivaria*, **35**, 24–37.

Gaved, M. and Mulholland, P. (2005) Grassroots Initiated Networked Communities: a study of hybrid physical/virtual communities, *Proceedings of the 38th Hawaii International Conference on System Sciences*, www.virtual-communities.net/mediawiki/images/4/45/22680191c.pdf.

Gilliland, A. J. (2014) Community Archives. In Gilliland, A. J. (ed.), *Conceptualizing 21st-century Archives*, Society of American Archivists.

Harris, V. (2002) The Archival Sliver: power, memory, and archives in South Africa, *Archival Science*, **2** (1–2), 63–86.

Hurley, C. (2005) Parallel Provenance (If these are your records, where are your stories?), www.descriptionguy.com/images/WEBSITE/parallel-provenance.pdf.

Ketelaar, E. (2008) Archives as Spaces of Memory, *Journal of the Society of Archivists*, **29** (1), 9–27.

Ketelaar, E. (2012) Cultivating Archives: meanings and identities, *Archival Science*, **12** (1), 19–33.

Millar, L. (2002) The Death of the Fonds and the Resurrection of Provenance: archival context in space and time, *Archivaria*, **53**, 1–15.

Nesmith, T. (1999) Still Fuzzy, But More Accurate: some thoughts on the 'ghosts' of archival theory, *Archivaria*, **47**, 136–150.

Nesmith, T. (2006) The Concept of Societal Provenance and Records of Nineteenth-century Aboriginal-European Relations in Western Canada: implications for archival theory and practice, *Archival Science*, **6** (3–4), 351–360.

Newman, J. (2011) Sustaining community archives, *Aplis*, **24** (1), 37–45.

Niu, J. (2013) Provenance: crossing boundaries, *Archives and Manuscripts*, **41** (2), 105–115.

Rydz, M. (2010) *Participatory Archiving: exploring a collaborative approach to Aboriginal societal provenance*. Unpublished Master's thesis, University of Manitoba, Canada, https://mspace.lib.umanitoba.ca/xmlui/handle/1993/4247.

Wurl, J. (2005) Ethnicity as Provenance: in search of values and principles for documenting the immigrant experience, *Archival Issues*, **29** (1), 65–76.

Popular music, community archives and public history online: cultural justice and the DIY approach to heritage

Paul Long, Sarah Baker,
Zelmarie Cantillon, Jez Collins and Raphaël Nowak

Introduction

This chapter explores the expanding range of community archiving activity concerned with the preservation of cultures, experiences and memories associated with popular music. Engendered by forms as disparate as jazz, rock, soul or country music, such is the variety of this field that a similarly expanding scholarly literature has emerged as a means of mapping and understanding its meanings and significance. While much of this activity takes a familiar physical form (Baker, 2017), here we explore the ways in which the digital enables the extension of such activity. In further democratising the nature of historical work and the archive, online practice is also suggestive of how popular pleasures are subject to a form of cultural justice, a concept which frames this chapter.

The nature of online community archives of popular music can be illustrated with reference to heavy metal, the most listened to genre of music on the streaming service Spotify (Van Buskirk, 2015). Affirming this popularity, *Wall Street Journal* reporter Neil Shah (2016) describes the genre as the real 'World Music', that 'Heavy Metal has become the unlikely soundtrack of globalization'. While record sales and tour receipts attest to the genre's economic power, its popularity is equally tangible in the activity of hundreds of thousands of individuals who contribute to the range of communities of interest associated with it. These are most visibly formed online at sites such as *Metal Wiki* (https://metal.wikia.com) or *Metal Travel Guide* (https://www.metaltravelguide.com), an 'evolving database of rock and metal clubs, bars, pubs, venues and more all added and reviewed by people like you!'

A key site discussed in this chapter is *Encyclopaedia Metallum: The Metal*

Archives (https://www.metal-archives.com), which, alongside the dynamic world of current activity, seeks to record the genre's global history. This archival intent is not uncommon among similar online communities. In relation to the metal genre, for instance, on Facebook one can find *Museo del Metal En Paraguay* (The Paraguayan Metal Museum), *MetalMusicArchives* or *Old School Metal, T Shirts And Memorabilia*, while on Twitter, the user Black Antiquarium presents 'Black Metal pics from '80s, '90s & present days'. One of the most ambitious projects to engage the metal community in building its collective history is the *Home of Metal* project. Funded by the UK Heritage Lottery Fund and Arts Council England, *Home of Metal* was founded with the aim of celebrating the genre, collating a digital archive of memorabilia and memories that calls explicitly to fandom's commitment: 'This is your opportunity to share your devotion by contributing to its legacy' (https://homeofmetal.com).

The practices represented by the projects outlined above are suggestive of a number of issues related to community archiving and public history. Some of these issues are signalled by the very ascription of terms such as history and heritage to the products of commercial music industries, traditionally dismissed as ephemeral if not wholly trivial as culture (Bryson, 1996; Weinstein, 2009). Certainly, the association of heavy metal with excess underscores this point. As we suggest here, by their very existence, projects that celebrate and preserve music and culture challenge such dismissals.

Our chapter seeks to frame the meaning and value of popular music heritage activity online in the context of this edited collection and for community archivists more widely. We outline how practices of popular music commemoration can be understood in relation to principles of public history and community archiving, and to the relationship between commerce and cultural value. Here, we summarise some of the ways in which this ever-expanding field might be categorised and understood. We then survey a number of projects that are focused on the reconvening of the geographically and temporally specific music communities of Manchester, UK. These examples manifest the thrust for cultural justice, an idea that we introduce below.

Community archives of popular music and the quest for cultural justice

Popular music as a product of modernity and mass culture is treated by its consumers as an anchor for meaning in terms of personal and social identity and is core to cultural memory and a literal sound of history. Community archives of popular music mobilise these memories and histories, capturing the material remnants of popular music's past and sharing knowledge in ways that 'promote and protect cultural ties that affirm collective cultural identities' in the community of interest (Banerjee and Steinberg, 2015, 43–4). These community archives override the cultural injustices marked by a lack of respect and recognition (Fraser, 1995) that have occurred through the trivialisation of music cultures and the marginalisation of popular music histories in authorised heritage activities and discourses. Fraser defines cultural *in*justice as:

> Rooted in social patterns of representation, interpretation, and communication. Examples include cultural domination (being subjected to patterns of interpreta-tion and communication that are associated with another culture and are alien and/or hostile to one's own); nonrecognition (being rendered invisible via the au-thoritative representational, communicative, and interpretative practices of one's culture); and disrespect (being routinely maligned or disparaged in stereotypic public cultural representations and/or in everyday life interactions).
>
> (Fraser, 1995, 71)

In response, and as Long et al. (2017, 3) have noted elsewhere, cultural justice is a 'critical concept that seeks to capture the manifest and implicit impulses of democratised practices, apparent in' community-led popular music heritage activities. As we highlight in the sections below, the activities of community archives of popular music indicate a desire to intervene in the representation, interpretation and communication of culture in ways that speak to the community of interest attracted to it.

Our emphasis on cultural justice in this chapter signifies a move beyond the emergent focus on social justice in archival studies and related heritage fields. Social justice 'specifically draws attention to inequalities of power and how they manifest in institutional arrangements and systemic inequities that further the interests of some groups at the expense of others in the distribution of material goods, social benefits, rights, protections, and opportunities' (Duff et al., 2013, 324–5). Cultural justice is an aspect of social justice that recognises the cultural fabric of a community of interest. It captures the extent to which an active engagement with culture, through the act of archiving, for example, can enrich the lives of those who produce and consume the forms of public histories arising from the types of DIY approaches to heritage outlined below. The activities of the activists and citizen archivists who establish physical and/or online popular music archiving initiatives emerge from a quest for cultural justice – a quest Ross (1998, 2) characterises as a 'passionate pursuit' driven by 'real love'. The DIY archive connects culture with the local and its community. It is driven by an ideal of cultural justice because it is underpinned by affective motives, with the aim of bringing the community of interest together.

Framing popular music heritage practice

Long (2015) argues that aspects of popular music consumption compare with those of the historian and archivist. Central to popular culture is, of course, the record, a redundant label that variously references the primary artefacts of music consumption: vinyl, tape, CD or digital file. Even the relatively uncommitted consumer speaks of their record collection – however small – and the most committed of collectors approach theirs as repositories, as important and culturally valuable as any state archive. Likewise, it is commonplace in popular culture to celebrate the content and affective structure of the record in mobilising personal and collective memory. As Ben Hecht lyrically suggested: 'Old Songs are more than tunes … They are little houses in which our hearts once lived' (cited in Steinhardt, 2006, 57).

In contrast with such perspectives, the business practices of the music industries are increasingly and consciously infused with the repertoire of the historian, curator and archivist. For example, in 2017, Canadian artist Neil Young made available in online form his extensive roster of songs – official releases, live recordings and studio outtakes – at *Neil Young Archives* (https://neilyoungarchives.com). The site's home page presents an interactive image of a brown enamelled filing cabinet. Its evocation of the pre-digital age is accentuated by peeling Kroy tape labels, and looking 'inside' the 3D cabinet's drawers, one finds file dividers and dog-eared record cards through which one can browse the artist's entire catalogue. Other examples include the 'curation' of London's Meltdown Festival by older, established musicians who typically programme other older, established musicians, and the glut of new 'archival' releases such as *The Bon Scott Archives* and *Miles Davis: The Archives.*

On one level, of course, this rhetoric and presentation is part of the business of generating continued value from the repackaging of material and the exploitation of artists who are deceased or whose commercial heyday is long gone. As consumer reviews of such materials and experiences attest, reflections on their commercial purposes and impact enjoin with questions of historical accuracy in their organisation and insights afforded by access to 'unheard' and reframed material and performances. As one customer suggests of the CD release of Neil Young's archive: 'At even half the price this would be overpriced. Still, the music remains mostly pretty damned good. I just wish I didn't have this sour taste in my mouth' (Williams, 2009).

This instance is but one of many examples that précis how consumers balance their recognition of the overtly commercial imperative behind popular music and their deeply affective devotions to it as a culturally meaningful and personally significant art form. As Weinstein (2009) argues of heavy metal music, for instance, understanding it as genre extends beyond its status as a marketing category for the music industries or one in which listeners are merely at the end of a commercial transaction. Weinstein writes that: 'It has a distinctive sound. It also has a stock of visual and verbal meanings that have been attached to it by the artists, audience members, and mediators who construct it' (2009, 5).

Beyond the commercial imperative described above, however, and notwithstanding the everyday practices of consumers, the *conscious* framing and presentation of the artefacts and practices of popular music in terms of history, heritage and archive is a relatively recent development. This is a feature of a wider public culture of preservation and commemoration outside of the control of the music industries alone that has seen the encroachment of popular music into the archive and museum. For instance, the aforementioned *Home of Metal* first exhibited at Birmingham Museum and Art Gallery in 2011 and returns there in 2019, while last year the British Library, which has its own popular music collections and dedicated curator, hosted *Punk 1976–78*. This development is at one with what Bennett (2009) describes as 'heritage rock'. This label refers to that process by which the music and artists of the 1960s and 1970s have become valued as more than icons of subculture and consumer fandom and are viewed as part of 'the essential character of late twentieth-century culture per se and an integral aspect of the way in which this era of history is to be remembered, represented, and celebrated' (Bennett, 2008, 266). Research responding to these developments addresses the meanings of popular music in relation to interpretations and practices of cultural heritage and its place in the archive (e.g. Brandellero et al., 2014). Such work explores when, why and where pop becomes an object of heritage (Roberts, 2014), its interactions with the museum (Leonard, 2007, 2010; Baker, Istvandity and Nowak, 2016) and the archive (Baker, Doyle and Homan, 2016; Long et al., 2017), and its role in relation to concepts of history, memory and nostalgia (Strong, 2015; Bennett and Janssen, 2016; Long, 2015).

Roberts and Cohen (2014) formulated a typology that describes the variety of heritage practices devoted to popular music. In this schema, *officially authorised* heritage is that which is sanctioned by government or associated cultural institutions. The British Library's various projects would be counted in this category, or the establishment of the *Heavy Metal and Hardcore Punk Archiving Project* at Bowling Green State University. Elsewhere, *self-authorised* heritage is established by way of the music and media industries, musicians, intermediaries and audiences that form the cultures of popular music. This category would encompass *Home of Metal*, 2016's *About The Young Idea* (an exhibition devoted to British band The Jam), or even the famous Rock and Roll Hall of Fame and Museum.

The *self-authorised* category incorporates the kinds of grassroots activities described by Baker and Huber (2013) as DIY (do-it-yourself) heritage institutions. Wehr (2012, 1) defines DIY in terms of how 'ordinary people build or repair the things in their daily lives without the aid of experts'. In music culture, DIY has resonance for its links with the practices of the alternative cultures of the 1960s, punk in the '70s and independent labels in the '80s. As Baker (2017) details more extensively, DIY captures the work of enthusiasts and volunteers in establishing popular music archives, museums and halls of fame. These operate beyond the scope of authorised projects of collecting and display, whether organised by cultural institutions or music businesses, understood as do-it-yourselves, do-it-ourselves or do-it-together enterprises (Chigley, 2014; Reilly, 2014; Collins, 2019). Examples include private museums operated by individual enthusiasts, such as KD's Elvis Presley Museum, located in the renovated garage of KD's home in Hawera, New Zealand, to more extensive organisations run by upwards of 50 volunteers, such as the Australian Jazz Museum in Melbourne, Victoria, or the Heart of Texas Country Music Museum in Brady, Texas, USA.

Roberts and Cohen's typology also allows for *unauthorised practice.* This category has an everyday nature, in which authorisation might not be sought or even identified as an issue, as its practice might not be considered by those involved to be about history, heritage or the archive at all. These ideas have been extended and applied by Baker and Collins (2015), who describe a continuum between on- and offline worlds and between the mainstream heritage sector and the DIY practices of communities of interest. Their typology is concerned with the archive in particular, with physical collections of music divided into categories of 'physical – authorised' and 'physical – do-it-yourself'. In acknowledging the impact of the digital in this field, they also recognise collections that they characterise as 'online – institutional' and 'online – community'. Their typology includes 'unintentional' archives, which they describe as those 'run by individuals or collectives who do not conceive of their practice as archiving' (Baker and Collins, 2015, 5). Whatever the global wealth of archives and public history practices devoted to preserving popular music cultures, much of it is very locally oriented and, in its physical form, out of reach to most. This activity is most accessible online, where its impressive variety of practices and quest for cultural justice becomes apparent.

DIY popular music archives online

Two questions arise in proceeding: how are these online sites communities and how are they archives? For Ernst (2013, 11), the capacity for storage and circulation of digital data is a manifestation of the logic of late capitalism, forming 'a part of a memory economy'. This economy is dependent upon the freely given labour of users of platforms like Twitter, WordPress, Instagram or Facebook that in turn underwrites the economic value of each. The efforts of users make such spaces sites of creativity and community, endowing them with cultural value. The digital thus offers imaginative and practical prompts for the building of archives and commemoration practices, online communities and their purposes enabled by its 'technologies of memory' (Van House and Churchill, 2008).

Like offline heritage sites, online worlds employ crowdsourced and user-generated materials in order to build and sustain communities. DIY projects are lacking the 'gilt-edged symbolic capital' of authorised cultural institutions (Roberts and Cohen, 2014, 284) and struggle to sustain themselves: physical sites require finances and human resources, while, increasingly, online sites encounter copyright and legal challenges for using material from the music industries (Baker and Collins, 2015). However, such enterprises are significant for the ways in which collection, curation and organisational criteria (or their absence) emerge from vernacular knowledge, collective authority and agreement on what constitutes the parameters of each community.

Long and Collins (2016) observe that the activities of online DIY archives appear coterminous with conventional aspects of music fandom, yet extend beyond it. Whether through the auspices of an originating individual or group, such sites engage diverse communities of interest and an extraordinary variety of contributors. To give three instances from Facebook: *london gay disco scene archives* has 12 members, *Reggae LP Archives* has 170, while *BRITISH ROCK'N'ROLL* boasts 1,700. *Encyclopaedia Metallum* gives the following statistics for its archive: 'There are currently 120793 bands, 334542 registered users and 96511 reviews' (https://www.metal-archives.com). While individuals may belong to many groups across the digital world, and although size of membership varies, the range of these enterprises is innumerable. Sites are organised around specific artists and genres whose moment is long past, including defunct bands and deceased artists. In terms of artists with lengthy and *ongoing* careers, their online presence is attended by sites created by fans that sometimes conflict with the desires of the artists themselves. For example, during his lifetime, the artist Prince sought to limit such activity; but after his passing, archival sites have emerged including *Prince Vault* (www.princevault.com), *Prince 365 Celebration 2018 Archive* (https://www.facebook.com/groups/500585307008497), and *The Prince Online Museum* (www.princeonlinemuseum.com).

Beyond the potentially hagiographic approach of such sites, many are devoted to particular time periods (e.g. the Facebook group *MUSIC & MEMORIES ARCHIVE (50s–80s) With Kevin & Annie*), genres (e.g. *PROG ARCHIVES*) or subcultures (e.g. *60s mods from east ham*). The titles of many of these groups attest to the way in which they share particular tastes and historical experiences, constituting an imagined community that is not built on any necessary historical proximity or exchange. Otherwise, many sites document activities connected with the geographic specificity of music cultures, such as record shops, performance venues and nightclubs. These examples are useful for highlighting how, while tangible artefacts and sites of music production define historical activities, the online archival community is invested also in the intangible. Thus, although contributors post links to music, scans of records and personal photographs or memorabilia, they retrieve the intangible – the atmosphere of a club night, for instance – by both reconvening communities of participants online and by building a repertoire of memory. Some contribute extensive memoirs in prose, others simply endorse, inflect or correct posts; many, by simply following a blog or joining a social media group, lend weight to this act of retrieval.

The wealth of such activity online is instructive for observing the dedicated and deeply affective ways that communities engage with music of the past and the practices in which they participated: at concerts and dance clubs, or simply in the role of being a fan. Certainly, some of this is couched in nostalgic yearning and value judgments and many express a covert and often overt judgment in their very title and purview, e.g. *Vinyl Days: When Rock and Roll was good!*. Nonetheless, we suggest that what is captured across this activity and the involvement of so many 'ordinary people' in self-authorised and unauthorised practice is a mode of democratisation enabled by technological change (Taylor and Gibson, 2017). Anyone can start a group and call it an archive, devoting themselves to celebrating any aspect of personal and collective history, thereby expanding the terms and content of the archive and its potential for cultural justice.

Thinking about such activities as a form of cultural justice recognises how communities devoted to music memory and its preservation are based on the appropriation of intellectual property that belongs to others. Popular music is taken to describe particular forms and genres, but relates also to the nature of its production and consumption: it is popular thanks to the action of its consumers. Beyond the purchasing of goods aimed at audiences, however – and music is not simply defined by sales – music's status as popular is conveyed by its imbrication into everyday life and culture. This takes many forms, such as particular songs becoming associated with cultural movements and other phenomena, or, at an individual level, with significant life events. In community archives – off as well as online – recorded music is the anchor that authorises prompts for memory and preservation, such as promotional photographs, ticket stubs from live concerts and, indeed, the memory-making that is shared by participants as they come together. Whatever the economic value produced by popular music, community archivists express cultural values through their actions. They do justice to popular memory and public history, validating the meanings of popular music and its role in defining the significance of particular places in time and space and the role of individuals and groups in them. Whatever the frivolous aspects of popular music, such sites evidence the serious nature of its pleasures and underline its place in people's lives.

Archiving the music heritage of Manchester, UK

What is singular about the communities of interest introduced in this chapter is the centrality of music and its attendant cultures to collective and individual identities and memory. While many sites are relatively disorganised as archives and about their purpose as such, in this chapter's final section we turn to consider how a set of community archives concerned with Manchester, UK, reveal an engagement with music as key to understanding broader social and culture issues and, indeed, the nature of commemoration and of the parameters of the archive.

Many authorised, self-authorised and unauthorised community and DIY archival projects serve Manchester's music memory. A number work between the off- and online worlds, physically engaging communities of interest and bodies that seek to aid· their sustainability. Some of these take advantage of the opportunities afforded by funds from organisations like the Heritage Lottery Fund (HLF). This chapter is itself evidence of how public historians in academia have paid attention to this practice more widely (see Baker, 2017).

In Manchester, the politics of music heritage and archival formation intersect with the dynamics of history more generally, of tensions between dominant narratives and those that have been neglected or actively suppressed. Key in addressing these themes is Manchester Digital Music Archive (MDMA), a crowd-sourced initiative 'for people all over the world to share Manchester music ephemera and memories, be they fans, musicians or involved with the music industry itself' (https://www.mdmarchive.co.uk). Established in 2003, MDMA is a volunteer-run organisation and registered charity. It embraces the plurality of popular music communities and their intersection with a range of social identities and cultural worlds. Its founders express a conscious engagement with the politics of history and archive formation that elucidates the character of the enterprises surveyed in this chapter:

> We are passionate about celebrating the hidden chapters and under-represented communities within Greater Manchester music. We believe that through crowd-sourcing artefacts we can democratise heritage and provide a platform for multiple versions of history to be shared. There is no hierarchy of 'merit' within our archive. The general public decides what is important and what is 'heritage'.
>
> (https://www.mdmarchive.co.uk/pages/our-work)

While archives organised on social media platforms are ordered according to the moment of posting and the attention they receive, MDMA is more formally structured. The invitation to contribute involves a number of organising principles. To upload an artefact (or rather, its digital reproduction), one is advised that 'We only accept items relating to Greater Manchester'. Contributions can then be tagged as anything from advert, audio file or autograph, to set list, ticket or video, supplemented by an identified year or more precise date. One adds the image, video or sound file and is then invited to give a story behind the deposit and to tag it further as band, DJ, venue or 'backstage bod'. MDMA offers a menu of artefacts and a browsable A–Z of its archive containing: '3487 Bands, 631 DJs, 1218 Venues, 105 Backstage Bods and 17244 artefacts contributed by 3136 members' (https://www.mdmarchive.co.uk).

MDMA has progressed its mission through projects that celebrate the hidden and under-represented, such as those dealing with inequalities focused on sexuality, gender and the intersection of race and class. For instance, 'Queer Noise: The History of LGBT+ Music and Club Culture in Manchester' is 'an online project that explores the hidden history of Manchester's LGBT music culture and club life' (Savage, 2017). This is conceived as a direct riposte to the 'dozens of books written about Manchester music and pop culture' (Savage, 2017) which represent 'official', familiar histories – of the Factory label or 'Madchester' (Halfacree and Kitchin, 1996) – and thus neglect queer issues and LGBT people. Queer Noise seeks 'to construct a proper people's history' and to 'reclaim' one aspect of music and club culture 'from the shadows'.

The history against which the Queer Noise project is positioned can be considered in relation to two dominant themes that galvanise other acts of retrieval. Firstly, Kate Milestone (2016) argues that the image of Manchester – at least in terms of the music culture formulated from within and without around the 'Madchester' era – relies upon a circumscribed set of reference points. She writes that: 'Part of Manchester's cultural identity is that of a masculine city in terms of its roots as a working class, industrial city … and high-profile bands such as Oasis and the Happy Mondays might be seen in these terms' (Milestone, 2016, 7). It is certainly the case that these bands and the culture they embodied continue to be disproportionately represented in the city's imaginary. The gender politics of this situation are addressed directly by MDMA's recent HLF-funded project 'Rebel Music: The Sound of Politics and Protest in Manchester', from which emerged a physical exhibition, 'Suffragette City: Portraits of Women in Manchester Music'. This attempt to recognise the achievement of women in the music industry is underscored by the centenary of the extension of the vote as a result of the suffragette movement. The photographic exhibition displays musicians, DJs, venue owners, sound engineers and record label managers. Lest this seem a conservative route to a regular mode of historical work, the exhibition prompts its inclusive and democratising approach to crowdsourcing contributions: 'Calling all female music fans, musicians, performers, DJ and industry bods! Why not add to the digital version of our Suffragette City exhibition? Just take a shot of yourself holding your favourite Manchester music artefact and upload it to our website! We'll do the rest' (Manchester Digital Music Archive, 2018).

A second theme to which MDMA projects are responding concerns the remaking of Manchester, the gentrification of its central spaces and its promotion as a cosmopolitan, 'entrepreneurial' city (Young, Diep and Drabble, 2006). In its new imaginary, areas like the relatively impoverished and disreputable Hulme and Moss Side have little place (Fraser, 1996). MDMA's attempt to address this absence is apparent in the online exhibition 'Moss Side Stories: The Hidden History of Hulme and Moss Side Club Culture'. This event originated from the prodigious amount of uploads to MDMA by an anonymous contributor who goes by the name 'Dubwise-er'. The majority of these posts convey this individual's lifetime love of live music, with contributions of concert flyers, photographs and newspaper articles as well as recollections of his activities in the 1980s in and around Moss Side. While Dubwise-er's posts were made over time, MDMA's tagging structure allowed curator Abigail Ward (n.d.) 'to group together these fascinating uploads and let them tell their own tale'. In the online exhibition, the geography, time and generic focus of this individual's interest come together to create an impressive collection, attesting to his archival energy: offline, in that he collected and preserved materials, and online, in his transfer of material, annotations and memories.

Dubwise-er's written story offers context and interpretation. His account is intensely personal, reaching back to his earliest memories of 'The protracted demolition of the Victorian back-to-back houses during the notorious redevelopment of Moss Side and Hulme in the 1960s and 70s' (cited in Ward, n.d.). This is a memory of 'never-ending vistas of destruction and derelict wastelands' (ibid.). Very quickly, music intrudes: 'I recall tagging along with elders on a day out to watch hippy-type bands play to that generation up on the big stage in Alexandra Park' (ibid.). In the same place a decade later, he would be inspired by benefits and rallies for Rock Against Racism, CND and Anti-Apartheid campaigns. Music is the core to his self-definition and his navigation of place: 'living in an area that was synonymous with reggae music, and like many of my generation I was drawn to much of what it had to offer, as it seemed to have a purpose and depth beyond the obvious chart fayre' (ibid.). Dubwise-er has the acuity of a historian in noting that, in spite of the wealth of musical creativity in Moss Side, 'it was mostly of the spontaneous and short-lived kind, and so much of it went undocumented and unrecorded, especially from the black musical perspective of sound systems and Blues' (ibid.). The nature of the culture was such that it 'passed into a faded, untold memory' (ibid.), its legacy recalled but intangible, save for records like his own and his and other memories.

This particular exhibition is, in turn, supplemented and extended by liaison with the Commonword Writers' Development Agency, which produced oral histories capturing the accounts of, among others, DJs, a club compere and the builder of a reggae sound system. These stories offer a candid picture of a history of place in which music is but one part of a set of pleasures, revealing a wider range of cultural interactions and social tensions. Posts and testimonies cover the formation of unlicensed drinking clubs – shebeens and blues – and 'the sense of community that was generated by the clubs of Moss Side and Hulme … and the strained relationship between the black community and the police, which culminated in the July 1981 Moss Side riot' (Ward, n.d.). As the curator claims, this material conveys a culture defiant in the face of economic hardship and oppression: 'a thread that runs through Manchester music as a whole' (Ward, n.d.). At its core is the thesis that music clubs are focal points for communities, important to individual lives.

Conclusion

As with any of the enterprises touched upon here, one might rightly ask of the archival work on Manchester: to whom does this material speak? As the Moss Side exhibition demonstrates, some of this is intensely local in its reference: to clubs, streets, housing developments and so on. Then there are musical references that may or may not prompt the same degree of recognition locally as they do nationally or even globally: after all, audiences for music are diverse and fractured. To a degree, this presentation evidences the way the MDMA archive speaks 'back' to those whose worlds it captures, so inviting contributions and corrections as it recognises and validates them: 'There are still many gaps, which we hope you will be inspired to fill' (Ward, n.d.).

The extent to which this, or other DIY music archives, speaks to potential 'users' in the same manner as formal institutions is a question that merits further research and consideration. Certainly, whatever level of organisation exists in such sites and the degree to which they emulate the archive proper, their existence and practices pose questions about power and hierarchies of value in how history and heritage are produced. As a result, many instances of popular music heritage practice on- and offline are inspiring and galvanising enterprises. However, lest we seem too uncritically celebratory, we might ponder how characteristics of music genre, consumption and subcultures are translated to commemoration and preservation activities. For example, if we turn back to heavy metal, there are critical assessments of the role of women in the music and culture of the genre. Likewise, aspects of the partisan and chauvinistic nature of music cultures might be echoed in their commemoration – witness the contentious assertion from *Home of Metal*, for instance, that the genre 'was born in the Black Country and Birmingham' (https://homeofmetal.com).

Perhaps such partisan displays and the potential challenges of such enterprises are a key aspect of their power. Either way, the principle of cultural justice can be understood to be at work in this sector, in recognising overlooked stories built by the community itself from the materials of its archive and their affective connections to it. In each case, their activity is an important assertion of their right to be documented and heard on their own terms.

References

Baker, S. (2017) *Community Custodians of Popular Music's Past: a DIY approach to heritage*, Routledge.

Baker, S. and Collins, J. (2015) Sustaining Popular Music's Material Culture in Community Archives and Museums, *International Journal of Heritage Studies*, **21** (10), 983–96.

Baker, S., Doyle, P. and Homan, S. (2016) Historical Records, National Constructions: the contemporary popular music archive, *Popular Music and Society*, **39** (1), 8–27.

Baker, S. and Huber, A. (2013) Notes Towards a Typology of the DIY Institution: identifying do-it-yourself places of popular music preservation, *European Journal of Cultural Studies*, **16** (5), 513–30.

Baker, S., Istvandity L. and Nowak, R. (2016) Curating Popular Music Heritage: storytelling and narrative engagement in popular music museums and exhibitions, *Museum Management and Curatorship*, **31** (4), 369–85.

Banerjee, D. and Steinberg, S. L. (2015) Exploring Spatial and Cultural Discourses in

Environmental Justice Movements: a study of two communities, *Journal of Rural Studies*, **39**, 41–50.

Bennett, A. (2008) 'Things They Do Look Awful Cool': ageing rock icons and contemporary youth audiences, *Leisure/Loisir*, **32** (2), 259–78.

Bennett, A. (2009) 'Heritage Rock': rock music, representation and heritage discourse, *Poetics*, **37**, 474–89.

Bennett, A. and Janssen, S. (2016) Popular Music, Cultural Memory, and Heritage, *Popular Music and Society*, **39** (1), 1–7.

Brandellero, A., Janssen, S., Cohen, S. and Roberts, L. (2014) Popular Music Heritage, Cultural Memory and Cultural Identity, *International Journal of Heritage Studies*, **20** (3), 219–23.

BRITISH ROCK'N'ROLL (2017), Facebook, https://www.facebook.com/groups/1399159883689390.

Bryson, B. (1996) 'Anything But Heavy Metal': symbolic exclusion and musical dislikes, *American Sociological Review*, **61** (5), 885–99.

Chigley, R. (2014) Developing Communities of Resistance? Maker pedagogies, do-it yourself feminism, and DIY citizenship. In Ratto, M. and Boler, M. (eds), *DIY Citizenship: critical making and social media*, MIT Press, 101–13.

Collins, J. (forthcoming, 2019) Doing-It-Together: citizen archivists and the online environment. In Popple, S., Prescott, A. and Mutibwa, D. (eds), *Remaking the Archive: communities, archives and new collaborative practices*, Bristol University Press.

Duff, W. M., Flinn, A., Suurtamm, K. E. and Wallace, D. A. (2013) Social Justice Impact of Archives: a preliminary investigation, *Archival Science*, **13** (4), 317–48.

Ernst, W. (2013) Aura and Temporality: the insistence of the archive, *The Anarchival Impulse in the Uses of the Image in Contemporary Art*, University of Barcelona, https://www.macba.cat/en/quaderns-portatils-wolfgang-ernst.

Fraser, N. (1995) From Redistribution to Recognition? Dilemmas of justice in a 'post-socialist' age, *New Left Review*, 212, 68–93.

Fraser, P. (1996) Social and Spatial Relationships and The 'Problem' Inner City: Moss-Side in Manchester, *Critical Social Policy*, **16** (49), 43–65.

Halfacree, K. H., and Kitchin, R. M. (1996) 'Madchester Rave On': placing the fragments of popular music, *Area*, **28** (1), 47–55.

Leonard, M. (2007) Constructing Histories Through Material Culture: popular music, museums and collecting, *Popular Music History*, **2** (2), 147–67.

Leonard, M. (2010) Exhibiting Popular Music: museum audiences, inclusion and social history, *Journal of New Music Research*, **39** (2), 171–81.

Long, P. (2015) 'Really Saying Something?': What do we talk about when we talk about popular music heritage, memory, archives and the digital? In Baker, S. (ed.), *Preserving Popular Music Heritage: do-it-yourself, do-it-together*, Routledge, 62–76.

Long, P., Baker, S., Istvandity, L. and Collins, J. (2017) A Labour of Love: the affective archives of popular music culture, *Archives and Records*, **38** (1), 68–79.

Long, P. and Collins, J. (2016) Affective Memories of Music in Online Heritage Practice. In Brusila, J., Johnson, B. and Richardson, J. (eds), *Memory, Space, Sound*, Intellect, 85–101.

Manchester Digital Music Archive (2018) Suffragette City – Portraits of Women in Manchester Music, *Eventbrite*, https://www.eventbrite.co.uk/e/suffragette-city-portraits-of-women-in-manchester-music-tickets-42212784575.

Milestone, K. (2016) 'Northernness', Gender and Manchester's Creative Industries, *Journal for Cultural Research*, **20** (1), 45–59.

Reilly, I. (2014) Just Say Yes: DIY-ing the yes men. In Ratto, M. and Boler, M. (eds), *DIY Citizenship: critical making and social media*, MIT Press, 127–36.

Roberts, L. and Cohen, S. (2014) Unauthorising Popular Music Heritage: outline of a critical framework, *International Journal of Heritage Studies*, **20** (3), 241–61.

Roberts, L. (2014) Talkin Bout My Generation: popular music and the culture of heritage, *International Journal of Heritage Studies*, **20** (3), 262–80.

Ross, A. (1998) *Real Love: in pursuit of cultural justice*, Routledge.

Savage, J. (2017) *Queer Noise: the history of LGBT+ music and club culture in Manchester*, Manchester Digital Music Archive, https://www.mdmarchive.co.uk/exhibition/id/77/QUEER_NOISE.html.

Shah, N. (2016) The Weird Global Appeal of Heavy Metal: from Indonesia to Latin America, Russia to Japan, metal is taking hold, *The Wall Street Journal*, (18 February), https://www.wsj.com/articles/the-weird-global-appeal-of-heavy-metal-1455819419?mod=e2fb.

Steinhardt, A. (2006) *Violin Dreams*, Houghton Mifflin Company.

Strong, C. (2015) Shaping the Past of Popular Music: memory, forgetting and documenting. In Bennett, A. and Waksman, S. (eds), *The SAGE Handbook of Popular Music*, SAGE Publications, 418–33.

Taylor, J. and Gibson, L. K. (2017) Digitisation, Digital Interaction and Social Media: embedded barriers to democratic heritage, *International Journal of Heritage Studies*, **23** (5), 408–20.

Van Buskirk, E. (2015) Which Music Genres Have the Loyalest Fans?, *Spotify Insights*, (2 April), https://insights.spotify.com/us/2015/04/02/loyalest-music-fans-by-genre.

Van House, N. and Churchill, E. F. (2008) Technologies of Memory: key issues and critical perspectives, *Memory Studies*, **1** (3), 295–310.

Ward, A. (n.d.) *Moss Side Stories: the hidden history of Hulme and Moss Side club culture*, Manchester Digital Music Archive, https://www.mdmarchive.co.uk/exhibition/id/76/MOSS_SIDE_STORIES.html.

Wehr, K. (2012) *DIY: the search for control and self-reliance in the 21st century*, Routledge.

Weinstein, D. (2009) *Heavy Metal: the music and its culture*, revised edn, Da Capo

Press.

Williams, I. (2009) *The High Cost of Neil Young*, review, Amazon (3 July), https://www.amazon.co.uk/Archives-1-1963-1972-Neil-Young/product-reviews/B001O12TO4/ref=cm_cr_arp_d_hist_4?ie=UTF8&filterByStar=four_star& reviewerType=all_reviews&pageNumber=1#reviews-filter-bar.

Young, C., Diep, M. and Drabble, S. (2006) Living With Difference? The 'cosmopolitan city' and urban reimaging in Manchester, UK, *Urban Studies*, **43** (10), 1687–714.

CHAPTER 7

Maison d'Haïti's collaborative archives project: archiving a community of records

Désirée Rochat, Kristen Young,
Marjorie Villefranche and Aziz Choudry

Introduction

This chapter documents a collaborative archives project at Maison d'Haïti, a Haitian community-based and cultural organisation located in the north east of Montreal, Quebec/Canada. Since 1972, the organisation has dedicated itself to the education and integration of immigrant individuals and families through its mission of promoting, integrating and improving the living conditions and defending the rights of Quebecers of Haitian origin and immigrants (Maison d'Haïti, 2018). In their 1981 activity report, members of Maison d'Haïti noted the importance of documenting and preserving their work. They stated that the newsletter was a precious tool because, in addition to providing information about the organisation's activities, it allowed them to make connections between the different programs and with other groups, served as a tool of reflection and animation, and acted as archives of their activities (Maison d'Haïti, 1981).

Beginning with explorations in the late 15th century, Canada became a settler colony primarily for British and French immigrants and their descendants through the dispossession of Indigenous Peoples and the invasion and occupation of their territories. A broader historical and contemporary feature of Canada's capitalist economy has been its systemic reliance upon exploitation through race, immigration status and shifting forms of 'unfree labour' (Thobani, 2007; Choudry and Smith, 2016). Racialised communities continue to fight and mobilise for their rights throughout Quebec and Canada. In doing so, they produce records that speak to the ways in which community is negotiated, built and rebuilt through time. The records and archives of community-based organisations encompass different types of records and entail various archival processes (Flinn, 2007; Flinn, Stevens and Shepherd, 2009).

Although there had never been a formal archives project before 2013, people who have been involved at Maison d'Haïti have, at different points, worked to preserve or organise older material. The current archival project and process began in January 2013 in parallel with the organisation's effort to build a new space to accommodate the community's growing and changing needs. Initiated by the director and a volunteer, the project has relied on the participation of volunteers and community members. Inspired by Bastian's (2003) concept of a community of records, the volunteer in charge of the project and the volunteer archivist are working so that the records in all their diversity – tangible and intangible – are understood and arranged as a community of records. They plan to eventually use oral history to contextualise, describe and add to the textual and photographic records.

This chapter is based on multiple conversations held between the authors at different moments over the years of the project, presentations done on the project by two of the authors, as well as academic literature that inspired the approach taken to process the archives. In the following sections, we will first present a short history of the organisation, its community and the content of the archives. Second, we will give an overview of the timeline and achievements of the collaborative archival process, as well as how it unfolded. Third, we will reflect on the approach taken to archive this 'community of records' by integrating and using oral histories. Fourth, we will highlight the importance of learning in and through such a project. Fifth, we will expose how community archives can be understood as part of constellations of archives, showing connections between individuals and organisations. Finally, we will address the necessity of working to preserve the archives of community-based organisations and of the space they need and can create.

From student project to community home: Maison d'Haïti

Maison d'Haïti was founded in the summer of 1972 as increasing numbers of Haitians made their way to Quebec, fleeing François Duvalier's dictatorship in Haiti (Mills, 2016; St-Victor, 2017). Political exiles had been in Montreal since the late 1950s, but with repression in Haiti reaching unprecedented levels of violence in the late 1960s, larger numbers of people left that country. Students, professionals and families spread out in countries around the Atlantic, in North and South America, the Caribbean, West Africa and Western Europe. Groups of resistance to the dictatorship formed throughout the diaspora, mobilising to try to overthrow Duvalier's regime (Mills, 2016; St-Victor, 2017) while imagining new politics for the country. Because of Duvalier's relentless attack on the Haitian left, the exiled diaspora partly consisted of members of different left groups and parties (Mills, 2016; St-Victor,

2017). They maintained connections between each other, across cities and countries, formed new groups, collectives and coalitions – which sometimes disagreed with one another. Those networks were sustained by movements of information, people and material. In Montreal, many also participated in local politics in a shifting Quebec context (Mills, 2010). In Quebec, the 1960s and 1970s were marked, amongst other things, by state restructuring and an expansion of social services, health and educational systems. There was also strong community mobilisation by citizens' committees, women, workers and neighbourhood associations and more, leading to the institutionalisation and emergence of Quebec's community sector (Mayer, 1994).

Maison d'Haïti began as a student summer project to provide support and orientation services to newcomers arriving from Haiti. Students provided translation services, accompanied people to immigration meetings, helped them find housing and much more. During its early years, it functioned as a platform from which a network of activists planned various activities and services to build and sustain a community life in Montreal while remaining involved in anti-Duvalier mobilisation. Maison d'Haïti offered immigration counselling, help with taxes and employment, medical assistance, language classes, organised sports teams and cultural events, as well as special events, information activities, picnics, carnival and Christmas celebrations and children's and family activities (Maison d'Haïti 1973, 1975).

By the mid-1970s, the organisation rented its first space, which also housed a medical community clinic, the Clinique Communautaire Haïtienne, in collaboration with Haitian doctors and nurses from the Association des Médecins Haïtiens à L'Étranger and the Ralliement des Infirmières et Infirmières Auxiliaires Haïtiennes. The clinic offered medical and reference services and organised information evenings for Haitian migrants who faced barriers in accessing or using health services (n.a., n.d.). The clinic occupied the space during the day and Maison d'Haïti ran its activities at night and during weekends. Moving from activities to classes, such as literacy classes, Maison d'Haïti soon developed full programs. Between 1975 and 1980, it refined and focused its main areas of work, setting priorities that still remain today: providing educational opportunities and support to newcomers through literacy and French classes and help with the immigration process; providing leisure opportunities for workers and families through special events and outings; ensuring the wellbeing and growth of youth through educational and leisure programs; and creating a space and educational opportunities for women through literacy and employment training programs. Its programs were always anchored in popular and community education. While maintaining constant connections with other Haitian diasporic resistance groups, Maison d'Haïti also worked closely with other community groups in Montreal.

During the 1980s, Maison d'Haïti continued to develop and expand its programs, but 1986 brought changes in its membership because of changes in Haitian politics. In February 1986, dictator Jean-Claude Duvalier was ousted. In the following months, many exiled Haitians returned to Haiti, including core members of Maison d'Haïti. Activities and programs continued in Montreal, while connections with Haiti and Haitian groups deepened throughout the 1990s. Maison d'Haïti supported Haitian organisations, responded to and mobilised in the face of turbulent political periods, such as the 1991 coup d'état and ensuing embargo. In the late 1990s, the youth and family programs expanded and in the early 2000s so did those for women. Meanwhile, the organisation continued to advocate for the rights of immigrants and newcomers and against the discrimination and racism faced by many community members and other immigrants.

In January 2010, the lives of Haitians in Haiti and abroad were shaken by a 7.1 magnitude earthquake which destroyed entire sectors of the capital and left between 200,000 and 350,000 dead. The impact across the diaspora was immediate. In Montreal, Maison d'Haïti and other Haitian organisations became central meeting points where people came for support, to try to find news of loved ones in Haiti and to start procedures to receive them. Maison d'Haïti's offices soon became too small, as more than 250 people daily came through the doors for months. The exploding needs of people and obsolescence of the offices prompted the board to launch a campaign to build a new building in 2011. In summer 2016, Maison d'Haïti moved into its brand-new space. 'A space of life and culture' was the motto that accompanied the construction project and aptly describes the sense of the new building.

The history of Maison d'Haïti and its community is intimately tied to life in Haiti. The repercussions of political events and natural catastrophes there – such as the 1986 fall of the Duvalier regime or the 2010 earthquake – are vividly felt in its daily activities, orientations and its records. While it was created primarily for members of the Haitian community, the organisation has always served more than just Haitian migrants. Now, its members include Haitian immigrants, Quebecers of Haitian origin, newcomers from other countries, residents of the neighbourhood, friends of the organisation (some of whom have been volunteers for 40 years) and more. Forty-six years after its opening, Maison d'Haïti now has a home that truly accommodates changing needs, while continuing to provide services to its community and participating in the revitalisation of the neighbourhood. For the first time, the archives have a dedicated space. The institutional memory continues to live between Maison d'Haïti's new walls.

A collaborative archiving process

The current project to organise and preserve the archives started in 2013 and emerged from a concern from the director and a volunteer to preserve the old documents produced and acquired by the organisation. But past members and employees had also worked before to preserve some of the older documents and photographs. Boxes and folders marked 'archives' were found in the depot, thematic folders and binders were arranged with old documents and the director kept important documents in her office. Although they were not arranged as an archives per se, Maison d'Haïti's records survived over four decades thanks to those who cared for them, stored them on shelves in different offices, in the depot and in the kitchen. Still a work in progress, the mission of the archives is:

> … to collect, organise, preserve, and make accessible the documentation produced and acquired by the organisation and its members as part of their activities. Its objective is to document and highlight the history of Maison d'Haïti and its members which include part of the Haitian Montreal community and of the St-Michel neighbourhood. [. . .] The archives is guided by the approach and working methods advocated by the organisation. It remains anchored in the community that created it to highlight its collective knowledge and resources in order to foster the socio-political engagement of participants and employees.
> (Maison d'Haïti, working document 'Mission et procédures')

The first summer of the project, a group of about five volunteers started to assess the types of records held by the organisation and inventoried part of the documents. While one of the volunteers was an archivist, those who formed the core group were not. This clearly influenced the non-standard methods used to sort through and organise the first boxes of documents. In addition to the records it had created, Maison d'Haïti had accumulated important publications that were connected to their activist and advocacy work. The documents produced by Maison d'Haïti were held alongside those of the groups they were connected to – whether diasporic, Haitian or Montreal-based. Together, these documents reflected the levels of collaboration intrinsic to their approach as well as informing their work. Questions quickly arose about whether it was necessary to separate the documents into a resource library and archives since the organisation had so far kept everything together. After looking at the ways in which documents were found, the labels on folders and boxes, it was decided to keep the existing thematic and chronological arrangement to organise the new material gathered. The themes echoed the organisation's main orientation and programs and organisational documents were often gathered with other thematic ones.

Professionally-trained archivists might shudder at the idea of volunteers reorganising what they found while weeding and putting records in boxes, but the volunteers who started had no archival background and this archives project was never about following standards. Rather, it sought to organise the archives to the best of the volunteers' abilities in a way that made sense for the potential users – community members and employees. As the project evolved, volunteers came and went, strategies and work methods changed depending on who was there and what else was happening in the organisation. The volunteer in charge also started her doctoral research based on the archives project. In total, there have been around 12 volunteers at different points for various time periods.

In 2014 and 2015, a few volunteers continued to locate, gather and weed the documents while storing them in boxes. As the project slowed down due to a lack of physical space to process and store documents, the inventory was also put on the backburner. During the same period, a volunteer archivist joined the team and started to work closely with the volunteer co-ordinating the project. Lots of discussions happened between them about what had been done, what was left to do and how to devise strategies where archival standards could be made to mesh with what had already been put in place. In Spring 2016, the project gained renewed momentum. As employees and volunteers prepared to move to the new building, they sorted out and boxed documents. The archives team had prepared an information sheet about records management and archives to ensure that staff knew what to do and so that important materials wouldn't be lost. After identifying boxes of inactive material and weeding, the archives team was left with about 80 boxes to go through again in the new building. The boxes were stored in the new meeting room and three volunteers spent the summer going through them, again weeding and rehousing them in new boxes.

As documents were laid out on the table and shelves, interesting encounters started to happen. The meeting room is on the second floor of the building, with the offices, kitchen, computer room and the teenage girl program's space. Located right in front of the stairs, glass windows allow people to see inside. As people went to the second floor, they were welcomed by a room full of archival records and boxes. Curious, many came in to ask questions or to sit and look at some material, which allowed for interesting discussions and experiences with the archives. One such encounter happened when a visitor – a past member – came through during a visit to Montreal from Haiti. As she sat to look at some pictures, at the top of the pile lay a photo of her as a teenager in the youth programs. Every day, community members came, asked questions, recognised documents and had conversations about the materials being sorted that day. Thus, this became a place where the community's collective memory was explored on a daily basis because of the work being done. This was such a beneficial experience for everyone involved that were it to be done again, we would be better equipped to record those spontaneous encounters and explorations of memory.

During 2017, the volunteer doctoral student worked on inventorying the first 20 boxes of textual material, listing audiovisual records and rehousing photos. With the archivist, they devised an inventory list, which was revised and corrected over time. The headings in our inventory are based on the ISAD(G) archival standards, with some community-specific additions. The inventory is currently a flat file Microsoft Excel database that we are continually transforming for better use and effectiveness. There were discussions about introducing specialised archival software, such as Access to Memory (AtoM). However, it was decided that it would demand too much maintenance and resources from the organisation to maintain such specialised software. Excel is also easy to navigate for potential users. Maison d'Haïti also obtained a grant from the provincial archives, Bibliothèque et Archives Nationales du Québec, to buy archival storage material. The archives are now housed in the computer room, in built-in shelves designed to store them. This room is a lively space where people come for computer classes and employment searches during the day, children come to do their homework in the afternoon and French classes are given at night to newcomers. Therefore, although the archival work no longer occurs in the meeting room, the archives itself lives in a room that will facilitate ease of access and conversation surrounding it. The objectives for 2018 are to finish the inventory of the first 24 boxes of documents and of nine boxes of photos, as well as to start oral histories, a point we will detail below.

The archives hold inactive records created or obtained by employees, volunteers and participants, as part of the organisation's activities since it was founded in 1972. The records are mainly in French and Haitian Creole, with a few in English and Spanish, and come mainly (but not solely) from Quebec and Haiti. They relate to the organisation's activities and programs, as well as its advocacy work on issues ranging from campaigns against discrimination and racism and for the rights of immigrants and refugees, to Haitian politics and women's movements, etc. There are publications by Maison d'Haïti (e.g. pedagogical material, newsletters, research, reports); administrative documents from programs, projects and events (e.g. planning and grant documents, minutes, correspondence, pamphlets, posters); documents from various advocacy campaigns and coalitions that the organisation initiated or participated in (eg. correspondence, pamphlets, posters, press releases); documents from the various local, national and international movements, associations and groups to which the organisation or some of these members have been affiliated (e.g. correspondence, minutes, pamphlets, posters, newsletters, newspapers); photos and audiovisual materials of activities and programs; and objects (eg. paintings, macarons or pinback buttons). As will be explained in the following section, soon oral history recordings and transcriptions will be added to the records, tying this community of records together.

Archiving a community of records: oral histories as description and memory frame

Maison d'Haïti archives project is anchored in a collaborative, community-based process. Although the processing work is done by only a few volunteers, it relies on the participation and labour – past and present – of many others. These include the employees who helped box and sort through material during the move, the people who help identify handwriting on documents and people in photos, and most importantly, those who created the records in the first place. The work of describing the archives relies on shared memories and stories of the organisation. The textual, photographic, graphic and audiovisual records, alongside the memories and stories that relate to them, constitute a community of records, exemplifying Bastian's theory of a community of records where the community acts '[…] both as a record-creating entity and as a memory frame that contextualises the records it creates.' (2003, 3–4). The collective memory and memories of the institution are partly held in those archives. This archiving process aims to ensure that memories and stories that people have and tell are interwoven with physical records, so that the arrangement and description reflects the community of records.

In addition to traditional archival material, the archives will include oral history interviews with Maison d'Haïti community members. The first series of interviews will be done by the doctoral student as part of her dissertation work, but, with the interviewees' consent, transcripts and recordings will be donated to the archives. Oral history offers a way to understand the people who sustained the organisation and what fuelled their work. It is a form of explanation and a way to document the creation of records that form the archives. These interviews will be included in the archives as part of a series of 'authority records', while excerpts will be used in descriptions for key files and series within the archives. Oral history thus becomes an explicit way to use community memory to describe and arrange its records and a way to document the memories of the archives' creators, which have previously been shared informally. While capturing these memories will expand the framework and understanding of the archives, integrating oral history transcripts as its own series means putting people's voices into the archives.

Using oral history as both a record and a way to describe other records means using the collective memories of the community to glue together the records, their context and their origins.

Further, the memories that will be documented in the oral histories will provide a context to the current order of the records. Over the years, the records in the archives have been shuffled, reshuffled and mixed up many times. Therefore, it is clear that the original order of the records, as we received them, will not give us a clue as to their context of creation and preservation, apart from the fact that the order has continuously changed, depending on who handled them and why – sorting, moving, weeding or organising thematically. At the same time, through previous rearranging of some of the archives, community members have made their mark. Through handwriting on labels and the arrangement of certain folders and boxes, as well as curated binders for programs, events and correspondence, we can see the arrangement work done by previous 'informal archivists'. Preserving these physical aspects of the archives will preserve traces of the labour that has gone into preserving and organising the records over time. Therefore, by arranging the archives with the community as our framework and maintaining the prior curated organisation of documents, we aim to create a meaningful arrangement, based on how best to ensure easy use of the archives by community members. Previous records maintenance, as well as the current structure of Maison d'Haïti, gave us the cues we needed to arrange the materials in a way that is meaningful to its community.

This archiving process does not aim to make an archives just for the sake of making one. Nor are we making an archives simply to preserve the records. Rather, we are organising it so that it maintains connections to its community of creation and inspires holistic growth in the future. That means thinking about users who are not familiar with archives, inviting people to come and explore, accepting that things might be moved or rearranged later depending on who will process the archives and inspiring conversations that ensure that the physical preservation of memories is user-friendly for this community. It means accepting that this archives lives, breathes, moves and grows and ensuring that members are not afraid to just walk into the computer room and pull a box from the shelf to explore. The daily conversations in the meeting room show that people not only see the value of the archives, but are willing to share their memories and materials in order to continue growing it. We have already received two donations to the archives of documents about programs, services and community work completed at Maison d'Haïti. By finding ways to make the archives easily searchable and accessible, the project aims to encourage learning from and engaging with it.

Community education and learning from the archives

The opportunities for learning in and through a community-based archives project are multifold and multidirectional. Learning can happen through the process of archiving, but can also arise from the archives itself, and the space it provides. As Flinn notes:

> … when informed by a radical public history agenda of not just reclamation and celebration, but also of reflection and explanation, then the community archives can represent not only the establishment of a place where the past is documented and passively collected but, crucially, also a space in which the archives can become a significant tool for discovery, education, and empowerment.
>
> (Flinn, 2011, 9)

We often think of more formal engagements with archives in relation to education – especially through research or exhibition, but the actual archiving of a community of records can elicit learning, whether formal, informal or experiential. At Maison d'Haïti, it has been a learning process for volunteers who have collaborated, as well as people who have engaged with the archives, even for a brief moment. Archival material has been used in at least four different programs and events in recent years, already fulfilling the archives' objectives of making the records accessible to community members and finding ways to include them in ongoing programs or educational activities.

In 2014, some of the archival material was used in two publications – a booklet and a timeline – produced for community educators working with youth. Created through a joint project between CIDIHCA (le Centre International de Documentation et d'Information Haïtienne, Caribéenne et Afro-Canadienne), a community-based documentation centre, and an academic at McGill's Department of Integrated Studies in Education, the publications provide an introduction to histories of Caribbean migration to and community organising in Quebec. Using material from personal, community and institutional collections, the project also partly aimed to launch a collective conversation about the archives of Caribbean community groups in the city, such as those of Maison d'Haïti. Excerpts of the booklet can be seen at https://caribbeanquebec.com/booklet.

On 15 and 16 October 2016, Maison d'Haïti's new building was inaugurated. Over 750 people came to discover the new space, representing the diversity of people who are connected to the institution. These included current and past members, participants, volunteers and employees, as well as people who had never set foot in the organisation but had supported its work from afar and curious neighbours. During one panel presentation, tables with records and photos were set up. Each table was hosted by participants of the young teenage girl programs, 'Juste Pour Elles'. Long-standing community members were present and many recognised documents like the newsletters at the archives tables. Some saw themselves, or their children, family members or friends, or people they knew in the pictures. As people recounted and shared their stories, these records sparked an inter-generational dialogue between themselves and the girls. Each interaction expanded on the information given to the girls who were then able to share even more history and spark more discussion about the materials with each new conversation.

In December 2016, the volunteer who steers the project worked with the animators of the teenage girl programs to develop an activity based on the photographs. The photos had been shuffled and reshuffled over the years and were stocked in a box in no specific order. Following conversations with the Director about the photographs, it was decided to create an arrangement that would speak to the community and that it would be most useful to arrange the photographs by date and event. During a series of workshops, armed with gloves and description cards, the teenage girls set out to sort some of the pictures. They helped arrange the photographs, putting doubles, or pictures of the same event and same format, back together. This inspired conversations about what they thought was happening in the pictures, when they were taken, (for 10- to 14-year-old girls, the 1970s looked like centuries ago!) and who was in the pictures. From those conversations, they slowly mapped out parts of the history of the organisation and its programs. The Director was also invited to some of the 'archiving sessions' to help identify people and events. After these sessions, each girl chose a picture for which she had to write a short description and create a poster related to the event it depicted. Those posters were then showcased at a public event in February 2017, attended by over 140 people. Throughout the workshops, the girls participated in discussions about what they would do if they were in charge of the organisation. They presented their ideas during the showcase. Having learned from the history of the organisation and created from its archives, they were now asked to project themselves into its future, to imagine how they would mobilise their community.

Finally, in September 2017, Maison d'Haïti's art educator started a project using some of the archival photos to develop a 3D environment to engage the public with the archives. Although the project is still in its early stages, a prototype was presented in October 2017. Using a 3D virtual reality headset, viewers can navigate a 360-degree environment created by the photos while listening to a short history of the organisation and the archives project narrated by the Director. This project aims to creatively use the archives to get people engaged with technology and the institution's history. In each of the above cases it is clear that Maison d'Haïti's archives has already had an impact on its programming and events. Through different forms of collaborations, the archives is expanding the collective memory and the community of records of this organisation.

Constellations, connections and collaborations: when community archives meet

The archives of community-based organisations reflect the connections between different groups and movements, whether they be of the same community in different diasporic spaces (e.g. Haitian organisations in Haiti and in the diaspora) or between different communities who rally together to mobilise for change in the same geographical space. Maison d'Haïti and its members are part of a constellation of organisations and activists that connect different places, communities and struggles. Mapping those connections and highlighting them in the archives is a way to put forth and highlight memories and histories of different moments of collaboration that sustain community organising. In the archive's inventory we decided to note these connections by building a list – as comprehensive as possible – of organisations that collaborated and coalitions in which Maison d'Haïti participated, which can be found in the records. We added sections to the inventory for institutions/groups and individuals to retrace networks.

We hope that in the future these connections will not just be noted in one archives, but in the archives of multiple organisations, making connections between groups explicit through their individual communities of records. Two community archives projects have recently begun in other Montreal organisations that also show the importance of mapping these connections. The first is at Head & Hands, a non-profit organisation that offers a harm-reduction, holistic and non-judgemental approach to youth social services in Montreal. This project aims to create an archives at Head & Hands through organising existing files, creating a records management plan, oral histories with the community and a robust collection policy going forward to ensure the growth of the archives into the future. The archives will be launched in time to commemorate the 50th anniversary of Head & Hands in 2020. The second is at the Jamaica Association of Montreal, which has been committed to the social, political, economic, educational and cultural integration of Jamaicans and Blacks in Montreal since 1962. This project aims to celebrate the Association's past presidents, members and larger community through creation of an archives, a history book and collection of oral history interviews, among other things. During the initial inventories and sorting taking place for both these projects, documents about coalitions or collaborative programs with Maison d'Haïti have already been identified. The reverse is also true, with traces of Head & Hands and the Jamaica Association being found at Maison d'Haïti.

Although still at an early stage, these findings suggest that as these projects and potentially other projects in Montreal continue, we are likely to find other points of connection between organisations. We may also find more information about the people who navigated within and between these communities. The archives of these groups represent constellations of communities of records that relate to different spheres of community organising in the city. Archiving them means not only working to preserve and make histories of activism and mobilisation better known, but it is also a way to participate in the continuation of collaborative work for a better, more just city.

Conclusion: seeing past and future

Archivist Eric Ketelaar writes:

> Communities of records need spaces. Archives as social spaces can help forming and hosting these communities. Archives serving as spaces of memory, where people's experiences can be transformed into meaning. Archives as a place of shared custody and trust [. . .].
>
> (Ketelaar, 2008, 21)

In an era where we increasingly rely on virtual space, it becomes especially important to create physical spaces where people can sit and talk together, face to face. Archives can provide that space. The over-reliance on technology obscures the fact that access to it is also not a given. It demands resources that community groups don't always have. All of us involved in community archival projects need to ensure that we respect and adapt our practices to the contexts we work in, which might sometimes mean bringing back older archival strategies and tools.

Community-based archival projects can open a collective space where the community that created the archives is involved in thinking about how to archive it, also ensuring the archives becomes a space of discussion, exchange and negotiation. When people other than archivists are involved in the archiving process, standards might be different, but happy mistakes are likely to happen, creating unlikely encounters and drawing people into the archives. Actions that take place in the community archives space, such as shuffling documents, inventorying records, trying to determine which ones to keep and which to discard, trying to understand what those records are about or who might know about them, create opportunities for people to share a moment, a conversation, a story, a memory.

At Maison d'Haïti, those encounters happened when volunteers were rehousing the material in the meeting room during Summer 2016 and they continue to happen in the archives' home in the computer room or whenever materials are used in a community activity. Having the archives in a multifunction room makes it alive. As people come in and out, they see volunteers inventory and process material, ask questions or offer help to move a box. The archives is slowly anchoring itself in the new space, becoming part of the daily life. Through encounters such as these, it opens a space where Maison d'Haïti's history is remembered, recounted and transmitted, where members revisit or learn their community's history, to continue making it.

References

Bastian, J. A. (2003) *Owning memory: how a Caribbean community lost its archives and found its history*, Libraries Unlimited.

Choudry, A. and Smith, A. (2016) *Unfree Labour? Struggles of migrant and immigrant workers in Canada*, PM Press.

Flinn, A. (2007) Community Histories, Community Archives: some opportunities and challenges, *Journal of the Society of Archivists*, **28** (2), 151–176.

Flinn, A (2011) Archival Activism: independent and community-led archives, radical public history and the heritage professions, *InterActions: UCLA Journal of Education and Information Studies*, **7** (2), Article 6, 1–20.

Flinn, A., Stevens, M. and Shepherd, E. (2009) Whose Memories, Whose Archives? Independent Community Archives, Autonomy and the Mainstream, *Archival Science*, **9** (1), 71–86.

Ketelaar, E. (2008) Archives as Spaces of Memory, *Journal of the Society of Archivists*, **29** (1), 9–27.

Maison d'Haïti (1973) *Maison d'Haïti Inc, Document No 4 Septembre 1973*, Maison d'Haïti.

Maison d'Haïti (1975) *Maison d'Haïti Inc. Centre Communautaire Haïtien, Programme 75–76, Document No 6 Octobre 1975*, Maison d'Haïti.

Maison d'Haïti (1981) *Rapport d'activités 1979–81*, Maison d'Haïti.

Maison d'Haïti (2018) Home page, Maison d'Haïti, www.mhaiti.org.

Mayer, R. (1994) Évolution des Pratiques Communautaires au Québec (1960–1990), *Canadian Social Work Review/Revue canadienne de service social*, **11** (2), 238–260.

Mills, S. (2010) *The Empire Within: postcolonial thought and political activism in sixties Montreal*, McGill-Queen's University Press.

Mills, S. (2016) *A Place in the Sun: Haiti, Haitians, and the remaking of Quebec*, McGill-Queen's University Press.

N.a. (n.d.) Pourquoi une clinique communautaire haïtienne?

Saint-Victor, A. (2017) *De l'exil à la communauté. Une histoire de l'immigration haïtienne à Montréal*, Master's thesis, Université du Québec à Montréal.

Thobani, S. (2007) *Exalted Subjects: studies in the making of race and nation in Canada*, University of Toronto Press.

CHAPTER 8

Indigenous archiving and wellbeing: surviving, thriving, reconciling

Joanne Evans, Shannon Faulkhead,
Kirsten Thorpe, Karen Adams, Lauren Booker
and Narissa Timbery

Introduction

Too often, Australia's mainstream discourse continues to be written and crafted to endorse and valorise the actions of an often-violent past, whilst disregarding the effects of the brutal systems of colonisation upon Indigenous Australian peoples. The authors acknowledge the diversity of Aboriginal and Torres Strait Islander peoples and communities across Australia and use the term 'Indigenous Australian' in this chapter to refer to the First Peoples of Australia. Various forms of trauma continue to impact upon many Indigenous Australian people, families and communities, contributing to ongoing discrimination and disadvantage (Atkinson, 2002). Cultural trauma is where a collective group is affected by a horrendous event that irrevocably marks memory and changes identity forever (Alexander, 2004). It is impossible to be an Indigenous Australian today and not be connected in some way to individual and collective experiences of invasion and colonisation.

As is so often the case, recordkeeping and archiving play a crucial role in the progression of colonial and oppressive regimes. Australia's government and collecting archival institutions manage this legacy, evidencing colonisation, not just in their archival holdings, but also in how these holdings are appraised, described, managed and made accessible.

As Indigenous Australians in the second half of the 20th century have sought access to records in institutional archives that document their lives, they have re-confronted not just the trauma in the records, but in the edifices and apparatuses around them. Moreover, when Indigenous peoples interact with archival materials that tell stories through a colonial lens, the trauma is not just an individualised one: it has collective impact in the here and now on both people and on Country. The term Country encapsulates deep and timeless cultural connections to land, environment and community and the depth and breadth of its meaning is hard to define for Western audiences. 'In Aboriginal English, a person's land, sea, sky, rivers, sites, seasons, plants and animals; place of heritage, belonging and spirituality; is called 'Country' (https://australianmuseum.net.au/glossary-indigenous-australia-terms).

Faced with the cultural genocide of colonisation, Indigenous Australians have utilised the strength and resilience of their oral traditions and other practices to retain connections to family, community and Country. These are the foundation of many community archives initiatives that are part of reclamation, revitalisation and continuation of language and culture, to come to terms with the ongoing ramifications from colonisation and contribute to reconciliation for the whole Australian community.

In this chapter, we begin with the 1997 *Bringing Them Home Report* as a significant turning point when the trauma in institutional archives and archival practices was revealed to all Australians. We then discuss the increased insight into the historical, social and political determinants of health and wellbeing for Indigenous Australians that has developed since. While much is written about the decolonisation of archives from social justice perspectives, our focus is to explore this area from a wellbeing perspective as a way to deal with the trauma of colonial archives for Indigenous Australians and for all those who interact with them. We introduce and use a Social and Emotional Wellbeing (SEWB) model to reflect on the enriched understandings of the interconnectedness of Indigenous archiving with wellbeing that has developed over the past 20 years. We examine continued challenges that exist for Indigenous peoples and communities in gaining access to institutional archives and to meaningfully address their inaccuracies and incompleteness. We look at how to foster continual decolonising of archival institutions, through embedding into archival frameworks, processes and systems rights of access, interaction and control for Indigenous Australians. We discuss the need for archival institutions to also learn how to better support and interoperate with Indigenous community archiving initiatives. We conclude with a summary of the key elements that we believe are essential for Indigenous community archives of the future. This requires embracing community participation in the formation and management of all archives, moving beyond improving access to embracing archival autonomy and self-determination, with flow-on effects for individual and community wellbeing and to further reconciliation across the Australian community.

Background

The brutal nature of colonisation is exemplified by the protection and assimilation policies that oversaw the forced removal of Indigenous Australian children from their families, communities, culture and Country throughout much of the 20th century. 2017 marked the twentieth anniversary of the landmark *Bringing Them Home Report*, the outcome of an Australian Human Rights Commission Inquiry that shone the spotlight on the identity, memory and accountability needs of those who had been forcibly removed – the Stolen Generations (Australian Human Rights and Equal Opportunity Commission, 1997). The Inquiry was charged with examining the adequacies and shortfalls of existing legislation, policies, practices and systems to support those who had been taken from their families and communities. With the report detailing the abuse suffered in childhoods under institutional 'care' and the lifelong ramifications of the denial of access to their Indigenous culture, it was also a time for private and public Australian memory-keeping institutions to begin a more critical examination of the evidence of forced removal within their holdings.

The *Bringing Them Home Report* highlighted the many difficulties faced by members of the Stolen Generations in seeking access to their records in order to piece together childhood experiences, establish identity and find their families. Its recommendations to make access to records 'easier and less hurtful' included challenging the Australian archival and recordkeeping community to work towards supporting Indigenous self-determination by providing Indigenous communities with opportunities 'to manage their own historical documentation'. These objectives recognise records in government and other institutional archives as intrinsic to the individual and community archives of Indigenous Australians and emphasise the importance of their decolonisation. Enabling Indigenous communities to access as well as have control over these records is 'one step in the process of recovering from the history of genocide' (Australian Human Rights and Equal Opportunity Commission, 1997, 299).

The *Bringing them Home Report* further promoted the significance of recognising the complex interconnections between Indigenous archiving, reconciliation and health and wellbeing for individuals, communities and Australian society as a whole. For generations, Indigenous Australian peoples have identified the need for a strong sense of identity and belonging, with the interconnectedness of past, present and future being the driving force for the return of Indigenous cultural materials and knowledge to their peoples to assist in addressing trauma and supporting wellbeing (Ley, 1991, 13).

Despite government policy and actions that removed cultural material from Country and banned cultural practices, knowledges and languages, Indigenous Australian peoples have found ways to maintain what they could, forget what they had to and pass on the knowledge required to survive.

Forgetting is a vital element of memory and collective memory, providing the ability to remember that which is important (Crane, 1997, 1380). Indigenous peoples also used it as a way of survival (Faulkhead, 2008). When facing cultural genocide over actual annihilation, communities needed to be pragmatic and resilient in making difficult decisions whilst retaining hope that lost/forgotten knowledge would somehow be located again. Inquiries, discussions, reports and research have reiterated the need to invest in mechanisms for securing and strengthening Indigenous culture as an integral part of addressing pressing health and social issues. The continued scrutiny and surveillance of Indigenous lives through quick fix responses, not only perpetuates ongoing discrimination and disadvantage, but through lack of agency and autonomy contributes to poorer health and social outcomes (Murphy, 2014).

Progressive policy-making is bringing together increased insight into the historical, social and political determinants of health and wellbeing for Indigenous Australians with deeper awareness, appreciation and responsiveness to the centrality of connectedness to kin, community, culture and Country (Commonwealth of Australia, 2017):

> 'Aboriginal health' means not just the physical wellbeing of an individual but refers to the social, emotional and cultural wellbeing of the whole Community in which each individual is able to achieve their full potential as a human being, thereby bringing about the total wellbeing of their Community. It is a whole-of-life view and includes the cyclical concept of life-death-life.
>
> (National Aboriginal Health Strategy Working Party, 1989)

This understanding builds upon human rights and Indigenous rights frameworks and both come about through, and foster the development of, strong and equitable partnerships with Indigenous Australian communities in tackling health challenges. For example, the *National Aboriginal and Torres Strait Islander Health Plan 2013–2023* is based on the four principles of Health Equality and a Human Rights Approach, Aboriginal and Torres Strait Islander Community Control and Engagement, Partnership and Accountability (see http://www.health.gov.au/internet/publications/publishing.nsf/Content/oatsih-healthplan-toc~overview).

Modelling of Indigenous perspectives of social and emotional wellbeing, such as that developed by Gee et al. (2014) for use in cultural competence education for mental health practitioners, show how perceptions of self are 'inseparable from, and embedded within, family and community' and placed within the context of continuing impacts of colonisation. Discussion of the practical usage of this model highlights the importance of mental health professionals knowing the history (and therefore engaging with the archives) of the Indigenous communities with which they work:

> These critical factors – such as a community's local history of colonisation and the extent to which a cultural group is able to resist assimilation, maintain cultural continuity, and retain the right of self-determination and sovereignty – will all significantly influence a community's capacity to retain their cultural values, principles, practices, and traditions. This, in turn, will differentially empower or impinge upon individual and family SEWB [social and emotional wellbeing].
>
> (Gee et al., 2014, 62)

Implicit in this discussion is the interconnectedness of Indigenous archiving with social and emotional wellbeing in and across individual, community and societal levels. As illustrated in Figure 8.1, this raises questions as to the roles archives of all kinds play in the strengthening or weakening of spirit and self.

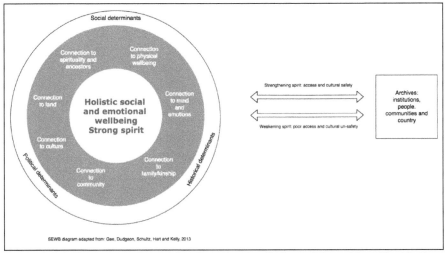

Figure 8.1 *Indigenous peoples social and emotional wellbeing and the archives. Chart by the authors* (adapted from Gee et al., 2014)

Trauma, healing and archives

Western methods of treating trauma often involve individualised psychological approaches through counselling or other therapeutic interventions focused on self. An Indigenous perspective moves beyond viewing trauma as an individual's medical problem and instead as a symptom of broader unresolved societal problems that continue to manifest as health and wellbeing issues (Corntassel, 2008; Atkinson, 2002). Dealing with the collective trauma resulting from colonisation requires broader communal approaches that incorporate cultural knowledge and traditional ways of healing (Corntassel, 2008). Involving Indigenous Elders or healers from within the communities to provide expertise as to appropriate cultural ways of dealing with the trauma of colonisation is a key strategy (Marsella, 2017). Holistic approaches that incorporate Indigenous knowledge are also supported by reviews and policies recommending good practice for strengthening Indigenous social and emotional wellbeing (Australian Institute of Health and Welfare, 2013; Australian Government, 2013; Department of Health, 2017; Victorian Government, 2017).

Indigenous Australian expressions of healing often refer to the spirit that resides within a person and its connection to multiple elements (Victorian Government, 2017). It is not uncommon to hear Indigenous Australian peoples refer to missing, broken, negative, low, weak, bad or wounded spirit to describe un-wellness and a strong, positive, energised, good and whole spirit for indicating wellness. Spirit is multi-dimensional and can refer to a person, family, community or to Country (Atkinson, 2002; Australian Government, 2013). Achieving a healthy spirit may involve delving into institutional archives in the quest for information to strengthen one's place, family, community and Country. In doing so, Indigenous peoples are taking a risk that they will find more trauma alongside answers, or in some cases, find nothing at all. Archival institutions can assist in this healing through creating protocols and processes that support people's journey rather than blocking their path. Restricting access to records may often result in individuals and communities being caught in a holding pattern with continuing trauma and negative impacts upon wellbeing. The inherent trauma in the stories and records adds further complexity, making them difficult to disclose and compounding the deliberate disruption to intergenerational sharing of stories of colonising actions and processes.

With increased desire and opportunity for archival access, ensuring cultural safety and personal and community wellbeing has become a growing concern. This is supported by anecdotal and intensifying evidence of the impacts this access can have upon individuals and communities. Issues pervade the archive world, such as: frustration with institutional barriers (McKemmish, Faulkhead and Russell, 2011); partnership tensions (Adams and Faulkhead, 2012); lateral violence (Australian Human Rights Commission, 2011); concerns about understanding, care and interpretation of records (Thorpe, 2005); offensive records and role confusion (Thorpe, 2014); and disappointment and despair at unfulfilled expectations of archival materials (Evans et al., 2012). In addition, Indigenous and non-Indigenous people utilising the archives for teaching and cultural revitalisation processes can be similarly challenged (Reynolds, 2005; Ma Rhea and Russell, 2012). However, there is little written about how wellbeing can be protected and cultural safety ensured.

Whilst government libraries and archives have been mandated with the task of making their records accessible to Indigenous Australians, there are bigger issues regarding connecting Indigenous peoples with their records and stories. Whilst members of the Stolen Generations, and Indigenous peoples more broadly, are now more able to access records relating to themselves, they currently have little agency over where and how the records are stored or who accesses them. Issues of ownership, copyright, rights over access control, de-accessioning and destruction of records are not being adequately addressed. Nor is the need to allow for amendments to records that are incomplete or incorrect. The majority of libraries and archives in Australia have not implemented policies to manage Indigenous Intellectual and Cultural Property (ICIP) rights (Kearney and Janke, 2018) and are yet to fully engage with Indigenous peoples and communities about appropriate protocols for the management of cultural records.

However, the Social and Emotional Wellbeing (SEWB) model clearly has implications for Indigenous wellbeing and archives. If Indigenous Australian peoples are seeking information on their histories of colonisation, then it is crucial that access to records in archival institutions is provided in appropriate ways. Without self-determination and ownership of one's own narrative, the archive and archival process have the ability to reiterate removal from family and dispossession of culture. Every person and community has the right to own their own stories and for them to become part of their individual, family and community archives. The potential via a people-centred participatory approach for archival institutions to be a decolonising rather than colonising force is manifold. But to do so requires an institution-wide commitment and an understanding of the rich landscape of contemporary Indigenous archiving.

Indigenous archiving

Indigenous Australian histories, stories and experience are now held across multiple and often fragmented places, including government, other institutional and community archives. In this contemporary context, a community archive encompasses oral and written records, literature, landscape, dance, art, the built environment and other artefacts. The archive exists within individuals, communities and lives within Country, both tangible and intangible. This is how Indigenous archives and memory have always existed, carried through generations orally, in performance, art, the environment and in place. Indigenous peoples who store their records in orality, in family and community, and in and on Country are blending this knowledge with institutional archival collections, providing opportunities for Indigenous stories and histories to flourish rather than being dispersed and disconnected (Faulkhead, 2009; Faulkhead, Bradley and McKee, 2017). In some cases, physical copying or digital repatriation processes are enabling institutional archival records to be reconnected with oral records in communities, allowing oral traditions to continue these stories intergenerationally.

Indigenous community archives are thus emerging as sites of truth telling and reconciliation, fuelling calls for national truth-telling to be a part of constitutional recognition. Two exemplars in the case of the Stolen Generations are Kinchela Boys Home Aboriginal Corporation https://www. kinchelaboyshome.org.au and The Cherbourg Memory site http:// cherbourgmemory.org. The opportunity for a national truth-telling of indigenous Australian peoples' history is continually being demanded as a way for reconciling Australia's indigenous and colonial past, present, and future. The latest was in the May 2017 First Nations National Constitutional Convention, convened to discuss constitutional reform to recognise Aboriginal and Torres Strait Islander peoples. The *Uluru Statement from the Heart*, 2017, seeks 'a Makarrata Commission to supervise a process of agreement-making between governments and First Nations and truth-telling about our history' (https://www.1voiceuluru.org/the-statement).

Repatriation and integration processes are vital in tackling the legacies of colonisation, particularly in addressing the resulting silences in the archive. Today, many Indigenous authors, artists, storytellers and archivists are sharing their stories and knowledge to reveal and heal the trauma in the archive (Jorgensen and McLean, 2017; Thorpe, Faulkhead and Booker, forthcoming 2019; Faulkhead, 2009; Vickery et al., 2007). They are demonstrating how archives can provide a platform to support the telling of Indigenous stories and become instruments of decolonisation. Positive narratives of Indigenous peoples, culture and history assists the wellbeing of the represented communities, whilst bolstering the education of next generation Australians to question the colonial, hegemonic and assimilatory narratives of the past. It assists in creating a possible future where complex Indigenous stories are part of mainstream Australian collective knowledge.

Indigenous archivists, in collaboration with other cultural heritage professionals, have also developed protocols to better guide the handling of Indigenous content in institutions and collections (Thorpe, 2013). The Aboriginal and Torres Strait Islander Library and Information Resource Network (ATSILIRN) Protocols, developed in 1995 and revised in 2005, aim to foster respectful collaborations with Indigenous Australian communities so that material is handled in culturally appropriate and respectful ways. They emphasise the need for such engagement to be reflected in governance, as well as operational processes, and that education and dialogue is required to enhance cultural competence and greater awareness of Indigenous Australian issues and needs.

A rich landscape of Indigenous community archival projects was showcased at the National Indigenous Research Conference organised by the Australian Institute of Aboriginal and Torres Strait Islander Studies (AIATSIS) in 2017. The projects embodied many of the principles of working with Indigenous communities – designed, developed and implemented in partnerships; time devoted to relationship building and mutual learning; respect for Indigenous cultural rights; representing Indigenous ways of knowing and being in system and process design – along with celebrating dynamic, vibrant and resilient peoples and cultures. It demonstrated a shift from debating the need to engage with the Indigenous community represented in records as can happen at other professional conferences, to showcasing the wide variety of ways in which such engagement can be carried out. (For the conference program and audio recordings of sessions see http://aiatsis.gov.au/news-and-events/events/aiatsis-national-indigenous-research-conference-2017).

The projects were both a reflection of how far Indigenous heritage and archiving projects had come, but also how far the cultural heritage sector still needs to go in enabling Indigenous communities to have (and sustain) control over their own historical documentation. In looking across the projects from a decolonisation perspective, many are still crafted around 'benevolent access' to specific archival material in cultural heritage institutions rather than developing shared models of ownership and stewardship for promulgating across other holdings and institutions. While it was important to hear the ways in which the barriers inherent in archival frameworks designed around the rights of a singular records creator (i.e. where records are described and controlled from the perspective of the person or body that created, collected or set aside the recorded material as evidence of the conduct of their activities) were negotiated in each case, it was also frustrating that future projects would have to go over the same ground and navigate the same hurdles. In some cases, there was also a sense of the instability of uneasy compromises that could so easily be rolled back with a change of personnel or management strategy. A further concern was the bespoke nature of the technological developments and a lack of interoperability between community and institutional systems. This could potentially put many Indigenous community archives projects at risk of obsolescence once resourcing comes to an end and/or the cost of re-development of custom-built database systems becomes too high.

With Indigenous community archival initiatives playing a part in the strengthening of spirit and connections as highlighted by the SEWB model, mechanisms to support and sustain them become vital. While a colonisation approach might see a collecting archive take on their responsibility in the face of sustainability issues, a decolonisation approach focuses on more complex and challenging questions of how they can be maintained within communities and/or – at the very least – under community control. Many would argue that to do so requires a shift to a participatory, post-custodial, post-colonial archival paradigm.

Ensuring the future for Indigenous archiving

Displacing systematic discrimination against Indigenous peoples created and legitimized by the cognitive frameworks of imperialism and colonialism remains the single most crucial cultural challenge facing humanity. Meeting this responsibility is not just a problem for the colonized and the oppressed, but rather the defining challenge for all peoples. It is the path to a shared and sustainable future for all peoples.

(Daes in Battiste, Bell and Findlay, 1999, 82)

Calls to transform archival frameworks, processes and systems for Indigenous Australian peoples were heard a decade ago in the findings from the Trust and Technology (T&T) research project. Funded through an Australian Research Council Linkage Grant, the T&T Project brought together recordkeeping and Indigenous Studies researchers at Monash University in partnership with the Public Record Office of Victoria, the Koorie Heritage Trust Inc., the Victorian Koorie Records Taskforce and the Australian Society of Archivists Indigenous Issues Special Interest Group to explore ways in which Koorie communities could archive oral memory and engage with existing government and institutional archives on their own terms (McKemmish et al., 2010). A draft position statement calling on the Australian archival profession, archival institutions and records authorities to address the archival and recordkeeping claims of Indigenous Australian peoples was one of the key outcomes of the project. It identified the need to reform legislation, policy, practices and technological systems to respect and enable the exercise of Indigenous recordkeeping rights (i.e. encompassing Indigenous cultural rights with other recordkeeping implications of the UN human rights charters) in support of reconciliation and self-determination (Iacovino, Ketelaar and McKemmish, 2009). A key section of this statement is reproduced in Figure 8.2 opposite to demonstrate its bold, far-reaching nature, along with its continuing relevance ten years later.

Recommendation to Archival Profession, Archival Institutions and Records Authorities

By far the largest obstacle to the realisation of Indigenous human rights related to the archival sources of their knowledge is that Australian legal and archival frameworks do not recognise Indigenous cultural rights as human rights, or provide for ownership rights for people who are considered to be the subject of records. Therefore the general effect of the laws of personal and intellectual property is that the organisations which create or receive and maintain records relating to Indigenous peoples exercise almost all control over them. In relation to government records, privacy, freedom of information and public records laws do give records subjects some rights over the collection, use and disclosure of information about themselves. However, these rights apply only to individual records subjects: they cannot be exercised by Indigenous peoples as a collective or by individuals in relation to deceased family members.

The legal and archival frameworks apply equally to anyone who is the subject of records in archives. Indigenous people are legally in exactly the same situation as everyone else. The *effect* of this framework, however, is not the same for everyone. The special claims of Indigenous people could be addressed by:

- Reforms to Australian archival legal frameworks to recognise Indigenous cultural rights in records, and consequent extension of existing international and national laws and protocols relating to Indigenous human rights and heritage to archival sources of Indigenous knowledge, e.g. United Nations *Joinet-Orentlicher Principles* (UN1999 & 2005), United Nations *Declaration of Indigenous Human Rights* (UN 2007), *Report on Australian Indigenous Cultural and Intellectual Property Rights* (ATSIC 1999).

- Australian archival institutions and records authorities should use a combination of information technology, legal and policy initiatives to extend the existing legal and moral rights of Indigenous individuals and communities relating to the control, disclosure, access and use of records.

- The adoption by the Australian archival profession and institutions of a participant model which involves repositioning record subjects as records agents - participants in the act of records creation. In a fully implemented participant model, every contributor, including the person who is the subject of the document, has legal and moral rights and responsibilities in relation to ownership, access and privacy.

- Expanding the definition of record creators in archival science to include everyone who has contributed to a record's creative process and has been affected by its action, thus supporting the enforcement of a broader spectrum of rights and obligations.

Figure 8.2   *Extract from exposure draft position statement: human rights, indigenous communities in Australia and the archives* (Iacovino, Ketelaar and McKemmish, 2009)

While those who developed this statement may despair at the lack of endorsement and uptake by the Australian archival profession as a whole, it still functions as a source of inspiration for those keen to explore the design and development of participatory recordkeeping and archival systems. A growing consensus is emerging that participatory requirements cannot be just tacked on to existing systems, but require a fundamental re-design (Evans et al., 2015). Models for shared stewardship (Gilliland and McKemmish, 2014; McKemmish et al., 2010), informed and influenced by human rights, decolonisation, continuum and critical theory discourses, to integrate, rather than segregate, community and institutional archives, are needed for currently marginalised individuals and communities to have archival autonomy – the ability to participate in societal memory on their own terms and with their own voice (Evans et al., 2015).

Participation begins with the ways in which these new models and systems are designed. Positive systemic change comes about where there is equity, enabling stakeholders to have voice and agency in design, development and implementation processes. Indigenous Australians have fought long and hard for inclusion in decision making that impacts on their lives and while there is still a long way to go, there is also evidence of where this is now a normative approach. Community engagement, partnering and control were a key feature of the community archives projects showcased at the 2017 AIATSIS conference discussed earlier. The challenge for the Australian archival community is to make this a feature of all their projects. It also extends to designing institutional systems as community systems, capable of respecting, representing and enacting multiple rights in records and embracing and enabling a plurality of perspectives to cohabit archival spaces.

In a participatory paradigm, the role of the archival and recordkeeping professional shifts from the benevolent provision of access to archival materials for Indigenous communities, to fostering the frameworks, processes and systems for the development of Indigenous community archives that can directly engage with institutional records. A participatory infrastructure would recognise the continua of orality and text, incorporate connections between people, Country, culture, community and history in a multiplicity of ways, and allow for remembering and forgetting in ways that promote and strengthen spirit and wellbeing. It would also interconnect institutional and community archives to overcome the current bifurcations (Evans, McKemmish and Rolan, 2017).

What might inform that reconfiguration? Thorpe (2017) has identified three key roles for an Aboriginal community archive, namely that 'it should be a learning place, a gathering and support place, and a place to connect with culture and heritage' (927) in order to enable archival autonomy, promote social and emotional wellbeing and support the self-determination of Indigenous communities. How can institutional archives become community archives? We suggest embracing the principles outlined below.

Acknowledging co-creation rights

Recognising the 'subjects' of records as co-creators is a first step in the development of models of shared stewardship. The right of Indigenous peoples to have control of their records held within archival institutions was emphasised in the reporting from the T&T Project and has spurred further research into rights-based models for recordkeeping (McKemmish, Faulkhead and Russell, 2011; Evans et al., 2017). Supporting co-creation rights requires acknowledgement of the power structures that currently exist and the ways in which they may inhibit equitable participation and mutual learning. Whilst it is a complex process to develop systems capable of representing and negotiating individual, community/collective and institutional rights, an investment in developing protocols and guidelines that complement and support Indigenous Australian community decision-making processes and governance structures is a way to begin to redress this imbalance in most archival institutions.

Embedding cultural protocols

Shared stewardship requires respect for cultural protocols to be at the core of archival systems. These protocols would be supported by appropriate governance structures to allow Indigenous people to lead decision-making about their records. For example, in collecting institutions, collection development and acquisition policies should be shaped and determined by community needs, with Elders providing advice on locally focused recording needs, including records that need to be maintained and preserved as ongoing memories and those that should not.

Cultural protocols would be a fundamental requirement of system design and archival management, not merely an add-on or a separate function, and be part of building and engendering trust. It would also include designing access systems that move beyond the traditional approach of material being either open or closed, to accommodate dynamic and contextual community access needs and extend to decisions about digitisation. Processes for embedding cultural requirements into processes and systems would enable mutual learning and help non-Indigenous practitioners to be less hesitant and fearful of community engagement.

Facilitating archival autonomy

Facilitating participation and enabling agency in archival processes requires the challenging and changing of colonial archival traditions. Bringing Indigenous and non-Indigenous archival practices together should be seen as an exciting challenge. Creating opportunities for mutual exploration of methods and models to embrace the complexities of dealing with sensitive, fraught or troubling records and the racist and discriminatory contexts of their creation and/or collection is fundamental to the building of inclusive models for managing archives. An example of this in relation to the needs of the Stolen Generations would be working with Indigenous communities on how a 'right of reply' to records could be embedded into systems, to acknowledge and address tensions and emotional impact that exists around racist, misused, inadequate and abusive terminology and language that is then replicated in description and access interfaces. This could lead to the development of ways in which materials could be described in culturally rich and appropriate ways to enhance their accessibility and be the start of the development of archival processes underpinned by Indigenous Australian ways of knowing.

Supporting cultural safety

Consistent with principles of wellbeing is cultural safety, which emerged from the field of health science and is a responsibility to 'provide care in a manner that is respectful of a person's culture and beliefs, and that is free from discrimination' (Australian Commission on Safety and Quality in Healthcare, 2009). Generally, cultural safety is considered the provision of a safe place where there is no assault, challenge or denial of a person's identity (Williams, 1999). To create change in health and wellbeing, leadership is needed. These leaders cannot work in isolation and require support to enhance their skills and knowledge, but, more importantly, to sustain their practice (Koh and Jacobson, 2009).

Cultural safety is an important issue for both users of archives as well as those that care for them. Archival institutions need to address the collective trauma archivists can experience and provide staff with ways to keep their 'spirit strong'. For example, one response could involve partnering with Indigenous communities to install memorials to recognise the archival trauma that exists in their responsibility and remit. Memorials can come in many formats and can act as places for reflection, contemplation and healing of spirit. Embedding cultural safety within the policies and practices of the organisation would be another way of demonstrating support and commitment to social and emotional wellbeing.

Sharing stewardship

Cultural heritage and archival institutions have the opportunity to develop a networked and co-ordinated framework to support shared stewardship and self-determination, acknowledging the value of archival material for communities and implementing operational changes to dismantle the inherited power structures of imperial and colonial recordkeeping and collecting regimes. The institutional inclination towards Western notions of ownership and preservation are often at odds with the goals of repatriation and revitalisation. Opening up archives comes about by relinquishing the idea that these processes and policies are not favourable to the institutional goal of keeping, cataloguing and display. Rather repatriation and revitalisation efforts provide the cultural heritage sector with new opportunities to respond to unethical and problematic collecting and curating histories and engage with communities and new audiences.

A national agenda that articulates pathways to mutual learning, shared stewardship and a relinquishing of control to deliver better outcomes needs to be developed in a format that works with the communities and practitioners who are already involved in repatriation and revitalisation efforts in order to best understand what is needed to move forward in policy. Cross sector communication and the consistent involvement of community in amending institutional policy and process is paramount to successfully shifting the focus of operations to support institutional accountability and community self-determination. Institutions would be made accountable for communicating information on their impact, in particular to ensure that services that are designed for communities are appropriate and transformational.

We call for leadership roles and decision-making roles to be created in the major collecting and cultural institutions to foster and enable Indigenous self-determination in archives. These leadership roles would be responsible for enacting the principles articulated in the ATSILIRN Protocols and the T&T Statement to consider the needs of records co-creators in all archival processes.

Conclusion

In this chapter we have discussed how colonial archives document histories of impact, dispossession and forced removal, as well as stories of resilience, political advocacy and community mobilisation. Trauma endured by Indigenous Australian peoples, and the cataclysmic effect on cultural knowledge and practice, moves inter-generationally through time and the archive is both a repository of evidence of these traumatic actions and a resource of materials to recover, reunite, redress and build anew. However, simply providing access is not enough, nor is it the full potential of what archival institutions can facilitate. We have argued that there is much to be gained in recognising and embracing the archives role in social and emotional wellbeing. Records in archival institutions are a source of lost or forgotten knowledge that can be brought back to Indigenous Australian peoples and communities to support healing and play a part in the continuation of inter-generational knowledge transmission for the world's oldest living cultures.

We call on archival institutions to look at how they can work together with Indigenous communities to develop culturally safe spaces in which multiple sources of evidence and memory can be brought together under community stewardship. The process of reconfiguring and reconceptualising the archive allows for the temporal and spatial shifting of narratives, in turn allowing for a plurality of perspectives to co-exist and connect. Our hope would be that not only would it help to heal the archive, but also to play a part in the reconciliation needed across Australian society to come to terms with our colonial past. Decolonising the archive is a concern for all.

References

Adams, K. and Faulkhead, S. (2012) Indigenous Research Partnerships: this is not a guide but it could help, *Information, Communication and Society*, **15** (7), 1016–1036.

Alexander, J. (2004) Toward a Theory of Cultural Trauma. In Alexander, J. (ed.), *Cultural Trauma and Collective Identity*, University of California Press.

Atkinson, J. (2002) *Trauma Trails Recreating Song Lines*, Spinifex Press.

Australian Commission on Safety and Quality in Healthcare (2009) *Roles in Realising the Australian Charter of Healthcare Rights*, https://www.safetyandquality.gov.au/publications/roles-in-realising-the-australian-charter-of-healthcare-rights.

Australian Government (2013) *National Aboriginal and Torres Strait Islander Health Plan 2013–2023*, Australian Government.

Australian Human Rights and Equal Opportunity Commission (1997) *Bringing Them Home: Report of the National Inquiry into the Separation of Aboriginal and Torres Strait Islander Children from their Families*, https://www.humanrights.gov.au/publications/bringing-them-home-report-1997.

Australian Human Rights Commission (2011) Cultural Safety and Security: tools to address lateral violence. In *Social Justice Report 2011*, Australian Human Rights Commission.

Australian Institute of Health and Welfare (2013) *Strategies and Practices for Promoting the Social and Emotional Wellbeing of Aboriginal and Torres Strait Islander People*, Australian Institute of Health and Welfare.

Commonwealth of Australia (2017) *National Strategic Framework for Aboriginal and Torres Strait Islander Peoples' Mental Health and Social and Emotional Wellbeing 2017–2023*, Department of the Prime Minister and Cabinet.

Corntassel, J. (2008) Toward Sustainable Self-Determination: rethinking the contemporary Indigenous-rights discourse, *AlterNative*, **25**, 105–132.

Crane, S. A. (1997) AHR Forum: Writing the Individual Back into Collective Memory, *American Historical Review*, **102** (5), 1372–1385.

Daes, Erica Irene (1999) United Nations Working Group on Indigenous Peoples at the UNESCO Conference on Education, July. As cited in Battiste, Bell and Findlay (2002) Decolonizing Education in Canadian Universities: an interdisciplinary, international, indigenous research project, *Canadian Journal of Native Education*, **26** (2), 82.

Department of Health (2017) *My Life My Lead – opportunities for strengthening approaches to the social determinants and cultural determinants of Indigenous health*, Australian Government.

Evans, J., Faulkhead, S., Manaszewicz, R. and Thorpe K. (2012) Bridging Communities: foundations for the interchange of ideas, *Information Communication and Society*, **15** (7), 1055–1080.

Evans, J., McKemmish, S., Daniels, E. and McCarthy, G. (2015) Self-Determination and Archival Autonomy: advocating activism, *Archival Science*, **15** (4), 337–368.

Evans, J., McKemmish, S. and Rolan, G. (2017) Critical Archiving and Recordkeeping Research and Practice in the Continuum, *Journal of Critical Library and Information Studies*, **1** (2), https://libraryjuicepress.com/journals/index.php/jclis/article/view/35.

Faulkhead, S. (2008) *Narratives of Koorie Victoria*, PhD thesis, Monash University.

Faulkhead, S. (2009) Connecting Through Records: narratives of Koorie Victoria, *Archives and Manuscripts*, **37** (2), 60–88.

Faulkhead, S., Bradley, J. and McKee, B. (2017) Animating Language: continuing intergenerational Indigenous language knowledge. In Anderson, J. and Geismar, H. (eds), *The Routledge Companion to Cultural Property*, 1st edn, Routledge.

Gee, G., Dudgeon, P., Schultz, C., Hart, A. and Kelly, K. (2014) Aboriginal and Torres Strait Islander Social and Emotional Wellbeing. In Dudgeon, P., Milroy, H. and Walker, R. (eds), *Working Together: Aboriginal and Torres Strait Islander mental health and wellbeing principles and practice*, 2nd edn, Telethon Institute for Child Health Research/Kulunga Research Network, https://www.telethonkids.org.au/globalassets/media/documents/aboriginal-health/working-together-second-edition/working-together-aboriginal-and-wellbeing-2014.pdf.

Gilliland, A. J. and McKemmish, S. (2014) The Role of Participatory Archives in Furthering Human Rights, Reconciliation and Recovery, *Atlanti: Review for Modern Archival Theory and Practice*, **24**, 79–88.

Iacovino, L., Ketelaar, E. and McKemmish, S. (2009) *Exposure Draft Position Statement: Human Rights, Indigenous Communities in Australia and the Archives*, Position Statement prepared on behalf of the Trust and Technology Project, Monash University, https://www.monash.edu/it/our-research/research-centres-and-labs/cosi/projects/completed-projects/trust/position-statement.

Jorgensen, D. and McLean, I. (2017) *Indigenous Archives: the making and unmaking of Aboriginal art*, UWA Publishing.

Kearney, J. and Janke, T. (2018) *Rights to Culture: indigenous cultural and intellectual property (ICIP), copyright and protocols*, www.terrijanke.com.au/single-post/2018/01/29/Rights-to-Culture-Indigenous-Cultural-and-Intellectual-Property-ICIP-Copyright-and-Protocols.

Koh, H. K. and Jacobson, M. (2009) Fostering Public Health Leadership, *Journal of Public Health*, **31** (2), 199–201.

Ley, John F. (1991) *Australia's Protection of Movable Cultural Heritage: report on the ministerial review of the 'Protection of Movable Cultural Heritage Act 1986 and regulations'*, Australian Government Publishing Service.

Ma Rhea, Z. and Russell, L. (2012) The Invisible Hand of Pedagogy in Australian Indigenous Studies and Indigenous Education, *Australian Journal of Indigenous Education*, **41** (1), 18–25.

Marsella, A. (2017) Ethnocultural Aspects of PTSD: an overview of concepts, issues, and treatments, *Traumatology*, **16**, 17–28.

McKemmish, S., Faulkhead, S., Iacovino, L. and Thorpe, K. (2010) Australian Indigenous Knowledge and the Archives: embracing multiple ways of knowing and keeping, *Archives and Manuscripts*, **38** (1), 27–50.

McKemmish, S., Faulkhead, S. and Russell, L. (2011) Distrust in the Archive: reconciling records, *Archival Science*, **11** (3–4), 211–239.

Minkler, M. (2000) Using Participatory Action Research to Build Healthy Communities, *Public Health Reports*, **115** (2–3), 191–197.

Murphy, M. (2014) Self-Determination and Indigenous Health: is there a connection? In Woons, M. (ed.), *Restoring Indigenous Self-Determination: theoretical and practical approaches*, E-International Relations, www.e-ir.info/wp-content/uploads/2014/05/Restoring-Indigenous-Self-Determination-E-IR.pdf.

National Aboriginal Health Strategy Working Party (Australia) (1989) *A National Aboriginal Health Strategy*, National Aboriginal Health Strategy Working Party.

Reynolds, A. J. (2005) *Wrapped in a Possum Skin Cloak: the Tooloyn Koortakay collection in the National Museum of Australia*, National Museum of Australia.

Thorpe, K. (2005) Indigenous Knowledge and Archives, *Australian Academic and Research Libraries*, **36** (2), 179–184.

Thorpe, K. (2013) *Protocols for Libraries and Archives in Australia: incorporating Indigenous perspectives in the information field*, Presented at the IFLA World Library and Information Congress, www.sl.nsw.gov.au/sites/default/files/ThorpeKirsten-Indigenousprotocols.pdf.

Thorpe, K. (2014) Indigenous Records: connecting, critiquing and diversifying collections, *Archives and Manuscripts*, **42** (2), 211–214.

Thorpe, K. (2017) Aboriginal community archives. In Gilliland, A. J., McKemmish, S. and Lau, A. J. (eds), *Research in the Archival Multiverse*, Monash University Publishing.

Thorpe, K., Faulkhead, S. and Booker, L. (forthcoming 2019) Transforming the Archive: returning and connecting. In *The Routledge Companion to Repatriation: return, reconcile, renew* [working title], Routledge.

Vickery, J., Faulkhead, S., Adams, K. and Clarke, A. (2007) Indigenous Insights into

Oral History, Social Determinants and Decolonisation. In Anderson, I., Baum, F. and Bentley, M. (eds), *Beyond Bandaids: Exploring the underlying social determinants of Aboriginal health, Papers from the Social Determinants of Aboriginal Health Workshop, CRCAH, Darwin*.

Victorian Government (2017) *Balit Murrup: Aboriginal social and emotional wellbeing plan 2017–2027*, Victorian Government.

Williams, R. (1999) *Cultural Safety – What Does it Mean for Our Work Practice?*, University of Tasmania.

CHAPTER 9

Community engaged scholarship in archival studies: documenting housing displacement and gentrification in a Latino community

Janet Ceja Alcalá

Introduction

This essay presents a community oral history and archiving project that documents housing displacement and gentrification against a Latino community in East Boston, Massachusetts, USA. We use this project as a case study to demonstrate how as archival educators we can become involved in and contribute to the development of social justice oriented archival practice by participating in community engaged scholarship. Community engaged scholarship focuses on the public good by forging partnerships with community groups to address pressing societal issues. This collaboration can serve as an example to archival scholars who are interested in combining community archiving with social justice principles and integrating them into their research and teaching.

Background to the project

On 3 August 3 2015, at 173–175 Maverick Street in East Boston, Massachusetts, ten families were displaced when the shared back wall of their apartment building collapsed (WBZ 4 CBS Boston, 2015). The building had structural code violations and a lack of maintenance that, according to Boston's Inspectional Services Department, is what likely led to the wall giving out (Lynds, 2015) (Figures 9.1 and 9.2). It turned out that the owner had hired construction workers to conduct maintenance on the property without the proper city permits. Just a month earlier, the tenants of the apartments had received letters first stating that their rents would increase from US$800 to US$2,000 per month and later that their leases would be terminated (Lynds, 2015). It is unclear if the illegal construction work was intentionally aimed at getting rid of the tenants, but that is what eventually happened. The landlord never renovated the living quarters and by November, when the landlord no longer had to pay for the tenants' temporary housing, the families had nowhere to go.

Figure 9.1 *According to Boston Real Estate, the two multi-unit buildings located at 173–175 Maverick Street each sold for US$1.9 million in 2018.* Photo by author

Figure 9.2 *The rehabilitated back wall that collapsed at 173–175 Maverick Street.* Photo by author

Around this time, I started working on a community oral history project in East Boston with Stand for Democracy, an interfaith group focused on issues in the Latino community. Some of the displaced families from 173–175 Maverick Street had sought refuge at Our Saviour's Lutheran Church where Stand for Democracy meets every week. The impact of witnessing this crisis, primarily affecting Latino families in the neighborhood, triggered the group's desire to document what was happening.

My role in the project was a natural fit stemming from my personal interest in and commitment to social justice issues, as well as my teaching and research interests in oral history and archiving at Simmons University's School of Library and Information Science (SLIS). To be clear, my participation in this group did not start from a desire to conduct research on housing displacement and gentrification. I was drawn to Stand for Democracy because of its Latino membership and my own search for community in a city marked by its highly segregated neighborhoods. This was an opportunity for me, as a Latina, to connect with local issues that were of personal and cultural interest. It was not until I was encouraged to lead the oral history project, called Eastorias, by other members of the group that I connected my whole self – Latina, archivist, educator, and so on – to help develop this project. I chose to lead it in service of the group and in solidarity with those fighting these issues firsthand. As a result, the project and the people helped guide me toward research that began with an ethos of collaboration and in which the group was already committed to participating.

Using this project as a case study, my intention with this chapter is to demonstrate how as archival educators, whether in library and information science or other higher educational settings, we can become involved in and contribute to the development of social justice oriented archival practice by co-developing scholarship in our communities. I begin with a discussion on the background of what's known as 'community engaged scholarship' and then go on to demonstrate its application through the Eastorias oral history project. Finally, I discuss how community engaged scholarship intersects with current research and teaching in archives.

Community engaged scholarship

Literature concerning community engaged scholarship in the United States often points to educator Ernest L. Boyer who wrote extensively on the topic in the 1990s when he was the president of the Carnegie Foundation for the Advancement of Teaching. In his seminal piece, 'The Scholarship of Engagement', he proposed that the traditional priorities of the professoriate be reframed as a scholarship of engagement that addresses the nation's most pressing social, civic, economic and moral problems (Boyer, 2016, 15). Boyer's visionary work is documented in the Carnegie Foundation report titled *Scholarship Reconsidered* in which the role of the professoriate was re-conceptualised to expand the scope of scholarship within and beyond the university setting. Indeed, Boyer's writings mobilised new forms of scholarship, including what is now popularly referred to as community engaged scholarship. While there is no one set definition for community engaged scholarship, work in this area often focuses on how the professoriate can propagate the common good through civic engagement and by solving problems of public concern. This usually involves developing equitable partnerships with communities outside of academia to address societal issues through research driven by a community's needs.

One manner in which community engaged scholars have sought to address the nuances of their research practice is by using a community engaged *continuum model*. The community engaged continuum can range from low intensive, where a researcher may work individually on addressing a community issue with little community input, to highly intensive where the researcher is collaborating horizontally on a community problem. Another way of thinking about this continuum is by introducing more inclusive and participatory principles into the research process, such as those compiled by Richard Reed (2015): inform, consult, involve, collaborate and empower (Figure 9.3). The *inform* goal involves conducting outreach to stakeholders about the project. *Consultation* takes this to another level by promoting two-way communication about the project, and *involvement* would incorporate community interests in the research design. The goal of *collaboration* implies full buy-in from the community through their interactions and investment in the project. Finally, *empowerment* refers to helping build capacity amongst the community to promote sustainability and empowerment through the results of the research project.

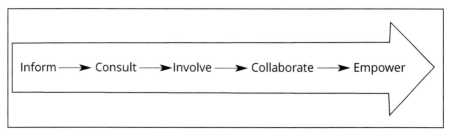

Figure 9.3 *Community engagement continuum model, adapted from Reed, R. (2015) Program Evaluation as Community-Engaged Research: challenges and solutions, Gateways: International Journal of Community Research and Engagement, 8 (1), 118–38*

Taking the community engagement continuum as a cue to give breadth and depth to the labour of archivists whether professional or organic, Desiree Alaniz and I have stated elsewhere how *community engaged archiving* should be understood as an archival approach that accounts for varied modes of practice in cultural heritage organisations and in autonomous environments (Ceja Alcalá and Alaniz, 2018, 153). (Another interesting framework worth noting is the Community Access to Archives Project led by the UK National Archives, focused on best practices for community-based online archive projects.) Mapping this variability in archival performance onto such a continuum provides a new conceptual tool for engaging with community archives. Most of all, by using the continuum model we are consciously working toward being accountable to the communities with which we partner.

We should not expect the continuum model to deliver neat results nor should we expect that our research will turn out to be a nicely packaged product. What the continuum model can do is act as a guide to help us map out different steps in the research process. As such, the continuum model is flexible and, most importantly, it can be practiced in ways that render community-based scholarship as something that is more than just one person's research pursuit, but a more broadly based and community-defined enterprise.

Geographical history of East Boston

Located northeast of Boston's downtown, across the harbor, East Boston is composed of five islands that were joined into one mass of land by the East Boston Company in the 19th century (Figure 9.4). Due to its oceanside geography, it was home to a major shipbuilding industry and later to textile and garment factories that employed local immigrant populations. Additionally, the East Boston Immigration Station, often compared to the Ellis Island of New York, was built in East Boston in 1920, likely for its proximity to the waterfront and high concentration of immigrants. It replaced the Long Wharf Immigration Center in downtown Boston, which had served as the central entry port into Boston by immigrants. During the same time period

Figure 9.4 *View of East Boston, Mass. Boston: O.H. Bailey & Co., 1879. Courtesy of the Digital Commonwealth, https://ark.digitalcommonwealth.org/ark:/50959/3f4634491*

when the immigration station was built, two major legislations were passed at the Federal level to restrict the number of immigrants entering the United States: the Emergency Immigration Act of 1921 and the Immigration Act of 1924 (National Origins Act and Asian Exclusion Act).

The first major wave of immigrants to East Boston, however, came much earlier with the Irish who were fleeing the Great Famine of the 1840s and Canadians who were hired to work in the shipyards (Global Boston). As transportation connecting East Boston to the city centre improved, new immigrant populations from abroad and the surrounding Boston area also found their way to East Boston. Some of these ethnic groups included populations from Portuguese, Russian and Italian heritage. By the late 1890s, Jews from Russia and Eastern Europe began arriving, as did a new wave of Italians who by the 1920s became the dominant population in East Boston. By then, immigration restrictions at the Federal level, and major changes in the manufacturing industries, greatly impacted immigrant spaces such as East Boston, as they no longer sustained a constant influx of migrant communities.

Until 1965, there was a preference for immigrants from Northwestern, Southern and Eastern Europe and tight restrictions on immigrants from Asia, Africa and the Caribbean (FitzGerald and Martin, 2015). Then the Immigration Act of 1965 banned discrimination in the issuance of immigrant visas based on national origins. It was not until the 1980s that populations from Southeast Asia and Latin America began settling in East Boston. Some of these populations held the status of refugees fleeing genocide, civil wars and other forms of violence. Today, Latinos comprise the largest immigrant demographic in East Boston, with the majority hailing from the countries of El Salvador, Colombia and Mexico (Boston Redevelopment Authority, 2013).

Migration patterns by populations from El Salvador, Colombia and Mexico to the United States can be linked to the significant violence and political and economic instability faced by each country in the late 20th century. Colombia saw growing drug violence given its coca production and drug trafficking cartels, and to some extent Mexico too was affected by this drug trade given its location as a major transportation corridor for drug exportation to the United States. Also, in Mexico, neoliberal economic policies since the 1970s, culminating in the North American Free Trade Agreement ratified in the 1990s, have devastated the agricultural sector, provoked periodic economic crises and led to migration to the north in search of better economic opportunities. In El Salvador, economic violence and political instability came as a result of the country's civil war, which was fought by the Salvadoran military government against leftist guerrilla groups. This bloody civil war led to major human rights violations that not only affected the guerrilla groups, but also civilians who lost their lives or sought refuge by emigrating out of their country. Here, the United States government was complicit in financially and politically supporting the Salvadoran government during this time period as part of the Cold War. Now these same migrant populations who call East Boston home, along with other Latino and low-income people, are once again being displaced. This time they are being displaced from their homes in East Boston as a result of gentrification – a phenomenon some are calling the new major civil rights issue of our time.

Gentrification is a term that was coined in 1964 by German-British sociologist Ruth Glass to describe the residential housing market changes in London that at the time were displacing working class people with the middle class. Recently, the term has been associated more generally with the transformational restructuring of space, the economy and society in urban areas (Smith and Williams, 1986, 225). These changes are made visible not only through residential housing changes, but also the redevelopment of land by investors targeting communities that have historically suffered from disinvestment and by rehabilitating spaces that had some prior industrial use. Ultimately, what results from these developments is the influx of new populations with greater income and capital accumulation. Patterns in environmental changes include new amenities, such as boutique grocery stores, expensive coffee shops and upscale art galleries, all of which are meant to cater to the new inhabitants. These environmental changes go on to displace populations of lower socioeconomic strata, who over time are unable to live in the neighborhood because of the rising costs of living. In the United States, systemic racism, socioeconomic segregation and unjust housing policies have disproportionately affected lower income people of colour, therefore making these populations some of the most vulnerable and affected by gentrification. Even so, these communities are often times at the vanguard of resistance against injustice (Figures 9.5 and 9.6 on the next page).

Stand for Democracy

Stand for Democracy formed in 2013 in response to the proposed construction of a casino in East Boston. Along with several other local organisations and activists, they mobilised to rally against the casino and as a coalition successfully prevented its construction. By the time I became involved in Stand for Democracy in 2015, membership had directed its attention to the pressing issue of housing displacement. A friend invited me to attend the group meetings, which are held weekly in the basement of Our Saviour's Lutheran Church.

What attracted me to the group was that its advocacy and organising takes on a spiritual dimension. Some members of the group are inspired by and

Figure 9.5 *New construction of luxury waterfront apartment buildings gentrifying East Boston.* Photo by author

Figure 9.6 *CityLife/VidaUrbana local action against housing displacement in East Boston.* Photo by author

philosophically oriented toward the tenets of liberation theology. Liberation theology is a Christian movement that grew out of Latin America in the 1950s and 1960s based on the social justice belief that the Roman Catholic Church should be fundamentally improving the lives of the poor. As a result, the

Church was viewed as integral in critiquing systemic socioeconomic injustices and encouraging oppressed populations to transform their lives through political and civic engagement. Stand for Democracy works alongside the Iglesia Nuevo Amanecer (a mission of the New England Synod of the Evangelical Lutheran Church in America) to provide leadership and spiritual support to the agencies that work out of the church building at 28 Paris Street. The Church has historically been an important meeting space for local community groups, a few of which are now well-established non-profit organisations, such as East Boston Community Ecumenical Council (EBECC) and Neighborhood of Affordable Housing (NOAH). For Stand for Democracy, this communal space has created important links with other community organisations that meet there, such as: City Life/Vida Urbana, a grassroots community organisation focused on racial, social and economic justice; the Massachusetts Coalition for Occupational Safety and Health, which works with underrepresented populations undergoing labour issues in the workplace; and the East Boston Community Soup Kitchen, an effort that began with local community members who wanted to address hunger and poverty in East Boston.

Unlike other groups, Stand for Democracy keeps its meetings and membership relatively fluid; in other words, there is no expectation that all members will attend each week, although people are welcome to do so. This flexibility provides the group membership with the liberty to come and go without the pressure to commit should this be an obstacle, as it can be for working class people. Because of this, the group's membership fluctuates anywhere from three to ten people depending on their schedules and interest in the activities taking place. The two Pastors who serve at the Church are of Norwegian heritage and were born and raised in the Midwest. They have been especially influential in supporting the group's mission and advocating on community issues beyond Stand for Democracy. The majority of the group are Latino, equally male and female, and whose ages range from their late 20s to 60s. Members hail primarily from countries that have been historically affected by United States foreign policy in Latin America: Guatemala, El Salvador, Colombia and Mexico. A few of us were born in the United States but identify more readily with the immigrant Latino community due to our generational status in this country. Our occupations are as diverse as clergy, service industry workers, musicians, students and educators.

Eastorias: documenting displacement with oral history

In many ways, members of the Stand for Democracy group had become my research mentors by way of their encouragement and participation in this project. At the same time, I was also their teacher as I designed the project using oral history workshop training sessions. Through this process we developed a vision statement, drafted questions that we wanted to pose to interviewees, addressed ethical considerations and learned how to use basic recording equipment.

In designing the oral history workshops, I focused the training on bearing witness to the plight of those being displaced by framing oral histories as *testimonio* (testimonies). The testimonio genre was readily used in Latin America in the 1970s and 1980s during popular liberation movements. A work from the time period that epitomises the testimonio as a collective voice is *Me llamo Rigoberta Menchú y así me nació la conciencia* (*I, Rigoberta Menchú: An Indian Woman in Guatemala*) written in 1983 by K'iche' Mayan and Nobel Prize winner Rigoberta Menchú. The testimonio as praxis affirms the agency of oppressed groups to speak for themselves and describe their own realities and truth as authorities. The testimonio's role, as scholar John Beverly states, is 'to intervene in the world – that is, in a place where the subaltern is not [visible]' (Beverly, 1996, 554). Methodologically, this is significant because the rhetoric of housing developers and politicians promotes urban renewal and regeneration, which denies and silences the reality of people's housing displacement and amplification of socioeconomic inequality. This is why the vision of Eastorias was drafted to address the following:

> We believe that by documenting our voices and histories we can be strengthened as a community, educate about displacement, denounce injustices, and create a new means of communication that reflects the courage of the Latino community. We want to create a space in which every person can share their story and hope.

After the training sessions, a total of five interviews were conducted by different members of the group. Most of those interviewed were Latino and were initially engaged by one of the pastors. The interviewees either had experiences with evictions or were actively involved in the East Boston community. Thus, major themes encountered in the interviews include their experiences with eviction as well as the type of activism that individuals have participated in locally. For instance, one of the interviewees who had been issued an eviction notice discussed his participation in activism and the importance of resisting these actions from landlords.

Another related theme is that of the mental health trauma that some interviewees faced as a result of being evicted. Other interviewees spoke about their arrival to East Boston and what made them leave their countries of origin. Unsurprisingly a recurring narrative is that of encountering violence or lack of opportunities back home. For instance, one interviewee mentioned how her family had fled El Salvador due to the death squads during the country's bitter civil war (1979–92). These narratives are invaluable as they evidence the effects of unjust living conditions, multi-generational mental health trauma caused by housing evictions and localised historical knowledge about East Boston and its transnational linkages to other parts of the Americas in the last 20 to 30 years.

A significant way in which community engagement intersects with teaching is by inculcating the research practices that we conduct with our students. With Eastorias I have worked one-on-one with SLIS Master's students interested in oral history and archiving practices. So far we have focused our attention on making the original interview recordings available online and creating interview summaries with time indices in the language of origin and, whenever possible, in both English and Spanish. This approach works in alignment with the testimonio genre by limiting the amount of contextual information so that, to the best of our ability, we allow each interview to 'speak for itself'. Our recent project efforts can be found online at https://eastorias.wordpress.com. The website is representative of a do-it-yourself approach to making the oral histories accessible as it uses the WordPress content management system, which offers free online hosting services.

One issue we have faced with the interviews is that of creating access specifically to the Spanish language interviews. This is a challenge because the project requires language fluency in Spanish and most of my students have been monolingual English speakers. This poses a language barrier that limits the ability to develop consistent workflows and establish stable processes for archiving. As a consequence, there is a growing backlog and ultimately a 'gap' in making the Spanish language interviews available on the website. This gap points to the importance of advocating for language diversity in the archival field, both with individuals who can process collections and individuals who design information systems to support access to multilingual and multimedia collections.

Language is an important dimension that has yet to receive the attention it deserves in discussions concerning social justice and inclusion strategies employed in archives. Perhaps most importantly, this imperfect archiving arrangement points to the need for developing collaborative relationships between community archiving projects and other cultural heritage organisations that can participate in enhancing archival processes and workflows. Such collaborations, however, will depend on the history of the community, the legacy of the cultural heritage organisation and the diligence of the people developing such social justice-based projects.

Community engaged scholarship in archival studies

On the subject of social justice in archival studies, Ricardo L. Punzalan and Michelle Caswell found that common social justice threads prevalent in the archival field addressed the inclusion of underrepresented and marginalised sectors of society, the reinterpretation and expansion of archival concepts, development of community archives, rethinking archival education and training and efforts to document human rights violations (Punzalen and Caswell, 2016, 28). Similarly, Marianne Beaulieu, Mylaine Breton and Astrid Brousselle found that social justice was a central tenet in their 20-year scoping review on the scholarship of engagement. Social justice principles were characterised in the literature as focusing on individual and social wellbeing, equity and civil democracy through the inclusion of vulnerable and marginalised populations into research, and finally, how the professoriate has a moral obligation to integrate scholarly achievement with the public good (Beaulieu, Breton and Brousselle, 2018, 5). Whereas Punzalan and Caswell found that the societal consciousness of 1960s and 1970s social movements in the United States influenced inclusion by way of archival functions (e.g. documentation strategy), Beaulieu, Breton and Brousselle discovered that including communities' participation in research through transformative action was a central component of scholarship. The shared principle of inclusion, though applied differently, is one important link shared between community engaged scholarship and archival studies.

Although perhaps not directly stated, many community archives studies to date have incorporated participatory principles that fall under the umbrella of the scholarship of engagement. An example of one such project includes 'Community Archives and Identities: Documenting and Sustaining Community Heritage', which was conducted in 2008–9 in the United Kingdom. This project focused on identity formation surrounding issues of race, colour, gender, sexuality and class in independent community archives. Andrew Flinn, Mary Stevens and Elizabeth Shepherd at the University College London (UCL) led the project and worked with four community archives – Future Histories, rukus!, Migrant and Refugee Communities Forum, and Eastside Community Heritage. From this research, Flinn, Stevens and Shepherd found that community archiving activities were political by documenting the unique histories and identities of these groups. This political work, moreover, was strongly interconnected with social movements (Stevens, Flinn and Shepherd, 2009). Several of the study's final recommendations align quite well with the principle of reciprocity that embodies community engaged research (Sandmann, 2008). For instance, these recommendations focused on how mainstream cultural heritage organisations could support community archives through capacity-building based on partnerships that promoted mentoring, training and internships to community archives; accountability to community archives through the organisation's recognition and remuneration for joint funding ventures; and maintaining equitable partnerships through trust building and long-term commitments. In addition to these recommendations, broader policy recommendations were also made at a national level (Stevens, Flinn and Shepherd, 2010).

Another application of community engaged scholarship is building community-based partnerships encouraging students to embark on community service that promotes civic responsibility via a classroom setting. Whereas I work one-on-one with my students, other scholars integrate their research into their course designs. For example, Andrew J. Lau, Kimberly Anderson and Anne J. Gilliland have discussed the impact of community engagement at UCLA's School of Information with local grassroots projects in a course titled 'Ethics, Diversity, and Change'. They state that community engagement 'helps to prepare future practitioners and researchers who are both competent in and philosophically committed to undertaking long-term community collaborations in diverse and often under-empowered settings; as well as providing mutually beneficial, low overhead entry-points for community organisations wishing to develop sustained partnerships with the university' (Lau, Gilliland and Anderson, 2011, 994). Integrating our students into these community processes creates a space for students to bridge theory and practice and also to become active participants in achieving results that can lead to community empowerment and their own empowerment as future archivists.

At Purdue University in Indiana, Kristina Bross's instructional approach to community engagement is a cross-disciplinary effort. She teaches a course titled 'Archival Theory and Practice' with colleagues in Rhetoric and Composition and History as a part of Purdue's American Studies program. For her, community engagement involves partnering with community archives and the university archives to have graduate students process local collections. As Bross notes, 'the final, and perhaps most crucial, requirement of the course is for students to translate their findings for a nonacademic audience of interested community members, to tell the story of our past to our neighbors' (Bross, 2016, 390). The end of the semester culminates in a 'neighborhood block party' where students present their research and service learning results to their community partners and a wider local audience. More recently, the issue of strengthening community engagement through such wide-reaching activities has been discussed by the Archival Education and Research Institute, Pluralizing the Archival Curriculum Group (Archival Education and Research Institute, 2011).

Conclusion

While Boyer's work did not directly articulate social justice as an aim of the professoriate, his work has brought to light how moral ethics are inscribed in higher education through faculty scholarship and its impact. Since social justice is indeed a value we can associate with ethics and morality, this ethical imperative is a crucial link between archival studies and community engaged scholarship. Here, the community engaged continuum is one way in which archival scholars can assess and reflect upon the ethical implications of their work.

My own intervention with Eastorias took shape through public service inspired by community and the ethical imperative to act and help transform the environment around me. In this case, my knowledge and teaching experience were used to serve Stand for Democracy, which has gone on to infuse my current research on displacement and gentrification through Eastorias and to expand my skills as an educator. For instance, as a result of the trainings, I was prompted to refresh an oral history course I teach by focusing it on community-based oral history and archiving practice. Additionally, in the second phase of the Eastorias project, I will have SLIS Master's students participate in the interviews to give them the opportunity to more intimately connect with the East Boston community. Finally, the Eastorias oral history project has gone on to influence my research in understanding how archivists can contribute to theories of gentrification. Here, the words of historian Suleiman Osman resonate when he calls on more scholarship on the periodisation of gentrification and notes how the study of this phenomenon often centres on discussions of class or economic lenses, but not on its histories (Osman, 2016, 218). Using oral histories to study what Osman refers to as the 'time' of gentrification could thus lead to a richer narrative that includes the role archives play in documenting the lives of migrants who have been doubly and triply displaced through the course of their lives as political and economic refugees.

References

Archival Education and Research Institute (AERI), Pluralizing the Archival Curriculum Group (PACG), (2011) Educating for the Archival Multiverse, *American Archivist*, **74** (1), 69–101.

Beaulieu, M., Breton, M. and Brousselle, A. (2018) Conceptualizing 20 Years of Engaged Scholarship: a scoping review, *PLoS ONE*, **13** (2), 1–17.

Beverly, J.(1996) The Margin at the Center. In Gugelberger, G. M. (ed.), *The Real Thing: testimonial discourse and Latin America*, Duke University Press.

Boston Redevelopment Authority (2013) *American Community Survey 2007–2011*

Estimate, East Boston Neighborhood. Place of Birth for the Foreign-Born Population, www.bostonplans.org/getattachment/c6b4a4f7-ed70-40a0-ace9-58874ac79df5.

Boyer, E. L. (2016) The Scholarship of Engagement, *Journal of Higher Education Outreach and Engagement*, **1** (1), 15–27.

Bross, K. (2016) Portable Pedagogy: neighborhood archives through graduate service learning, *American Quarterly*, **68** (2), 397–400.

Ceja Alcalá, J. and Alaniz, D. (2018) Toward Community Engaged Archiving: building a digi-rasquache archives. In Salvatore, C. L. (ed.), *Cultural Heritage Care and Management: theory and practice*, Rowman and Littlefield, 153–67.

FitzGerald, D. S. and Cook-Martín, D. (2015) The Geopolitical Origins of the U.S. Immigration Act of 1965, *Migration Information Source*, Migration Policy Institute, https://www.migrationpolicy.org/article/geopolitical-origins-us-immigration-act-1965.

Global Boston (n.d.). East Boston, https://globalboston.bc.edu/index.php/home/immigrant-places/east-boston.

Lau, A. J., Gilliland, A. J. and Anderson, K. (2011) Naturalizing Community Engagement in Information Studies, *Information, Communication and Society*, **15** (7), 991–1015.

Lynds, J. (2015) Boston Inspectors Looking in to Maverick Building Collapse. East Boston Times-Free Press, https://www.eastietimes.com/2015/08/20/boston-inspectors-looking-in-to-maverick-building-collapse.

Osman, S. (2016) What Time Is Gentrification?, *CICO City and Community*, **15** (3), 215–19.

Punzalan, R. L. and Caswell, M. (2016) Critical Directions for Archival Approaches to Social Justice, *The Library Quarterly*, **86** (1), 25–42.

Reed, R. (2015) Program Evaluation as Community-Engaged Research: challenges and solutions, *Gateways: International Journal of Community Research and Engagement*, **8** (1), 118–38.

Sandmann, L. R. (2008) Conceptualization of the Scholarship of Engagement in Higher Education: a strategic review, 1996–2006, *Journal of Higher Education Outreach and Engagement*, **12** (1), 91–104.

Smith, N. and Williams, P. (1986) Alternatives to Orthodoxy: invitation to a debate. In Smith, N. and Williams, P. (eds), *Gentrification of the City*, Allen & Unwin, 1–10.

Stevens, M., Flinn, A. and Shepherd, E. (2009) *Activists in the Archives: making history in a diverse society*, A summary of the report of the AHRC project, 'Community Archives and Identities: documenting and sustaining community heritage', University College London, 1–12.

Stevens, M., Flinn, A. and Shepherd, E. (2010) New Frameworks for Community Engagement in the Archive Sector: from handing over to handing on, *International Journal of Heritage Studies*, **16** (1–2), 59–76.

WBZ 4 CBS Boston (2015) *Families Displaced after Wall Collapse at Boston Apartment*

Building, https://boston.cbslocal.com/2015/08/01/families-displaced-after-wall-collapse-at-boston-apartment-building.

CHAPTER 10

Post-x: community-based archiving in Croatia
Anne J. Gilliland and Tamara Štefanac

Who will keep my city, my friends, who will bring Vukovar out of the dark?
There are no backs stronger than mine and yours, and therefore, if it's not too
much bother for you, if any youthful whispering remains in you, join. Somebody
has touched my parks, benches on which your names are still carved, a shadow
in which you gave and received your first kiss – somebody has simply stolen
everything because, how to explain that there is even no Shadow any more?
There is no more window shopping in which you took small pleasures, there is
no cinema in which you watched the saddest film, your history is simply obliter-
ated and now you have nothing. You have to build it all over again. First your
past, search for your roots, then your present, and then if you have any strength
left, invest it into the future. And as for the city, don't worry about it, it has been
all this time inside you. It has just been hidden. So the executioner doesn't find it.
The city – it is you.

(Siniša Glavašević, Croatian reporter on Radio Vukovar, 1991)

Introduction
The Republic of Croatia declared independence from the Socialist Federal
Republic of Yugoslavia (SFRY) in June 1991 and was quickly plunged into
war as Croatian Serb populations revolted and the Yugoslav National Army
and Serb paramilitary groups attacked along the states' ethnically mixed
borders. Eastern Croatia saw some of the most brutal early fighting. Each
lunchtime during its 87-day siege, Croatians across the country tuned their
radios to listen to Siniša Glavašević's report from inside the border city of
Vukovar, the first European city to be completely destroyed since World War
2. His poignant, reassuring yet defiant invocations continued until the radio

went silent. Several hundred soldiers and civilians, Glavašević among them, were summarily executed by Serb forces when the city fell. His body was exhumed from a mass grave on a farm at Ovčara outside Vukovar in 1997.

Glavašević's words paint a picture of the daily life and spaces of this previously vibrant, multi-ethnic Danube city that preserves its citizens' most intimate moments and personal pleasures in ways that no official archive can replicate. His words bridge its community's past, their terrible present and their drive for survival into the future, reminding all listeners that a city is not simply a geographic space and a complex of physical structures, it is also a state of individual will, identity and experiences that no amount of external force can kill. His words speak to a refusal of a community to cease existing and of resistance to the physical annihilation of its people, its landscape and its cultural markers.

The 1991 siege of Vukovar has become a defining moment for contemporary Croatia in terms of personal, community and national identity, memory and narratives. Since 2015, every Croatian schoolchild is required to spend a night in the city and to visit Ovčara and the many survivor-initiated memory projects and memorial sites that have emerged in and around Vukovar since the war. Collectively, these community-initiated projects have not only an affective power, but also a national profile and political presence that is probably unparalleled in Croatia.

Much of the recent community archives literature in the English language centres around community-based collections of multiple forms and provenance that are committed to promoting community needs, archival presence and voice. Many have overt activist or social justice agendas, focusing on historically marginalised or oppressed groups, countering dominant narratives and often eschewing professional staffing, best practices and relationships with elite institutions as inappropriate to their community orientation (Gilliland and Flinn, 2013). Most resonate with affect in ways that have until recently remained largely unaddressed in archival discourse.

This chapter considers how such a framing of community archives holds up in the social and political conditions of post-Yugoslav and post-conflict Croatia – conditions that we have dubbed here 'post-x' – where the 'facts and figures' as well as memory relating to historical events are regularly contested by the country's various communities. While certainly not all Croatian community memory or documentation endeavors are related to the war, many *are* related to broader ethnic and nationalist agendas and all must contend with current regulatory and professional structures that provide scant support for community archiving as either a concept or a practice. And although the Croatian archival profession has yet to respond to the kinds of shifts in archival thinking that have been wrought elsewhere by postmodern and other 'post-' critical ideas, in this chapter we argue that Croatia's post-x conditions have been stimuli for a range of instantiations that fit within and extend our understandings about the nature and roles of community archives in different socio-political contexts.

The chapter begins with a review of definitional, legal and regulatory considerations relevant to community archiving in Croatia (because of these considerations, the authors refer interchangeably to community entities, community-based initiatives and community archives throughout). Then, in order to support reflection on the political, professional and affective 'space' in which community archiving exists, the chapter presents descriptions of exemplars of community-based initiatives derived from ethnographic fieldwork and interviews that the authors conducted between 2015 and 2018. That fieldwork focused on the conditions and contexts that precipitated a range of community-based documentation, memory and other heritage initiatives, and on how they function within the greater national and archival landscape with regard to autonomy questions, identity and memory politics and civil society. The chapter concludes with a brief discussion of what Croatian experiences might offer to wider understandings of community archives and their possibilities and directions.

It is important to acknowledge here, especially since this chapter is addressing how different community memories and perspectives are presented and respected, that not every community in Croatia will see causes and events associated with the war in the same way.

Definitional, legal and regulatory considerations

In Croatia, even though entities with characteristics of community archives have increasingly emerged since Croatian independence, there is still no accepted linguistic or professional conception of a 'community archive'. This situation begs some fundamental definitional, legal and regulatory questions about the status and nature of and future possibilities for community archives within the Croatian national and archival landscape.

That there is no equivalent term in the Croatian language for 'community archive' is a reflection of inter-related socio-political and professional factors. Among the more obvious are the dominant ethno-centric focus and political sensitivities around what constitutes a 'community' given the country's history of ethno-religious divisions (most prominently Catholic Croats, Orthodox Serbs and Muslims, and other 'national minorities' such as Hungarians, Germans, Italians and Roma). Croatian law recognises specified national minorities, but this legal acknowledgment does not necessarily extend to others who might self-identify or organise as a community, such as those who might continue to identify as Yugoslavs, or based on a characteristic other than nationality, ethnicity or religion. Applying the concept of a 'community archive' to refer to initiatives emanating out of ethnic and ethno-religious populations in Croatia risks running into similar issues of politicisation and identity to those pointed out by Elizabeth Crooke (2010) with reference to Northern Ireland, another region with a history of identity and memory politics along ethno-religious lines.

The history of multiple reversals in power and majority status between historically antagonistic ethnic communities in the region also complicates the notion of community archives as a means of achieving voice and redress. The recently independent and democratic state of Croatia is attempting to promote a reconciled population and national identity, even while its national narratives are clearly aligned with certain kinds of community identity and memory projects and not with others. National desire for reconciliation between communities, however, can also be in tension with those communities' own desires to promote and preserve their distinct identities, histories and politics in their own ways.

Croatian legal, regulatory, funding and professional structures do not explicitly address 'community archives' because in the perception of the public, and indeed of many professional archivists, these kinds of entities are more akin to documentary projects than to 'real' archives. Nevertheless, these structures circumscribe the organisational and professional autonomy to which community-based archiving may aspire. In civil law jurisdictions such as Croatia, which operate much more through codified statutes than do common law countries, and especially in the former SFRY and Eastern Bloc countries, 'archives laws' and parallel 'museum laws' as well as regulations setting out implementation procedures remain common. Croatia's Archives and Museum Laws, revised versions of those first implemented in the SFRY and mandating state registration of such institutions, distinguish between archives and museum materials and lay out different archival or curatorial practices for each (Štefanac, 2017). Materials that might be relevant to both kinds of institutions should be allocated to one or the other. This means that a community archive should be registered as either an archive or a museum, with no possibility of straddling both, or indeed other forms of heritage or memory institutions. Institutions founded through these procedures are officially acknowledged by the State Archives, while other initiatives that might be more conceptually or structurally fluid are not considered by the State Archives to fit into this framework or choose not to fit.

An additional structural consideration is that the law also distinguishes between several categories of archives – public, specialised and private (the category into which a community archive would likely fall) – and those who are the creators, holders or custodians of the materials. Although 'cultural goods' must be registered with the state and professional archivists are required to report to the state any knowledge they have of the existence of such materials in any location, many of what otherwise might be considered to be community archives are basically recognised as creators. They therefore have only some basic obligations – and only if they have been identified or recognised as archives, a process that can seem quite arbitrary.

If a community archive decided not to go through the official registration process, likely nothing would happen to it, but it would not be treated by the state as an institution and the people developing it would not be perceived as a community or recognised as archivists. It would also have to apply for state or local funding through procedures designated for NGOs and not through the procedures established for archives or museums, which receive the majority portion of available resources. In fact, many community entities see few benefits to becoming a recognised private archive. Doing so would require them to employ trained, credentialed staff and professional best practices and state funding would likely not significantly increase, leaving them still needing to look elsewhere for resources. As Mokrović (2014) has noted, there is instead a growing tendency to create webs of institutions such as documentation centres and museums that use the rubric of 'private' or 'community', but exist outside the public archival system.

Different forms of community-based archiving in Croatia

Historically, many populations had their own cultural and arts associations. These primarily cultural but sometimes ethnological entities produced and collected different kinds of documentation that reflected their identity and history as a Croatian national minority. These collections, which can still be found in historic sites and local or ethnological museums, might include the research papers of ethnologists, ethnomusicologists or linguists who were studying ethnic identities and cultures, as well as other documents and photographs. They were also artifact-heavy, including such items as instruments or clothing that reflected ethnic identity.

A more contemporary form of state-sponsored community archiving is commonly carried out by national archives of countries with significant numbers of economic and/or political emigrés, displaced populations or ethnic populations separated by national borders. Such initiatives can have several different motivations – raising funds for projects in the homeland (e.g. digitising archival holdings, restoring heritage sites, general investment in the state); promoting national identity and culture among the diaspora; identifying records and other forms of documentation about emigration or exilic experiences and communities residing outside the country; and even locating or recovering records or other historical materials that could be used to support particular political movements or territorial claims within the home country. For example, the State Archives of Macedonia, another former SFRY, sent a representative to Australia between 1995 and 2002 to gather archival material in Australia from Macedonian emigrés. She collected more than 5,000 documents from individuals and families, Macedonian citizen and political organisations and religious communities for 18 different 'emigration' fonds (Santovska, 2018).

The Croatian State Archives reaches out to and works with the Croatian diaspora regionally and around the globe. Other efforts extend to two other categories of ethnic Croats outside Croatia: Croats in Bosnia and Herzegovina and what are termed 'Croatian national minorities' in neighboring countries. Diaspora communities are also supported through the government Central State Office for Croats Abroad and tend to be stratified by the region from which those Croats originated or settled, by the national identity of the era when they emigrated or by the politics of opposition that led them to leave their homelands. These strata shift with political change at home and generational change in the diaspora. However, it is important to note that these diasporic communities are often themselves initiators of heritage organisations and independent community archives in the countries where they have settled. Examples include the Dalmatian-American Club in San Pedro, California, the various Croatian cultural societies in New Zealand or the Jugoslav Socialist Federation, founded in Chicago in 1905 and functioning until 1952.

Part officially-sponsored, part web of institutions, ICARUS-HRVATSKA was founded in 2016 by Vlatka Lemić, former National Archivist of Croatia, as an offshoot of the Vienna-based ICARUS, an autonomous consortium that promotes international co-operation and digital standards, strategies and infrastructure-building across archival institutions (ICARUS, n.d.). Through its establishment, Lemić sought to open up more space for individual, community and institutional initiatives and collaboration than is currently possible given the structural limitations of existing archives and the increasingly conservative and nationalist leanings of the major Croatian political parties and the government's Ministry of Culture (which controls funding and the appointments of senior administrative appointments for those institutions). Lemić stated her 'clear and poignant' vision for the organisation:

> We want to gather positive ideas and proactive people as a base for this profes-
> sional network. We want to promote and implement hands-on activities where
> existing institutional frameworks are not in place yet. I know that the real driving

forces behind innovative impacts are people – individuals who share common visions, have the drive to accomplish changes and bring like-minded communities, associations and institutions together.

(ICARUS, 2016)

ICARUS-HRVATSKA launched the Topotek digital initiative in Croatia in the same year and has since extended it to include other multi-ethnic and multicultural regions of the former SFRY such as the Autonomous Province of Vojvodina of Serbia. Topoteka are place-based or thematic digital resources that contain, collate and describe, using internationally accepted standards, digitised cultural heritage content of different types relating to particular local communities within Croatia and contributed by archives, museums, libraries, associations and individual members of the public. To build Topoteka, ICARUS-HRVATSKA has organised public events in local communities where content is brought, digitised, described and uploaded. This is not merely a top-down initiative, since the Topotek structure is available for communities to build their own archives in order to promote their own histories and culture and sometimes to encourage tourism, a mainstay of the economy of many Croatian locales.

Since Croatian independence in 1991, at least two additional and often intertwined strands of community-based documentary and/or memory entities have emerged, several different examples of which are presented below. One strand is documenting post-Socialist urban culture and originated out of civil society ideas about the strengths and duties of a democratic society after Croatian independence and the establishment of a multi-party system and market economy. Civil society is a post-communist or post-Socialist notion introduced by David Rockefeller in 1970 whereby citizens come together as communities linked by common interests and collective activity to form a third societal influence besides the state and the private sector. The other strand focuses on specific ethnic or regional communities, frequently, although not exclusively, with an emphasis on the experiences, collective memory and legacy of the 1990s wars. While all these entities face autonomy and sustainability challenges under the legal, regulatory and archival structures already outlined, identity and memory politics are particularly in evidence with the post-war initiatives.

The Centre for Documenting Independent Culture

The Centre for Documenting Independent Culture is an example of the first strand, where archiving is being used not simply to reflect the development of the independent culture scene, but also as a strategic tool of activism. The

Centre is part of the ABC of Independent Culture, one of Croatia's first NGOs. It has been located since 2011 in the Booksa Klub, a literary club and community gathering place in central Zagreb for different NGO actors and the public. The small ground floor and mezzanine hold the Centre's collections, digital access initiatives and digitisation activities, as well as a café-bar that hosts various literary and critical programs. It has a single designated archivist, Dunja Kučinac, also a community member, who began working as a volunteer and then on a part-time student contract in 2010 when she was still a student in art history and comparative literature.

The Centre considers urban culture as encompassing aspects such as art, including street art and murals, performance, and environmental activism. Part of its mandate is to encourage other independent culture organisations to self-document and self-archive because no mainstream archive or museum organisation is doing so. Most of the organisations originate from the 1990s, some from the anti-war campaign (Bilič, 2013) but the majority from the late 1990s when the war was over, at which point, Kučinac observed, 'the atmosphere became unbearable and had to erupt somewhere, and so a space was created'. At the end of the 1990s, she continues, the Open Society Foundation funded some organisations, but:

> They were struggling to make a space for something that cannot be identified
> with the 'right' identity in Croatia – nationalism, religion, Croatian culture.
> Instead they were counter-culture, anti-war – making a space for speech . . .
> After 2000 and the change in government the social democrats came and the
> climate changed a bit and some laws were passed regarding NGOs. They slowly
> started to find spaces, network with each other, and to see themselves as actors
> in the socio-cultural and some even in the political sphere. The scene started to
> get stronger. The organisations empowered themselves through their networks
> and Klubtur– a cultural network of NGOs – provided funds and other support.
> It was more or less on stable ground.
>
> (interview of Dunja Kučinac by Anne J. Gilliland, 2016)

She ruminates that documenting is presumably one phase of building one's identity and presumably also in some sense it is exclusionary: 'it is, by definition, self-defining and so who might it be excluding? Maybe something that mightn't be the best fit for that organisation, since most organisations are experimental, progressive, critical or innovative' (Kučinac, 2016).

In 2009, the Centre began collecting oral histories, mapping independent human rights organisations and hosting public talks and then publishing them on the non-profit web portal Kulturpunkt.hr (https://www.kulturpunkt.hr), which 'systematically [follows and represents] the work of the independent cultural scene, with a focus on contemporary arts and critical art practices, as well as media and civil society' (Kulturpunkt.hr, n.d.). These activities resulted in an extensive archive of interviews with people from the independent cultural scene that emerged after Croatian independence. It became apparent, however, that even with the oral histories, the Centre was missing the more physical evidence of independent culture. At the end of 2011 it began to collaborate with another NGO that ran a bookstore but was financially struggling. Today it is primarily oriented towards collecting both documentation and material objects created by different organisations involved in urban culture, such as curators' collectives, anarchistic initiatives and performers' groups. They collect almost everything that these organisations produce except their business records. The Centre uses its portal to bring in different perspectives, make the archive a bit cooler and obtain media coverage and it has collaborated with a student radio station on a weekly show featuring something from the archive that can be connected to a current event or organisation.

The Centre has used its space to collect materials that otherwise would get lost. These organisations are well networked so the Centre's first activities were to call them all and begin to collect material. It then found itself without funds to process the material and so work stopped until the end of 2012, although the Centre was able to buy some basic furniture during that year and obtained a small grant that enabled it to describe the materials in a database. The following year the Centre received some more funds and bought professional software that was being used by several museums in Croatia. Kučinac notes that the open source and hacking communities complained that the software wasn't open source but the organisation wasn't thinking strategically at the time and wanted the support of the software company. The Centre makes that software available to other organisations that wish to use it at the Centre and also offers training in how to use it.

Living from grant to grant, the Centre and its individual digitisation initiatives and innovative cultural and art practices have received funding from the Ministry for Culture and a similar fund administered by the City of Zagreb and by the National Fund for the Development of Civil Society, as well as various foundations that cover staffing and basic infrastructure costs. The Centre remains chronically under-capacitated, however, and thus emphasises being maximally collaborative, since sharing resources is essential to sustainability. For example, Kučinac has worked with Nikola Mokrović in Documenta. He digitised the anti-war campaign zine and some Klubtur magazines and gave them copies. While both entities are gathering oral histories, she thinks it is unlikely that their efforts might overlap because her Centre does less work with human rights movements.

The Centre is also trying to assist organisations in Serbia to establish their own archives by offering workshops and they have been exchanging videos between Serbia and Kulturpunkt. Kučinac notes that in Serbia there is a very different independent cultural scene. There is no network, no awareness and no one actively documenting. The Centre is helping them to discuss this and find solutions and raise awareness and motivation and received a private grant for developing a portal with Serbia from CCULT (European Union Committee on Culture and Education).

Kučinac observes that how groups think about their materials varies a lot according to their situations. Mostly they are glad that someone is doing something and they feel good about the Centre collecting their material. A few might worry about the accessibility of their books and products – perhaps they want people to buy directly from them – but it can be easier for users to come to the Centre than to find the organisation in question. Some organisations interact with their collected material when they are doing a historical or new project. A few are obsessed with collecting or saving. Most are focused on current and future projects because of funding exigencies.

Anniversaries have also begun to occur that provide an opportunity for organisations to reflect on their own pasts and how things have changed, especially since the late 1990s. Some organisations are now less DIY and politically engaged. Many of the people who started them in their twenties are now in their forties and are handing them over to younger people. She believes this is a good moment to document the older people's knowledge and to ensure succession planning and transition but it is hard to find young people to come into an established organisation to volunteer and be as enthusiastic as the people who were starting something they needed that wasn't there before. New people also lack necessary skills. The government will pay the salary for the first year of employment for young people, but after that staff funding and training is still needed (interview of Dunja Kučinac by Anne J. Gilliland and Tamara Štefanac, 2018).

Documenta – Centre for Dealing with the Past

Documenta was founded in 2005 by the Centre for Peace, Non-Violence and Human Rights Osijek, Centre for Peace Studies, Civic Committee for Human Rights and the Croatian Helsinki Committee as a civil society organisation that works with other civil society organisations, government institutions and similar centres outside Croatia:

> … in an attempt to encourage the process of dealing with the past and
> establishing factual truth about the war and to contribute to shifting the

discussion from the level of dispute over facts (the number of killed people, etc.) towards a dialogue on interpretations. The key reason for making this attempt was the silence about and falsification of war crimes and other war-related events in the period from 1941 to 2000, which has influenced the recent past of Yugoslavia, as well as post-Yugoslav societies.

(Documenta, n.d.)

It sees itself continuing work that was begun by other civil society organisations in the 1990s that had very close ties with the anti-war movement and human rights groups. For example, the first co-ordinator of the Croatian Antiwar Campaign in 1991 was Vesna Teršelič, who today is Documenta's director. Nikola Mokrović, Documenta's archivist, also sees Documenta as countering the:

> ... growing tendency towards the mythologization of the war while many of its consequences and problems remain unresolved ... Space for different interpretation was narrowing with the war becoming more and more a sacred entity – and the whole background – war crimes trials, missing persons, establishing rights of various statuses (especially of civilian war victims), all the relevant data not being transparently put forward and available.
>
> (response by Nikola Mokrović to questions posed by Anne J. Gilliland and Tamara Štefanac)

Instead, Documenta sought to promote public facts-based dialogue among the various involved actors as well as good and equitable practices under the rule of law (Documenta, n.d.). Recognising the social and political complexities of constructing historical narratives, Documenta decided that by conducting oral histories with people who played a variety of roles and who came from different social and ethnic groups was a way 'to go beyond the positive (written) history and give space for subjective stories and memories to be told, recorded, and thus remembered' (Documenta, n.d.). Mokrović notes that:

> ... the basic idea is literally to establish, problematize and discuss how we remember, how the culture – or politics – of remembrance is being created. This whole complexity is understandable only with a grasp of all the political changes which these areas witnessed, roughly with the beginning of the First World War, intensified with the Second World War and ending with war in Yugoslavia [1991–2000, in Croatia 1991–1995].
>
> (response by Nikola Mokrović to questions posed by Anne J. Gilliland and Tamara Štefanac)

As its activities progressed, Documenta evolved from being principally a human rights organisation to being a form of documentation/research centre focused on systematically supporting research, advocacy and other human rights-related needs. It has approached the creation and archiving of documentation as one of the mechanisms that can help society to deal with the past, although its activities are controversial because of the fundamental divides and historical disagreements between different communities. Mokrović mentions that there were very dynamic debates between 2011 and 2013 about transforming some part, or all, of Documenta into a public research institute. But he argues that:

> ... changing this status would bring different kinds of responsibilities, some of which presuppose [Documenta] losing independence in performing its policies. And of course, we could argue that Documenta's work has been evolving in a positive way through the appropriation of knowledge gained through performing everyday activities and projects. We could especially trace this development in areas where the methodology of work and technical skills are very tangible.
>
> (response by Nikola Mokrović to questions posed by
> Anne J. Gilliland and Tamara Štefanac)

Documenta is funded through different EU projects, donations from foreign countries and philanthropic organisations, as well as by the Croatian State through the National Foundation for Civil Society Development. Since 2010 it has been co-located with several other civil society organisations and NGOs in Human Rights House Croatia, a complex of two formerly abandoned old buildings that were acquired through an agreement with the city government and subsequently renovated. Documenta has been officially recognised as a creator/holder by the State Archives and so must follow their professional guidelines with regard to the creation and management of archival materials. This is not a concern for Documenta, which believes this to be very important if the evidentiary materials it holds are to be kept safe and be widely trusted. Its holdings are organised in fonds that reflect Documenta's programs. The most extensive are Human Losses and War Crime Trials Monitoring and the Oral History Program, which comprises predominantly digitally-born videos with accompanying translations, annotations and metadata. The archive also holds materials generated by smaller programs and the records of Documenta's own business activities. To facilitate analysis, much of these holdings has been digitised.

The number of employees has ranged from a few in the beginning, to 25 in its most productive period and to around ten full-time employees today, depending on the availability of funding and Documenta's involvement in international projects. Many employees have worked for Documenta for several years. It also has a number of volunteer staff coming from different social networks and receives many requests each year from other countries to host interns. It has found this to be the optimum size staff for a civil society organisation. Any larger and co-ordination becomes too challenging because it needs network relationships to be formalised.

Since its founding, Documenta has always had a professional archivist on staff. Mokrović, who has a background in political science and was previously executive editor of *Politička kultura* (*Political Culture*), came to Documenta in 2010. He himself has written on the subject of community archives in Croatia, concluding that the conditions are ripe for more such entities but that there needs to be some kind of structural independent or private space in which they can exist. Of Documenta's staff, Mokrović says:

> Motivation for work/participation in this field always comes from some kind of personal (that is, personal-political) motivation. We could argue that most of the people here have a similar understanding of the tragedies that occurred during the nineties, and a similar idea of how to handle this burden. Also, some of them were close and direct witnesses of these events, and/or were already at the time enrolled in similar kind of antiwar/peace/human rights groups.
>
> (response by Nikola Mokrović to questions posed by
> Anne J. Gilliland and Tamara Štefanac)

Mokrović identifies four major challenges moving forward, some similar to those identified by Kučinac. The first is knowledge transfer between generations and difficulties in recruiting new and younger educated people with the necessary political sensibility, especially when Documenta is not a stable and secure working environment. The second is difficulties in competing against larger, more sophisticated proposals for EU and other funding. A third challenge is maintaining a consistent workforce and knowledge transfer across projects that may last several years. The fourth challenge is the political atmosphere – 'with growing misunderstanding of the role of civil society, the space for autonomous work and public dialogue is shrinking' (Mokrović, 2018). He observes that while Croatian society has been going through the process of normalisation, the space for different interpretations is decreasing as the Croatian political landscape moves further to the right. Expressing different opinions is seen as enmity towards core ideas and national 'truths' that have purported consensus. Thus, civil society organisations, as in other European so-called 'illiberal democracies', are increasingly excluded from the political sphere. Organisations such as Documenta are accused of working on the destruction of the state, all the while receiving state funds, or of being foreign agents that are using foreign money to undermine the state.

The Serb National Council's Archive of Serbs in Croatia

The impulse to preserve community identity in a way that is defined by members of the community itself can be traced back to the aforementioned actions of cultural-artistic organisations and their efforts to preserve and secure their own traditions, values and historical perspectives. In the post-war period, this impulse was reinforced by the Constitutional Law on the Rights of National Minorities that was first enacted in 1991 and in which such activities are treated as an expression of human rights. Article 7 of this law accords special rights to national minority communities such as 'cultural autonomy through the preservation, development and expression of their own culture, preservation and protection of their cultural heritage and tradition'. State funds are provided to finance projects run by the communities, such as religious or ethnic minorities. An important argument for why such proactive support is needed can be seen in the case of the Roma, a populous underdocumented minority community, large numbers of whose members were murdered in Croatian fascist concentration camps during World War 2. Almost no records or other documentation of their presence can be located in mainstream archives or museums of Croatia (Štefanac and White, 2013).

One project that has grown over time into a formal institution and which refers to itself as a private community archive is the Archive of Serbs in Croatia, founded in 2006 as one of the organisational units of the Serb National Council (SNC). The SNC comprises representatives of a number of Serb cultural, municipal and political community organisations as well as the Independent Democratic Serb Party, the Association of Serbian Refugees and Expellees from Croatia and church municipalities of the Serbian Orthodox Church in Croatia, as well as ethnic Serb members of the Croatian Parliament. It acts as a political, consulting and co-ordinating body and a form of self-government institution supporting the cultural autonomy of Serbs of Croatia in matters regarding human, civil and national rights, as well as issues of identity, participation and integration into Croatian society.

Located one floor up in the Beth Israel building in Zagreb, the Archive has been involved in collaborations with the Croatian State Archive. It is still in the process of inventorying its archival holdings in accordance with guidelines from the State Archives, but 90% of the library materials have been cataloged. SNC funds the Archive, whose projects are also funded by the Council of National Minorities, and the Archive holds some of the Council's business records going back to the SNC's founding after the Erdut agreement in July 1997. The SNC is a frequent target of criticism from Croatian far-right elements and was also criticised in 2012 by the Serbian Democratic Forum, a non-partisan NGO that is a member of the SNC, for alleged non-transparent and illegal management of funds allocated by the Croatian Government for the development and work of Serb organisations and institutions in Croatia. These records, therefore, are potentially important in terms of demonstrating the accountability and transparency of the SNC.

The majority of the Archive's holdings, however, consists of materials in various media that have been donated or collected as part of the Archive's efforts to document the national minority of Serbs and their cultural, economic and historic position in Croatia. Among these are materials from Serb associations and prominent individuals in the Serb community such as the late sculptor Vojin Bakić. Croatian Jewish publisher, historian and politician Slavko Goldstein, who identified as Yugoslav, also left his papers to the Archive. The Orthodox Gymnasium gave them books. The Archive also collects materials that can present historical counter-narratives to the official state narratives and proactively undertakes fieldwork in the community to create additional documentation. It holds exhibitions, is open to anybody to use and is committed to ensuring easy access to its materials (Serb National Council, n.d.).

An example of the work of Serb community associations that directly engages records can be found in the hinterland of Zadar County in Dalmatia, an ethnically mixed region that saw fierce fighting during the war but that now is a prominent source of Croatian tourism revenue. Some of the people who were displaced from Serb villages have been seeking to return but need the records that prove their ownership of property in the destroyed villages. Without a certain base village population, the county is not obliged to provide services or prioritise removing remaining landmines and may argue that there is nothing there for young people who will only leave anyway. Without property records it is impossible to reclaim one's home and without reclaiming it, the population of the village will not increase and basic infrastructure will be denied. Without basic infrastructure, return is much less desirable. And so the situation is circular. At the edge of the village of Islam Grčki is an ancient castle belonging to an old Serb family. The castle, a registered historic monument, has been renovated by a local Serb community organisation with funding from the Ministry of Culture, as well as from other sources, to support cultural and tourist activities. The association has pledged to use revenue generated through those activities to support returnees to the village, including helping them to obtain the property records they need to reclaim their homes (Kula Jankovića, n.d.).

Vukovar memorial institutions

There is insufficient space in this chapter to do more than introduce the several forms of memorial institutions that were initiated as community projects by survivors after the end of what Croatia calls the Homeland War (Domovinski Rat) of 1991 to 1993. In 1995, the Croatian Association of Inmates of Serb Concentration Camps was formed and opened the Centre for the Investigation of War Crimes with the declared goal of collecting materials on the camps that could prove how members of their community had suffered. The Memorial Centre for the Homeland War, which connects all memorial sites in Vukovar and the surrounding area (including the Memorial Home of Croatian Defenders at Trpinjska Street, the Memorial Home Ovčara and the Place of Memory in Vukovar Hospital), was founded by Vukovar's Croat defenders-veterans and their families and the Ministry of Defence, together with several public entities such as the City of Zagreb, which funded its infrastructure. In 2013, all the sites officially gained the status of public institutions.

Vukovar's early initiatives and projects, as well as their current continuations, place the memorial and evidential aspects of records and artifacts at the centre of their collecting, research and exhibition activities. Vukovar itself remains only partially restored, with its now iconic shell-pocked water tower also preserved as a memorial. In this state it is increasingly becoming a prominent locus for dark tourism and is far from the vibrant city that Glavašević so wished to see remembered . . . and restored. The memorial institutions and projects ensure that the siege is seen as the city's defining moment and reinforce the national narrative of Vukovar as a space that defines the Croat community and resilience and indeed Croatian national identity. At the same time, however, for those dedicated staff and volunteers who manage these public sites, it is a daily reminder of the horrors of the siege, the war and the loss of loved ones, some of whose personal effects, retrieved from mass graves, are displayed on a bed of farm straw in the memorial at Ovčara and some of whom remain missing.

The effect of these initiatives is almost overwhelming, not only is it deeply embedded in the consciousness of Croatian society, it is also experienced deeply by those who work for the initiatives. While some say that they could not cope if they stopped doing this work and that for them it is a form of therapy, one staff member recounts how, when he finishes up at work each day, he has to leave it all behind or it would engulf him. At the same time, these initiatives are also a reminder of the many other bloody conflicts in which the families of the citizens of Vukovar have participated and suffered across the last century and one has to wonder what their individual and cumulative impact might be on communities and a country that still have so much healing to do. One young docent had been a child during the siege.

Welling up with tears, he remarked that each generation of males in his family in recent memory – his brother, father, grandfather, great-grandfather – had been caught up in conflicts and imprisoned in a camp. 'Every 50 years it happens in this space', he said. He thinks it is an inevitability for himself and his children.

Conclusion

Community entities in post-x Croatia complement and provide a counterpoint to the official archival system and to official historical narratives. They are also integral to civil society efforts. Indeed, Glavašević's plea, 'Who will bring my city out of the dark?' could almost be read as a mantra for their efforts to re-illuminate, revitalise and provide a voice for diverse elements within Croatian society today. At a fundamental level, all these cases conceive of their activities as a form of activism, whether their motivations are in concert with or oppositional to dominant historical and political narratives as these are seen through the eyes of impacted communities. They might reinforce the presence and promote the voice of a minority or traumatised community or instead be dedicated to building civil society and independent culture across communities. What is particularly striking is the leadership role that they have taken upon themselves, whether that be within their own community, across organisations, nationally or even trans-nationally.

Another way to look at these cases is in terms of how they view their roles as witnesses, testifiers, gatherers of evidence, even societal repairers. Predominantly, they do so through commemoration and memorialisation without challenging their own communities' historical truths or seeing these initiatives as a vehicle for reconciliation. Documenta is an exception in this respect in that it is built around putting plural perspectives into dialogue. When tragic or contested memories of events become reified, however, as they may well do through community initiatives, especially those that fit within government-promoted narratives, then it may also become more difficult for the communities to move beyond those events. Independent culture entities, by comparison, are more focused on capturing artistic and cultural expressions and providing an independent reflection on history. The trade-off in this focus is that they often don't see their scope as extending to the more traditional archival role of preserving their own organisational records, which might provide future evidence of these movements.

One might ask, at this point, what this discussion and these examples add to wider conceptualisations of community archives and their possibilities and directions. A few aspects stand out in particular. Firstly, how independent and autonomous can community archives realistically be, especially in a small country with strained economic resources, strong alignments between community memory and politics and a strong regulatory and political grip on the cultural sector? In the SFRY, cultural organisations were accustomed to being regulated by the state and dependent upon it for funding. While the initiatives discussed here may be community-based and may aspire to independence, regardless of their legal status, they remain largely dependent upon funding from state and local authorities, especially if they do not have philanthropic, diasporic or EU support from outside the country. Funding that is essential to their sustainability and profile is much more likely to be forthcoming when the stories that community archives tell, or the activities they support, fit within wider political and social agendas. At the same time, however, most of these entities also rely upon webs of strategic organisational and personal relationships where there are common needs or goals. These webs serve as an important sustainability mechanism that can provide them with some of the structure, support and visibility that operating outside state structures does not.

Secondly, what kinds of relationships and inter-dependencies may form between community archives and the tourism industry? Croatia is a country that is predominantly dependent upon tourism. In the wider critical heritage literature there has been discussion of ways in which heritage organisations have colluded with tourism interests to keep out or submerge undesirable elements such as refugee presence or ugly history (The Editors et al., 2015). The case of Islam Grčki, however, provides an interesting counter-example where cross-community cultural heritage and tourism is strategically imbricated with the revitalisation and restoration of a community and decimated scenic site that otherwise might not be a priority for the local Croatian authorities, even with the current legal protections for minorities. However, as the Vukovar experiences suggest, community initiatives may also devolve into dark heritage projects that ultimately may lead a community to an unhealthy dependence upon dark tourism and an inability to move past trauma (Drvenkar, Banožić and Živić, 2015).

Finally, community archives are usually thought of as activist entities addressing the interests, experiences and absences of a specific community, but what role might they play in wider movements for fundamental changes in society? This question is certainly not a new one when one thinks of the role of community archives within the LGBTQ movements or in challenging white supremacy through the Black Lives Matter and other civil rights movements. What perhaps this discussion surfaces are the possibilities for community archives to play an overt role in support of embattled civil society movements. Both the Centre for Documenting Community Independent Culture and Documenta view activist engagement in civil society to be a fundamental part of their mission and have also received funding from organisations interested in promoting civil society. This in turn has led them to cross community lines and refuse simplistic identifications with 'the right identity', suggesting that certain kinds of community archives might also ease the tensions in post-x nations caught between the twin needs for national reconciliation and support for community identity and self-determination.

The authors would like to thank all the organisations with which they have worked on this study and particularly Dunja Kučinac, Vlatka Lemić and Nikola Mokrović for all their input.

References

Bilič, B. (2013) Between Fragmenting and Multiplying: scale-shift processes in Serbian and Croatian antiwar activisms, *Nationalities Papers*, **41** (5), 801–814.

Crooke, E. (2010) The Politics of Community Heritage: motivations, authority and control, *International Journal of Heritage Studies*, **16** (1–2), 16–29.

Documenta, https://www.documenta.hr/en/30.html.

Documenta, *Croatian Memories: unveiling personal memories on war and detention*, https://www.croatianmemories.org/en.

Drvenkar, N., Banožić, M. and Živić D. (2015) Development of Memorial Tourism as a New Concept – Possibilities and Restrictions, *Tourism and Hospitality Management*, **21** (1), 63–77.

The Editors et al. (2015) A Discussion on the Global and the Universal, *Grey Room*, **61**, 66–127.

Gilliland, A. J. and Flinn, A. (2013) Community Archives: what are we really talking about? In Stillman, L., Sabiescu, A. and Memarovic, N. (eds), *Nexus, Confluence, and Difference: community archives meets community informatics*, Proceedings of the Prato CIRN Conference held on 28–30 October 2013, Centre for Community Networking Research, Centre for Social Informatics, Monash University.

Glavašević, S. (1991) PRICA O GRADU, http://os-sinise-glavasevica-vu.skole.hr/upload/os-sinise-glavasevica-vu/images/static3/1468/attachment/3._Prica_o_gradu.pdf.

ICARUS, https://icar-us.eu.

ICARUS (2016) *Foundation of ICARUS HRVATSKA*, https://icar-us.eu/english-foundation-of-icarus-hrvatska.

Kula Jankovića, https://www.kulajankovica.hr.

Kulturpunkt.hr, https://www.eurozine.com/associates/kulturpunkt-hr/?subpage=self-description.

Santovska, V. (2018) A Personal Experience of Collecting Archive Material about the Macedonian Emigration, *Macedonian Archivist*, **22**, 79–86.

Serb National Council, *Archiving*, https://snv.hr/eng/what-we-do/archiving.

Štefanac, T. (2017) *The Conceptualization of Archival Materials Held in Museums,*
    Doctoral thesis, University of Zadar.
Štefanac, T. and White, K. L. (2013) The Representation, Rights, and Identity of
    Croatia's Roma Community: exploring archival implications. In *Proceedings of the
    Records, Archives and Memory Studies Summer School and Conference, held May 2013,*
    University of Zadar Press, 163–182,
    www.unizd.hr/Portals/41/elektronicka_izdanja/RAMS_tisak_konacno.pdf?ver=2
    016-10-20-104937-423.

Index